CROW
AFTER
ROE

CROW
AFTER
ROE

HOW "SEPARATE BUT EQUAL" HAS BECOME
THE NEW STANDARD IN WOMEN'S HEALTH
AND HOW WE CAN CHANGE THAT

ROBIN MARTY AND JESSICA MASON PIEKLO

PUBLISHING

BROOKLYN, NEW YORK

Printed in the United Sates of America.
First Paperback Edition
10 9 8 7 6 5 4 3 2 1

Please direct inquiries to:
Ig Publishing, Inc
392 Clinton Avenue
Brooklyn, New York 11238
www.igpub.com

Library of Congress Cataloging-in-Publication Data

Marty, Robin.
  Crow after roe : how "separate but equal" has become the new standard in women's health and how we can change that / Robin Marty and Jessica Mason Pieklo.
      pages cm
  Summary: "2013 will mark the fortieth anniversary of Roe v. Wade, one of the most divisive rulings ever to shape American politics. In recent years, attempts to overturn Roe v. Wade have reached a fevered pitch. Since 2010 hundreds of bills banning or creating roadblocks to abortion access, contraception, and basic women's health have been proposed across the United States, with nearly one hundred new laws going into effect. The goal is to create a law that will eventually be brought before the most conservative Supreme Court ever to occupy the bench, in order to overturn *Roe v. Wade*. *Crow After Roe: How "Separate But Equal" Has Become the New Standard In Women's Health And How We Can Change That* takes a look at twelve states that since 2010 have each passed a different anti-abortion or anti-women's health law, and how each law is explicitly written to provoke a repeal of Roe v. Wade. "-- Provided by publisher.
  ISBN 978-1-935439-75-2 (pbk.)
  1. Women's health services--United States--History. 2. Women--Health and hygiene--United States--History. 3. Pro-choice movement--United States. 4. Birth control--Law and legislation--United States--History. 5. Abortion--Law and legislation--United States--History. I. Pieklo, Jessica Mason. II. Title.
  RA564.85.M3923 2013
  363.46--dc23
                                        2013003847

"To those who need care but can't access it, and to those working tirelessly to change that."

CONTENTS

FOREWORD

"The right to an abortion may be a matter of standing law, but its legal underpinnings are being hacked away at an alarming rate, so that many women in this country, particularly the young and poor, are having to resort to desperate measures we never thought we would see again... In many ways, we are back to where we were then, with a two-tiered system: women who have the means to travel to get a safe abortion could do so, and the others suffered illegal, unsafe abortions or unplanned pregnancies."

When I wrote these words in my 2004 book *The War on Choice: The Right-Wing Attack on Women's Rights and How to Fight Back*, I had spent three decades leading the charge on the frontlines of the battle for women's rights. Reproductive rights are both personal and political to me—as they are to each and every human being. And they are not just about abortion, as the predominant media narrative implies, but also a panoply of health and justice choices concerning sex and family planning.

As a teenage mother in Texas long before *Roe* was decided, I struggled to obtain the type of control over my body and future that could only come from access to the birth control pill that came our way in the 1960's. As executive director of Planned Parenthood of West Texas in the 1970's just after abortion was made legal, I saw firsthand how reproductive choice truly was the most fundamental human and civil right for my generation and the generation of women and girls to follow. During the 1980's and 1990's in Arizona, I had the satisfaction of growing one of the largest Planned Parenthood affiliates in the country.

And as President of Planned Parenthood Federation of America from 1996 through 2005, I was able to help give more girls and women the means to create their own destinies and make their own responsible reproductive choices by gaining insurance coverage of contraception, getting FDA approval of emergency contraception and the early abortion pill Mifepristone, and more, despite intense opposition at every turn.

But over those years I also experienced some of the greatest assaults on the rights and access to abortion and birth control women had ever faced. Without access, rights are meaningless. I wrote *The War On Choice* as a call to action to illustrate how the Bush administration was circling the wagons around reproductive rights and health care access, promoting ineffectual, medically inaccurate abstinence only sex education programs and implementing gag rules while cutting family planning funding and evidence-based sex ed. Bush had recently signed into law the first-ever federal law criminalizing a standard medical procedure, the federal abortion ban its proponents deliberately misnamed "partial birth abortion."

"We must not just fight back," I warned; "We must fight forward." Yet reproductive rights have eroded much, much further since then.

The 2008 election of President Barack Obama ushered in not (as many assumed) a time for reclaiming bodily autonomy, but instead the further elimination of abortion coverage in insurance plans to assist women in paying for procedures. Women's groups were either naïve in thinking that having "our side" in power in the White House meant restrictions on reproductive rights and health care would come to an end, or they were co-opted by a president who withdrew campaign promises to prioritize the Freedom of Choice Act while attempting unsuccessfully to find "common ground" with anti-choice forces. After women's advocates lost the battle to keep further restrictions on abortion coverage out of the Affordable Care Act, the right-wing smelled weakness and unleashed a tidal wave of measures to hack away at access to abortion and contraception. From 2010 on, with the election of Tea Party ultra-conservatives across the country, hundreds of anti-choice state laws were proposed, with some states literally making abortion access available in name only.

There was backlash, of course, as women and men of like mind awakened to the threats that seemed more personal each day. The 2012 election showed us that reproductive rights mattered not just to those who had fought for them in the past, or those who lived in progressive, liberal states, but to the nation as a whole. But will that message make it to the White House, and even if it does, could it already be too late?

To turn the tide, the next generation must be engaged. Those of us who have long been in the fight must advocate for new voices to rise up, and to push on with a vibrant new agenda, not merely defend past wins. As you will see in the following pages, the anti-choice right has leveled a volume and variety of attacks never before seen in this nation, and they will not stop until *Roe* is overturned and women are second-class citizens again. But we can stop them if we change our tactics and bring the struggle for reproductive justice out of the "women's issues" ghetto focusing only on abortion, and into the mainstream conversation with a narrative that clearly recognizes that abortion is just the tip of a much larger ideological iceberg about women's place in the world.

We must also face the fact that privacy is not and has never been a strong enough legal justification for reproductive rights. Therefore, it is essential to bolster jurisprudence affirming women's civil rights to make their own childbearing choices, and to pass laws such as the Freedom of Choice Act that demonstrate grassroots support for women's full equality under the law.

I've been directly involved in the fight for abortion rights since the year after *Roe v. Wade* was decided and I have seen many peaks and valleys. I have seen history repeat itself in part because of the general political cycles and shifts in party control. Yet the one thing that remains unchanged is our need to remain on the offensive, even when we are under assault, and even more so when we are allegedly in power. An aggressive agenda, one where we play from an offensive, not a defensive stance, is what we need today to reassert our rights to bodily autonomy. We must win back abortion rights for every woman, not just those who can be seen as victims due to sexual assault, not just those who can afford to travel to another state or country, to spend three days waiting, or to jump through the humiliating hoops that state legislatures force upon them.

Reproductive self-determination continues to be the most fundamental human and civil right in our society. During the fortieth anniversary of *Roe v. Wade*, we must commit to undoing our two-tiered system of access to reproductive health care. We must work together with more strategic action and less reaction to reaffirm that the right to choose unequivocally belongs to each woman and girl, regardless of race, location or economic status. We must be freedom's vanguards. Without that pledge, *Roe* won't see another forty years.

—**Gloria Feldt**, President of Planned Parenthood Federation of America 1996-2005, and author of *No Excuses: Nine Ways Women Can Change How They Think About Power*

INTRODUCTION

The pinnacle of reproductive rights decisions, the 1973 Supreme Court ruling in *Roe v. Wade* established that any woman, regardless of means, race, income or class, had the right to determine whether or not she wished to remain pregnant. *Roe* declared that, until the point of fetal viability—the ability of a fetus to survive outside the uterus—the right of a woman to control her own body outweighed any interest that the state might have in legally defining an embryo, fetus or any other such entity as "life." By recognizing the choice of whether or not to have an abortion as a federal and constitutional right, *Roe v. Wade* was pivotal in providing a generation of women with the structural support for achieving economic and civic equality.

The constitutional protection of a woman's decision to terminate her pregnancy is derived from the due process clause of the Fourteenth Amendment. This clause offers both procedural protections and substantive rights, the most familiar of these substantive rights or liberties (the terms are used interchangeably in case law describing the evolution of substantive due process analysis) being those recognized by the Bill of Rights. In *Roe,* the Supreme Court famously found a woman's right to control her reproduction to be part of the "penumbra" of the right to privacy. This was largely the framework that the courts embraced in the years following the decision, understanding that fundamental recognition of someone's humanity must include the recognition of that person's right to make decisions that control his or her health and destiny.

In the wake of the *Roe v. Wade* decision, the principle that women had a fundamental right to bodily autonomy seemed like settled law. And it largely was, until the early 1990s, when there was a shift in the focus and concerns of reproductive rights jurisprudence, which offered an opening to individual states to initiate a new wave of restrictive anti-abortion laws. The key case in this shift was *Planned Parenthood v. Casey*. "Liberty finds no refuge in a jurisprudence of doubt," wrote Justice Sandra Day O'Connor in the opening of the plurality opinion of the 1992 decision, which affirmed the role of the Fourteenth Amendment in protecting a woman's right to bodily autonomy and privacy but also dramatically reduced those protections from what they had been under *Roe*. A woman's right to control her body must fall, O'Connor wrote, into the same sphere as other intimate personal liberties, areas where the government simply should not tread:

> It is a promise of the Constitution that there is a realm of personal liberty which the government may not enter. We have vindicated this principle before. Marriage is mentioned nowhere in the Bill of Rights and interracial marriage was illegal in most States in the 19th century, but the Court was no doubt correct in finding it to be an aspect of liberty protected against state interference by the substantive component of the Due Process Clause in *Loving v. Virginia*, 388 U.S. 1, 12 (1967)[1]

But instead of simply reaffirming the right of a woman to control her body as one of personal liberty, in *Casey*, O'Connor placed that right in opposition to the rights of the state to protect potential life. And it is this opposition, this tension, that has come to define the legal battle over reproductive rights in the two decades since *Casey*:

> The woman's liberty is not so unlimited, however, that from the outset the State cannot show its concern for the life of the unborn, and at a later point in the fetal devel-

opment the State's interest in life has sufficient force so that the right of the woman to terminate the pregnancy can be restricted.

With that, O'Connor and the plurality signified a shift away from abortion as an aspect of a woman's civil rights and embraced a state's interest in protecting potential fetal life. This shift gave anti-abortion advocates the opening they were looking for, as *Casey* permanently tilted the balance of rights, prioritizing the state's interest in regulating procreation over a woman's right to control her body. Individual states were now free to restrict abortion rights so long as those restrictions did not create an "undue burden" on a woman's "right to chose abortion." As the federal courts had done with slavery and Jim Crow laws in the nineteenth century, *Casey* established a two-tiered system made up of those who had access to the basic trappings of citizenship, and those who did not.

What is an "undue burden"? That's a question that anti-abortion activists have been asking for the past two decades as they test the limits of the *Casey* ruling. Relying on what appears to be Supreme Court Justice Anthony Kennedy's growing discomfort with the discordance between his Catholic faith and his lack of advocacy for ending abortion, within the past few years several states have offered laws designed as test cases to see just how far they can extend the what they refer to as the rights of a fetus. "*Roe v. Wade* mandates that abortion be legal in the fifty states of the USA. It does not require that abortion be accessible," is the battle cry of anti-abortion activists and the fulcrum on which the current war over reproductive rights rests.[2] "Legal but not accessible" is the goal of those who rally against a woman's right to control her reproductive health; "legal in name only" may be the end result of the onslaught of anti–women's health bills that have exponentially hit state houses throughout America since the 2009 inauguration of President Barack Obama. After the Republican Tea Party election wave of 2010, these bills only became bolder, and there's no reason to think the legislative efforts to undermine choice will slow down anytime soon.

Fueling the state laws seeking to restrict abortion rights is an ever-increasing supply of undisclosed political donations made possible by the Supreme Court's attack on campaign finance reform, which culminated in the 2010 *Citizens United v. Federal Election Commission* decision. That ruling, and the explosion of "super PACs," corporate entities largely exempt from financial disclosure requirements, that followed in its wake, was made possible by attorney James Bopp Jr., one of the foremost legal and tactical minds behind the anti-abortion movement and the author of the "incremental" approach to ending legal abortion altogether. The explosion of anti-abortion legislation would not have been possible to the same degree without the undermining of our campaign finance laws, and Bopp is at the center of it all.

Anti-choice advocates have long said that overturning *Roe v. Wade* would send the issue of abortion back to the states, thus providing each state the opportunity to decide whether or not it wants abortion to be legal inside its borders. As the issue has grown in importance, thanks to the dominance of religious conservatives in American politics, presidential and congressional candidates have tried to play both sides of the debate, advocating a states' rights position while also supporting a federal ban on the procedure. Meanwhile, at the state level, governors campaign on promises to pass backup legislation that will either reinforce the ability to access a pregnancy termination or immediately make the procedure illegal should the Supreme Court ever reverse the Roe opinion.

Less noticed and more deliberate, however, has been the new stealth method of ending abortion rights by eliminating the protections of *Roe* in the first place. With the increased restrictions in Republican-led legislatures across the country, *Casey's* "undue burden" limit has receded incrementally. States that were once without mandatory waiting periods are now seeing bills proposed that mandate twenty-four-hour waiting periods between a consultation with a doctor and the actual termination of a pregnancy. Those that already had one-day waiting periods are seeing that period extended to three days. States that allowed minors to obtain abortions without involving their parents are now ordering girls to notify their parents in advance, while those that already had parental notification laws in place are now proposing parental consent, sometimes from both parents, as well as limiting the ability to obtain a judicial bypass. Dozens of states have made getting an ultrasound as well as listening to a government-sponsored script describing the image and warning about the possibility of depression, suicide, breast cancer and other medically disproven "side effects" of abortion a prerequisite to termination. Others forbid abortion prior to viability of the fetus even if the fetus has a terminal condition or the woman's health is at risk. One state has even made providing medication to cause an abortion early in the first trimester so onerous that no providers will offer the medication, RU-486, out of fear of losing their licenses, eliminating the entire practice of medication abortion. Another is trying to shut down its only abortion clinic, making safe, legal abortion an utter impossibility. Wendy Long, the 2012 Republican challenger to New York Senator Kirsten Gillibrand, notoriously told a local news outlet that if "*Roe v. Wad*e were overturned tomorrow, nobody would even notice, because the states are legislating their own laws about abortion, completely independent."[3]

While access to abortion will always be a reality for women in California, New York, Washington and other states that value a woman's right to control her body, in places like Texas, Arizona and Kansas, it's a different story. As the Center for Reproductive Rights reported in its 2004 study *What if Roe Fell?*, only twenty states (at the time) would have safe, legal abortion if *Roe* were overturned. The other thirty states would have limited access, and twenty-one of those would likely have no access at all based on their own trigger laws or previous state court verdicts:

> Anti-choice forces are counting on a changing Supreme Court and have been working tirelessly to pass anti-choice legislation in hopes that such legislation will be challenged in court, eventually forcing the Court to reexamine, and overturn, *Roe*. Given their near misses in the past . . . these anti-choice forces are especially determined to be successful this time at overturning *Roe*.[4]

If "nobody would even notice," it would only be because in many states, restrictions prior to having an abortion have become so onerous that access has become a matter of where a woman lives or how much money she has. While safe abortion will always be available for those with economic means, just as it was before *Roe*, for women without the same opportunities—those in rural areas, those who are poor, and especially women of color facing both of those issues—the ability to obtain an abortion is already limited and becoming more so on a daily basis. In addition, rather than assisting these women by helping them prevent unintended pregnancies in the first place, the same politicians and activists working to end abortion are also trying to eliminate women's ability to access contraception, either by extinguishing family planning funding, targeting and closing reproductive care clinics, or denying medical attention and birth control, under the name of conscience rights. As a result, not only have we hit a point where abortion is literally legal in name only for many women, but we could soon see the same thing happen to contraception, followed by access to even basic health care services for the most vulnerable women. Rather than solidify women's right to bodily autonomy, the impact of the legal challenges to *Roe*, along with the coordinated legislative attacks on the contours of "choice," has been to segregate out the delivery of reproductive health care for women into an essentially "separate but equal" model that simultaneously threatens the very foundation of those rights. The result is twofold: abortion opponents create several avenues of challenging and undoing *Roe* altogether while leaving women with an increasingly restricted protocol of care endorsed by the courts as necessary for the state to "help" women exercise autonomy over their bodies.

By drafting laws that range from banning abortion at different points prior to viability, as in Nebraska and Ohio, to banning certain types of abortions, as in Wisconsin, legislators are inserting themselves as authorities on medical best practices and turning providers into criminals. In Indiana, they are seeking ways of criminalizing women for "endangering" their pregnancies, while in Idaho, prosecutors have taken steps toward jailing women for procuring their own abortions. Washington, DC, Texas and Kansas have all found different means to use funding as a way to cut off women's access to reproductive health services, while South Dakota, Oklahoma and Mississippi use "informed consent" and "women's safety" as means to deny women the right to choose. Arizona simply bans everything and hopes one of its laws will eventually make it to the Supreme Court.

After forty years of judicial precedent that has incrementally rolled back abortion access, and with a panel of Supreme Court justices who appear more willing than ever to reopen an issue once considered settled law, women's reproductive rights have never been more vulnerable. And thanks to a handful of state legislators determined to make their political names and reputations by advancing legislation meant to crumble the protections offered by *Roe*, the United States may fragment into opposing factions of pro– and anti–women's health states sooner than anyone could have imagined. To prevent that from happening, advocates of women's rights need to move away from merely defending a woman's right to choose and return to an aggressive stance that demands bodily autonomy for all women, regardless of race or class.

Anti-choice activists have set the battleground in states like Nebraska, Wisconsin, Idaho, Indiana, Ohio, Texas, Kansas, Arizona, Oklahoma, South Dakota and Mississippi, as well as Washington, DC. In these places, they have used the legislatures to create laws that have practically regulated abortion out of existence, and padded the judiciary with abortion-hostile justices to control any legal challenges. But in examining each individual prong in the attack on *Roe v. Wade*, it becomes clear that the assault is not simply on women, but on women who have the least means to fight back by, and for, themselves. Together, those who support women's rights can and must create a game plan to bring the battle back to these places and across the country as a whole in order to ensure an equitable health care system that offers reproductive justice for all.

1. WHERE IT ALL BEGAN: NEBRASKA—"THE GOOD 'LIFE'"

As you cross the bridge that separates it from neighboring Iowa, Nebraska, whose state motto is "The Good Life," welcomes you into a land of cornfields, the College World Series, and an un-wavering belief held by many of its residents that just as there is no contradiction in being a registered Democrat who hasn't voted against a Republican candidate in decades, there is also no contradiction in believing the government's interference should be outlawed in every instance except when it comes to a woman's right to choose.

So when State Senator Danielle Conrad stood in front of the state's unicameral legislature in Lincoln in March 2010, she no doubt knew she was already the champion of a lost cause. The Pain-Capable Unborn Child Protection Act, a new and unprec-edented piece of legislation introduced by Nebraska senator (and speaker of the legislature) Mike Flood and extensively advocated for by Nebraska Right to Life, the state's powerful anti-abor-tion lobbying group, had already been sponsored by twenty-two members of the legislature—nearly half of its forty-nine sena-tors. Even if she couldn't defeat the bill, Conrad wanted at least to expose the medical fallacies, distortions and legal snares resid-ing in its language, as well as its intent to try to end abortion under the guise of "saving babies from excruciating pain."

"It was important to create a legal record," Conrad said, ex-plaining why she put so much effort into countering the bill. "If Nebraska Right to Life supports a bill it is going to become law. But it needed to be shown that there was not unanimous consent, that the evidence presented wasn't undisputed, and the variety of issues that weren't being taken into account when the law was crafted."[1]

In many ways, Nebraska was an obvious choice to fire the opening shot in the battle to overturn *Roe v. Wade*, as the state offered several advantages when it came to testing a piece of model anti-abortion legislation before it was fed to other restriction-friendly states across the country. First, owing to Nebraska's unicameral legislature, the Pain-Capable Unborn Child Protection Act would require only one body to vote it through, eliminating the risk that it would be derailed by critics or watered down with amendments in a compromise between the house and senate. Also, the small number—Nebraska has the smallest legislature in the country—of lawmakers to woo, many of whom already opposed abortion in nearly every circumstance, made passage of the bill certain, something the Right to Life activists needed in order to build their momentum as they began their push to challenge *Roe*. The hearings on the bill would provide them a platform to voice their talking points on a fetus's alleged ability to feel pain, their justification for why *Roe v. Wade* should be reviewed and reconsidered.

Furthermore, there was the added bonus of potentially eliminating the practice of Dr. LeRoy Carhart. A long-term provider of abortions in Nebraska, Carhart became the sole practitioner to openly perform later-term abortions in the Midwest after the 2009 murder of Dr. George Tiller in Kansas. A thorn in the side of anti-abortion activists in the Cornhusker State since the late 1980s, Carhart had fought vehemently against restrictions meant to undermine a pregnant woman or teen's ability to access an abortion, including parental notification laws and bans on certain types of later-term abortion procedures. Anti-abortion forces had been trying for years to force Carhart to close up shop. On the day a parental notification law was passed in 1991, for example, Carhart was the victim of a mysterious fire at his farm, which killed many of his horses and a few house pets.[2] While the fire department said it could not determine the cause of the blaze, Carhart received a letter the following day at his clinic in which the anonymous writer took credit for the fire and cited the abortions Carhart performed as the reason. It was that act of violence that turned Carhart from a doctor who provided abortions into an unapologetic activist.

In 2000, Carhart filed his first lawsuit to try to halt Nebraska's attempts to restrict abortion, suing the state for outlawing a type of procedure used primarily in later-term abortions. Dubbed "partial-birth abortion" by abortion foes, the term didn't adhere to an exact medical procedure per se but was vague enough to potentially criminalize any kind of dilation and extraction (D&E) abortion, a type of procedure usually performed once the patient is sixteen weeks or beyond. In an additional affront to a woman's right to choose, the bill also took a direct and determined swing at *Roe v. Wade* by not allowing an exception for the health of the mother. The reason, according to the state legislature, was that there is no such thing as a medically necessary abortion.

Carhart brought suit against Don Stenberg, the then Republican attorney general of Nebraska, challenging the partial-birth ban on several fronts, including the lack of a women's health exception. Carhart argued that without such an exception, the law failed even the lowered "undue burden" standard for permissible abortion restrictions first articulated in a dissenting opinion by Justice Sandra Day O'Connor in *Akron v. Akron Center for Reproductive Health* and later adopted in *Planned Parenthood v. Casey.* Those cases ruled that states were allowed to put "reasonable" restrictions on pre-viability abortions as long as they did not place extreme hardship on women trying to obtain them.

Carhart's challenge was successful in federal district court as well as in an appeal filed in the Eighth Circuit Court of Appeals. When the Supreme Court agreed to review the lower court decisions, it represented one of the first true tests of the *Casey* "undue burden" standard as well as an opportunity to survey the cultural shift in the high court away from viewing abortion access as a component of a woman's liberty and toward protecting the liberty of potential fetal life.

Justice Stephen Breyer delivered the majority decision in *Stenberg v. Carhart*, striking down the Nebraska law, but it ultimately turned out not to be the victory pro-choice advocates had hoped for, as the decision established a legal standard that would later be leveraged by conservatives to chip away at women's ability to access abortion care. Citing *Casey*, Breyer wrote that any abortion law that imposed an "undue burden" on a woman's "right to choose" was unconstitutional and that, in this case, the Nebraska law failed because it caused those who sought or procured abortion to fear prosecution, conviction and imprisonment. Though it was not apparent at the time, the focus of the court's analysis had permanently shifted, as no longer would it first consider the individual liberty rights of a woman. Instead, it would assume a legitimate state interest in protecting fetal rights, then balance the woman's rights against that. Women had officially become a secondary consideration in the debate over abortion access.

Justices Ruth Bader Ginsberg and Sandra Day O'Connor each wrote concurring opinions. Ginsberg's concurrence stated unequivocally that the state could not force physicians to use procedures other than those they felt were safe based on their own judgment and training. Importantly, she tied this prohibition on state action to the individual "life and liberty" protection under the Constitution. It was an analytical framework Breyer had either accidentally or intentionally disregarded in his majority opinion. Justice O'Connor agreed with Ginsberg's concurrence and reinforced that any law that sought to regulate out of existence a particular medical procedure would have to be applied only to prevent unnecessary partial-birth abortions and would have to include an exception for the health of the woman. Since the Nebraska law did not, O'Connor said it could not stand.

Justice Anthony Kennedy wrote the court's dissenting opinion, arguing that the Nebraska ban was permitted under *Casey* and that the state had a legitimate interest in protecting prenatal life. Because the State of Nebraska had concluded that partial-birth abortions were never medically necessary, Kennedy argued there could be no "undue burden" on a woman's "right to choose" since she would never be in a position to "choose" this procedure in an emergency. The rest of the conservative wing of the court added predictably blistering dissents. Justice Antonin Scalia even referred back to his earlier dissent in the *Casey* ruling, calling the standard "unprincipled" in its origin and "doubtful" in its application. Scalia wrote that he believed not only this decision, but also *Casey*—and by implication *Roe*—should be overturned, suggesting that "undue burden" was so broad as to allow pro-choice activists to claim any regulation of abortion would be "burdensome," making states unable to regulate abortion. It was an argument that turned both logic and decades of constitutional jurisprudence on their heads.

While the court ultimately struck down the Nebraska partial-birth ban by a five to four majority, the victory for pro-choice advocates would be short-lived. Over the next ten years, a more conservative Supreme Court, an entirely different Department of Justice and a repudiation of decades of legal precedent would reveal just how tenuous the basic protections of *Roe* had become.

In November 2003, President George W. Bush signed into law the federal Partial-Birth Abortion Ban Act, a copycat version of the law that had been struck down as unconstitutional in Nebraska three years earlier. It was challenged almost immediately by abortion rights advocates, including Planned Parenthood and LeRoy Carhart. Because of the near-identical nature of the two pieces of legislation, several lower courts, including the Eighth Circuit, found the Partial-Birth Abortion Ban Act unconstitutional, relying on the reasoning and the precedent established in *Stenberg*. When the Supreme Court agreed to review the case in 2006, it became clear it wanted to revisit *Stenberg*, if only to address the differences between states enacting specific abortion procedure bans and the federal government doing so. By this time, the court had become more conservative than the one that had ruled on *Stenberg* just a few years prior, primarily because Justice O'Connor had retired and been replaced by abortion foe Samuel Alito. With this change in its makeup, the new court made clear that it wanted an opportunity to revisit abortion rights, and the Bush administration's top lawyer, Alberto Gonzalez, was going to make sure it had its chance.

Justice Kennedy wrote the majority opinion in *Gonzalez v. Carhart,* upholding the constitutionality of the partial-birth ban and ruling that Dr. Carhart and Planned Parenthood had failed to show that Congress lacked authority to outlaw this specific abortion procedure. Abortion had once again become an area of federal concern; despite the Supreme Court's increasing interest in limiting the power of the federal government, when it came to abortion, the conservative justices had no issue with Congress prohibiting specific medical procedures and dictating practices to doctors across the country. Furthermore, once again showing a willingness to defer to legislative assertions that D&E abortions were never needed to protect the health of a pregnant woman, Kennedy also held that a health exception was unnecessary—correcting what the anti-abortion wing of the court perceived as the greatest flaw in the *Stenberg* decision. The court also determined that Congress was entitled to regulate in an area where the medical community has not reached a "consensus," thus granting anti-abortion foes an opening to drive the "evidence" behind legislation targeting reproductive health care and choice.

Most significantly of all, the court decided to "assume . . . for the purposes of this opinion" that the principles of *Roe v. Wade* and *Planned Parenthood v. Casey* governed. In other words, the majority signaled that *Roe* and *Casey* were in effect . . . for the moment. For court watchers everywhere, this was a visible and blatant nod to anti-abortion forces signaling that *Roe* could be overturned in its entirety by the court if the right case were brought before it. Justice Kennedy wrote that he believed the lower courts had wrongly decided a central premise of *Casey* in ruling that a woman's right to choose abortion superseded a state's ability to place burdens on abortion in the interest of preserving fetal life. Since the federal ban fit that state interest, Kennedy wrote, it did not create an undue burden on a woman's right to choose. Kennedy held that "ethical and moral concerns," including an interest in fetal life, represented "substantial" state interests which could be a basis for legislation pertaining to all stages of pregnancy, not just after viability as posited in *Roe* and limited in *Casey*. This effectively erased the pre-viability/post-viability distinction and rendered meaningless any previous understanding of how an "undue burden" on a woman's right to chose would be measured.

However, it was in its explanation of its abandonment of *Stenberg* that the conservative shift in the court became most apparent. The court held that the state statute at issue in *Stenberg* was more ambiguous than the later federal statute at issue in *Carhart*, despite the nearly identical language and findings supporting both laws. More strikingly, the majority avoided all previous abortion case precedent by not analyzing the federal ban under a "due process" standard. Instead, they simply stated that the court disagreed with the conclusion of the Eighth Circuit that the federal statue conflicted with due process considerations, without explaining how it arrived at this conclusion.

Justice Ruth Bader Ginsberg led the dissent, joined by Justices David Souter, John Paul Stevens and Stephen Breyer. She argued passionately that the ruling was an "alarming" one that ignored Supreme Court abortion precedent and "refuse[d] to take *Casey* and *Stenberg* seriously." Referring in particular to the court's holding in *Casey*, Ginsberg sought to reground the court's abortion jurisprudence in its previous acceptance of women's personal autonomy and equal citizenship rather than the more nebulous and shifting approach centering around privacy. "Thus," she wrote, "legal challenges to undue restrictions on abortion procedures do not seek to vindicate some generalized notion of privacy; rather, they center on a woman's autonomy to determine her life's course, and thus to enjoy equal citizenship stature." Due process cannot be ignored, according to Ginsberg, unless the court disregards women as full and equal citizens under the law.

Ginsberg also took issue with the lack of a health exception in the federal ban, writing that "the absence of a health exception burdens *all* women for whom it is relevant—women who, in the judgment of their doctors, require an intact D&E because other procedures would place their health at risk." In general, her dissent criticized the usurpation of medical decision making by legislators and the minimization of "the reasoned medical judgments of highly trained doctors . . . as 'preferences' motivated by 'mere convenience.'" While Justice Kennedy's majority opinion in *Carhart* did not explicitly overrule *Roe* or *Casey*, in her dissent, Ginsberg made it clear that it might as well have. "*Casey's* principles, confirming the continuing vitality of 'the essential holding of *Roe*,' are merely 'assume[d]' for the moment . . . rather than 'retained' or 'reaffirmed.'" Ginsberg concluded by criticizing the majority for abandoning the principle of stare decisis, by which the rules set forth in previous judicial decisions are adhered to, writing that "a decision so at odds with our jurisprudence should not have staying power." But staying power is exactly what the *Carhart* decision has had.

By 2010, emboldened by an explicitly sympathetic Supreme Court, with John Roberts having replaced William Rehnquist as chief justice (while he joined with the anti-abortion wing of the court, Rehnquist had not been a judicial conservative the caliber of Roberts), anti-abortion activists turned their attention to their next crusade: fetal pain. The Pain-Capable Unborn Child Protection Act, like many abortion restrictions, was created by pro-life activists and lawyers as a piece of model legislation that could be fed to friendly legislators to propose in local governments across the country—in particular, in conservative, abortion-restriction loving states in the Midwest and South.

Written by lawyers from the National Right to Life Committee, the Pain-Capable Unborn Child Protection Act was considered the next logical step in "fetal pain" legislation, building off a 2003 Minnesota law that mandated that abortion providers must offer women seeking abortions the following statement: "Some experts have concluded the unborn child feels physical pain after twenty weeks gestation. Other experts have concluded pain is felt later in gestational development. This issue may need further study."[3] Further study was in fact done, with a 2005 article in the *Journal of the American Medical Association* concluding that, after reviewing multiple studies, "evidence regarding the capacity for fetal pain is limited but indicates that fetal perception of pain is unlikely before the third trimester."[4] Despite this finding, at the end of January 2010 Nebraska speaker Mike Flood, one of the state's most actively anti-abortion senators, introduced the Pain-Capable Unborn Child Protection Act, a bill Nebraska Right to Life called their "priority legislation for 2010."[5]*

A young senator who had quickly made a name for himself as a politician to watch, Flood was named to *Time* magazine's "40 Under 40" list in 2010 as part of "a new generation of civic leaders ... already at work trying to fix a broken system—and restore faith in the process."[6] Elected in 2004 from Norfolk, Nebraska, and becoming speaker just three years later, Flood claims he wrote the Pain-Capable bill not as a challenge to *Roe* but "to stop Dr. LeRoy Carhart of Bellevue from becoming the region's main provider of late-term abortions."[7] Mary Spaulding Balch, the state legislative director for National Right to Life in Nebraska, was more blunt about the intentions of the bill. "I think National

---

*The Royal College of Obstetricians and Gynaecologists published their own study in June 2010 that confirmed it was "apparent that connections from the periphery to the cortex are not intact before 24 weeks of gestation and, as most neuroscientists believe that the cortex is necessary for pain perception, it can be concluded that the fetus cannot experience pain in any sense prior to this gestation."

Right to Life wants to see something go to the Supreme Court that would provide more protection to the unborn child," she told the *Omaha Word Herald* in February 2010. "What I would like to bring to the attention of the court is, there is another line. This new knowledge is something the court has not looked at before and should look at."[8]

Introduced on January 21, 2010, the Pain-Capable Unborn Child Protection Act was declared a priority bill on February 19, allowing it to fast track through the unicameral legislature. Senator Danielle Conrad, who became the face of opposition to the bill, filed numerous amendments to try to add exceptions for fetal anomaly and health of the mother, all of which were defeated. Only one change to the ban ultimately made it through—an allowance for abortion in the case that the procedure could save the life of another child in utero. This extremely narrow exception was created to address the testimony of Tiffany Campbell, a South Dakota woman who discovered late in her pregnancy that her fetuses suffered from a rare condition known as twin-to-twin transfusion syndrome. Fetuses with this syndrome are identical twins who, due to chromosomal issues, share a placenta with abnormal blood vessels that connect the umbilical cord and the shared circulatory system. It is a condition that in its most severe cases can kill both fetuses before birth. According to Campbell, one twin's heart was doing the work for both, and the effort of driving blood through two bodies was weakening him to the point that both would die. As her husband, Chris, explained to NPR in 2009, "Brady's heart was doing all the work. He was pumping all the blood, and he was starting to show the effects of the strain . . . and he was really at severe risk of cardiac arrest."[9]

After meeting with several doctors, it was determined that the only option was to abort the second twin, allowing the first twin's heart to do less work and keep Tiffany out of danger, too. "It was awful," Tiffany told reporters. "How do you give up on one of your children? But we were forced to make a decision. We don't regret our decision. We regret having to make that decision to choose one child over the other. We live . . . every single day with what we did. But then we look at Brady and say, 'Wow, he would not be here otherwise.'"[10]

After that experience, Campbell began testifying at anti-abortion hearings, explaining the real-life consequences of restrictions that don't take into account the medical condition of the fetus unless the mother carrying it is in imminent danger of losing her life. She spoke out first against South Dakota's proposed full abortion ban ballot initiative in 2008 and two years later at the Nebraska fetal pain hearing. "We could let nature run its course and pray miraculously by the grace of God that both our boys would survive or we could abort the sicker of the two and give one of our sons a fighting chance to survive. We decided to abort one of our sons at twenty-two weeks," she told the legislature during testimony on the bill.[11]

While the exception allowed women in Campbell's situation to choose an abortion, it did not offer any such protection for those whose fetuses had other life-threatening complications. Women whose fetuses had severe birth defects, for example, would not have the same option under the Pain-Capable Unborn Child Protection Act, despite the low likelihood of the baby's survival after birth. There was no exception for fetuses with anencephaly, a neural tube disorder that causes a fetus to grow despite missing part or all of its brain, a condition that is incompatible with life even if the baby survives birth. There was also no exception for fetuses with trisomies, which create fatal defects of the heart that would force those fetuses that did survive outside the womb to live short, painful lives for the hours or days they would be on life support. There was no exception for fetuses with severe gastroschisis, a condition wherein a fetus's intestines grow outside the abdominal cavity and need to be surgically inserted back inside the abdomen via surgery after birth, even though the organs are sometimes so damaged that they cannot be repaired.

Most important, the law did not allow a medical exception for cases like that of Nebraska resident Dawn Mosher, whose fetus was diagnosed with the severest possible form of spina bifida, another neural tube disorder in which the spinal canal doesn't fuse closed.[12] Should her fetus have survived birth (Mosher had an abortion), the baby's short life would have been filled with the kind of suffering that Flood, his supporters and the National Right to Life movement claimed they created the bill to protect babies from feeling.

Although exceptions for nonviable fetuses were proposed during the hearings on the bill, Flood dismissed them all, saying that although he did not want to "hurt people" with his ban, all fetuses are humans who deserve to be born, whatever "disabilities" they had. "I also ask the question, why does a baby that's going to be born with a disability become a better candidate for an abortion? Does their disability make them less human? Are they less deserving of the state's protection?"[13] Senator Conrad quickly rebuked the speaker: "We are not talking about engineering perfect pregnancies. We are talking about pregnancies incompatible with life."[14]

The testimony for the first fetal pain bill in the country set the stage for what would become the basic pattern in every other state that proposed legislation based on the same model. Anti-abortion medical experts would first present "evidence" that a fetus could feel pain by twenty weeks. In the Nebraska case, the expert witnesses were Dr. Jean Wright, chair of pediatrics at Mercer University School of Medicine, and Dr. Kanwaljeet (Sunny) Anand of Arkansas Children's Hospital Research Institute and the University of Arkansas College of Medicine. Dr. Wright had been a featured speaker at the Focus on the Family Conference of Medical Professionals and Spouses in 2008.[15] A "traditional family values" organization launched in 1977 by Dr. James Dobson, Focus on the Family is against abortion in any form and even some types of contraception they claim are "abortifacient"—an erroneous belief that said contraception can cause a fertilized egg not to implant in the womb. By 2010, Wright and Anand had become the go-to experts when it came to using fetal pain as a basis of passing anti-abortion laws. Both had testified in front of Congress to support the Partial-Birth Abortion Ban Act, using their experiences in dealing with micro preemies and surgery done in utero as a basis for their claims that a fetus can feel "extreme" pain by, at the latest, twenty weeks post-gestation. As evidence of their assertion, Wright and Anand referred to fetuses in utero "recoiling" from needles and to an increase in stress hormones that quantify fear and pain. However, most mainstream medical professionals consider these reactions to be involuntary reflexes that cannot be attributed to actual experience of pain since they can be seen in patients in vegetative states as well.[16]

National Right to Life's Balch summarized this "expert" medical testimony to *LifeNews*. "By twenty weeks after fertilization, unborn children have pain receptors throughout their body, and nerves link these to the brain. These unborn children recoil from painful stimulation, which also dramatically increases their release of stress hormones. Doctors performing fetal surgery at and after twenty weeks now routinely use fetal anesthesia."[17] Wright and Anand's testimony that pre-term babies in neonatal intensive care units often react to IVs and shots by crying or turning away was followed by a litany of rhetoric from supporters of the bill in the legislature. A few senators apologized that they could not eliminate abortion altogether but praised the bill as an excellent "first step." One senator declared that people on both sides needed to stop using the "F word" (i.e., fetus) because it was "offensive and demeaning." "He/she is an unborn child," he said. "He is someone's son. She is someone's daughter. He is someone's grandson. She is someone's granddaughter."[18]

The hearings grew even testier as senators began to debate the lack of a mental health exception to the bill. The omission was especially noticeable because Nebraska was concurrently debating and passing a bill that would mandate that abortion practitioners inform women that an abortion could be a mental health risk, and that a doctor must determine whether a woman was of "sound mental health" before allowing her to terminate a pregnancy. Senator Brenda Council of Omaha, an opponent of the fetal pain ban, pointed out the hypocrisy of lawmakers arguing in one bill that doctors were the sole decider of when a woman was mentally fit enough to receive an abortion, but in an another bill have their decisions on a patient's mental health rejected in favor of forcing a woman to carry her child to term. "I'm disturbed about the absolute blatant disregard of this legislature for the health and well-being of the mother," Council stated during the hearing.[19]

After three rounds of hearings, the unicameral legislature overwhelmingly voted to enact the Pain-Capable Unborn Child Protection Act on April 13, 2010. Only five senators voted against it—including Council and Conrad. It was signed into law by Governor Dave Heineman later that day. Only one amendment made it through to final passage—a six-month moratorium on the bill to allow both sides to prepare for the lawsuit likely to follow. Most expected Dr. Carhart to challenge the bill both on its constitutional merits and on its obvious targeting of him as a provider. Carhart didn't challenge. Instead, he began to practice at a new clinic in Germantown, Maryland, and considered the idea of performing later-term abortions in Council Bluffs, Iowa, just across the river from Omaha. The Iowa legislature responded to the news of his possible move by attempting to pass a ban on the opening of any new abortion clinics in the city of Council Bluffs. The bill eventually stalled out as the house fought to turn it into a full twenty-week fetal pain ban. However, by that point Carhart had given up on trying to open a clinic in the state.

In the weeks and months that followed, pro-choice activists and anti-abortion supporters waited for a challenge to the Nebraska fetal pain ban, assuming that someone somewhere would have a case that would instigate it. None ever came. Instead, over the next two years, numerous states began proposing, and in some cases passing, their own versions of the law. Some, like Iowa and Arizona, strayed from the model legislation and based their bills not on twenty weeks post-fertilization but on twenty weeks LMP (last menstrual period), thereby moving the date of the ban prior to the point that many women will even have had a scan to see if there are genetic issues with their fetus. (Arizona's ban passed[20]; Iowa's did not.[21]) In 2011, an Idaho woman named Jennie McCormack sued to challenge the state's own twenty-week fetal pain ban, but the suit was dismissed for lack of standing, as her abortion had occurred before the law went into effect. She and her lawyer then launched another suit against that ban, as well as another ban on abortion in the state, which went to the Ninth Circuit for review. The following year, Arizona's ban would be challenged by the Center for Reproductive Rights, which called it an unconstitutional ban on abortion prior to viability. The district judge disagreed, and that case also moved up to the Ninth Circuit, which put a temporary restraining order on the ban while it was being reviewed.

In the meantime, abortion opponents would have to look for a new type of law to challenge *Roe*, which they would do in Ohio, South Dakota, and Wisconsin.

2. OHIO: HEARTBEAT BAN CAUSES HEARTBURN IN ANTI-ABORTION ACTIVISTS

It started with balloons on Valentine's Day. The Ohio legislature was about to receive a major delivery, and it wasn't a bouquet of roses, or chocolates. Instead, anti-abortion activist Janet Porter had chosen February 14, 2011, as the day to begin the push for a never-before-considered bill that, if passed, would virtually eliminate abortion in the Buckeye State.

The concept behind HB 125, commonly known as the heartbeat bill or the heartbeat ban, was simple enough: if a woman went in to get an abortion and a fetal heartbeat could be detected, she would not be allowed to have the procedure. To launch the campaign to create one of the strictest anti-abortion bills in the United States, Porter's group, Faith2Action, in conjunction with a variety of other pro-life action groups, sent thousands of heart-shaped balloons to the Ohio statehouse as a thank you for those who had sponsored the legislation and a warning to those who stood in its way. Attached to each balloon was a small card that read HAVE A HEART. PASS THE HEARTBEAT BILL.[1] After the heart-shaped delivery, the wordplay flew fast and thick across the statehouse floor on Valentine's Day 2011. One representative who "fought his way through a sea of balloons to get to the podium" said, "As much as I don't like balloons, this bill really gets to the heart of the matter!" while Republican bill sponsor Lynn Wachtmann remarked, "After all, Ohio is the 'Heart of it all,' so it's only fitting that we protect our fellow human beings with beating hearts."[2]

In many ways, Wachtmann was the ideal representative to spearhead the heartbeat ban. Referred to among colleagues as

Captain Caveman, he was the nominal head of the "Caveman Caucus," a group of Ohio legislators so conservative that they were mostly ignored by the rest of the Republican party until sweeping gains in the 2010 election gave them numbers and power. Wachtmann was proud to live up to his "caveman" nickname. "To me, what it meant was the way that we were willing to keep butting our heads against the wall for what we believed in," he told the *Cleveland Plain Dealer* in January 2011.[3] This stubborn tenacity was just what Janet Porter needed to get her bill onto the docket; in spite of the ban's numerous supporters in the legislature, the bill wasn't a hit with the entirety of the pro-life movement. Many, in fact, regarded it as a waste of time, effort, resources and, most especially, money. Leading anti-abortion activist James Bopp Jr. testified against the bill, arguing that it could provide the Supreme Court the opportunity to consider abortion restrictions through the lens of equal protection guarantees in the Constitution. "If this view gained even a plurality in a prevailing case, this new legal justification for the right to abortion would be a powerful weapon in the hands of pro-abortion lawyers that would jeopardize all current laws on abortion, such as laws requiring parental involvement for minors, waiting periods, specific informed consent information, and so on," Bopp warned. "A law prohibiting abortion would force Justice Kennedy to vote to strike down the law, giving Justice Ginsberg the opportunity to rewrite the justification for the right to abortion for the Court."[4] The risk, it seemed, was too great for even a grand opponent of choice like Bopp.

Also notably opposed to the ban was Ohio Right to Life, which worried that the bill would either sidetrack other anti-abortion bills they believed had a greater chance at becoming enacted law, such as a twenty-week "fetal pain" ban and a twenty-four-week "viability" ban, or actually become law, get challenged in the courts, make it to the Supreme Court and then be used to reaffirm the right to abortion that *Roe v. Wade* already upheld, making it more difficult to overturn the ruling later on. "Timing is everything," said Mike Gonidakis, executive director of Ohio Right to Life. "I don't want to get set back one hundred years because we pushed too hard to take down [*Roe v. Wade*]."[5] To Porter, the lack of support from Ohio Right to Life had to be the most disappointing part of pushing the legislation, as she had spent nearly a decade as the legislative director of the group.

Porter wasn't the only one disappointed with Ohio Right to Life's opposition to the heartbeat ban. The group's former president, Linda Theis, urged unity on the bill, which she called "an engraved invitation to overturn *Roe*."[6] Dr. Jack Willke, founder of Ohio Right to Life and perhaps best known as the physician behind Missouri congressman Todd Akin's belief that rape victims can't get pregnant, went as far as to resign as a board member due to the group's failure to support the heartbeat ban. Willke quickly became one of the biggest advocates of the bill, putting all of his support and influence behind it.[7]

The bill may have been one of the most heavily opposed abortion restrictions in the legislature, but the efforts to get a vote on it ranged from mildly theatrical to completely over the top. For example, in March 2011, just weeks after the Valentine's Day balloon delivery, a pair of pregnant women came to the hearings and allowed ultrasounds to be performed on them so that the fetal heartbeats within their bodies could be heard by committee members. "For the first time in a committee hearing, legislators will be able to see and hear the beating heart of a baby in the womb—just like the ones the heartbeat bill will protect," explained Porter. [8] The spectacle itself didn't go very well, as only one of the two "witnesses" was able to provide testimony. The nine-week-old fetus, on the other hand, was "barely audible."[9] Audible heartbeat or not, the bill was passed out of committee by a vote of twelve to eleven on March 30 and was sent to the full house.

It was there that things began to stall, as Ohio Right to Life continued to apply pressure on legislative leaders to kill the bill, advising them that if they passed the ban it would do more harm than good. By May, House Speaker William Batchelder was still trying to find a compromise that would make all of the factions of Ohio's anti-abortion movement happy. "Obviously, we don't want to send a bill out that has caused division within the right-to-life movement, but by the same token we have to make sure that it doesn't come to the floor in a format that isn't as good as we can do because it will undoubtedly end up in the Sixth Circuit [Court of Appeals]," he explained.[10]

Though no real compromise was ever found, the house passed the bill nevertheless. On June 28, 2011, the heartbeat ban officially cleared the first chamber of the Ohio state legislature by a fifty-four to forty-three vote. Overjoyed, supporters waited eagerly for the senate to vote on the bill next. However, the senate recessed without taking any action on the bill, saying they would consider it once they returned to session in the fall. Porter prepared for their return with a rally on behalf of the ban, complete with luminaries from the anti-abortion movement and even heart-shaped cookies.[11] By November she became even more proactive, as Faith2Action joined with other supporters to create a new group specifically for the purpose of lobbying for the heartbeat ban. Ohio ProLife Action was formed, joining together members of Faith2Action with the angry ex-members of Ohio Right to Life. Linda Theis became the new group's president, Jack Willke its vice president.

One of the new group's first endeavors was to broadcast a commercial asking Ohioans who wanted abortion made illegal to call their senators and demand that they support the heartbeat ban. The ad, which ran on Fox News, featured a school bus pulling up to two children at a bus stop. A voiceover said that passing the heartbeat ban "will save the equivalent of a school bus full of children every single day." The ad then cut to the image of a bus full of children, with THE HEARTBEAT BILL WILL

SAVE 70 OHIO CHILDREN EVERY DAY at the bottom of the screen, followed by a plea to call politicians and ask them to vote for the bill.

In December, a three-day senate hearing was conducted to discuss the bill, with both supporters and opponents testifying. The opposition argued that the most dangerous aspect of the bill was that it would ban abortion at a point at which many women don't even yet know they are pregnant. Because a heartbeat can be detected in some cases as early as eighteen days after conception, and most women don't even miss their period until fourteen days post-conception, the window for obtaining an abortion would be almost impossible to hit. Dr. Lisa Perriera, a member of Physicians for Reproductive Health and Choice, said as much in her testimony:

> This bill is effectively a ban on abortion, since the heart-beat is usually detected between the fifth and sixth week after the last menstrual period, often before a woman even realizes that she is pregnant. Banning abortion has never stopped abortion from happening; it has only made abortion unsafe or more difficult to obtain. World-wide 48 percent of abortions are unsafe. As a physician I do not want to go back in time and see unsafe abortion in Ohio.[12]

Perriera, who served low-income women in the state through her work at Preterm, an abortion clinic in Cleveland, was especially concerned about the effect that a virtual ban would have on her own patients. "It would have presented a lot of issues. It would have required women to travel to other places to have abortions if they wanted to have them," she said. "But the patients that I care for are of so little means already, it would have forced them to continue their pregnancy. We would have had a lot more women that are having babies that don't want to have them. It's not a way to bring children into the world."[13]

Kellie Copeland, executive director of NARAL Pro-Choice Ohio, attended the hearings and later reported the impact that the testimony of Perriera and several other physicians had on the committee. "I think one of the things that got, in particular, the chairman of the senate committee was the number of physicians who came and testified," she recalls. "He asked one of the doctors who is with the Ohio State medical center what would happen if this bill passed, in terms of [the doctor's] colleagues, and I think the doctor really shocked him because he said that doctors who are residents in Ohio now are leaving because of the bills they already passed."

Copeland was referring to four bills that had passed the year before, which, among other things, banned later-term abortion without providing a health exception and prohibited abortion from being covered by insurance plans. "The chairman physically sat back in his seat," Copeland said. "He was really shocked by that. Every doctor who testified after that, the chairman asked them the same question and they said the same thing. The doctors were leaving the state in droves. It's a bad environment already and the heartbeat bill would make it impossible. Ohio already has an ob-gyn shortage, that's pretty commonly known. So to have doctor after doctor testify that 'if you pass this, we're leaving,' I think it really shook them up. I don't think that's something they expected to hear. They should have, of course."[14]

Although the testimony obviously moved the senators to be cautious about the bill, it was the behavior of those who supported the ban that was the final straw. Eager to calm senate president Tom Niehaus's worries that the bill was not clear enough, the backers proposed some adjustments. Those "adjustments" ended up being twenty proposed amendments. As a result, Niehaus called off the rest of the hearings. "These eleventh-hour revisions only serve to create more uncertainty about a very contentious issue," he said. "We've now heard hours of testimony that indicate a sharp disagreement within the pro-life community over the direction of this bill, and I believe our members need additional time to weigh the arguments." The bill was officially tabled until 2012.[15]

With no idea of when a vote would be scheduled in the senate, the heartbeat ban supporters began 2012 on a mission to get a vote on the bill and were willing to use any kind of tactic to make that happen—including those involving children and stuffed animals. In January, ProLife Action bused fifty children to the capitol to lobby for a hearing on the heartbeat ban. One young boy, only eight years old, chastised the senators, saying, "I'm here to save babies with beating hearts. And I want to tell the senators to pass the heartbeat bill right now. And when I mean right now, I mean right now."[16] The children didn't come empty-handed, either: each one brought along a stuffed bear to give to a senator. The bear came complete with a recorded heartbeat.

Although the event got the attention of the media, the senators were less than impressed. Nearly all of them tried to return their bears, saying they were concerned that the amount the animals cost exceeded the maximum they were allowed to receive in gifts without reporting them on their financial disclosure forms.[17] The bears and children were also seen as manipulative ploys by some senators. "I'm not at all supportive of the bill, and I'm not supportive of them sending kids in my office with a teddy bear that mimics a heartbeat, either," Democratic Senator Shirley Smith told the *Huffington Post*. "I thought that was a very cheap exploitation of kids. I would rather them come in my office and ask to sit down and talk about it, rather than send a kid into my office. I didn't like it at all."[18]

Kellie Copeland also heard from many legislators who were concerned about children being used as pawns in the group's anti-abortion message. "I think a lot of our folks looked at the flowers and other things as stunts. I think that was how it was received in a lot of the senate offices as well," she said. "The one that got a little different reaction was when they had the children come and lobby and deliver the teddy bears. One of the senate staffers told me that it kind of disturbed them because some of the kids were quite young. Their family walked them to the door of the senate office but didn't go in with them. She told me that the kids that walked into her office looked pretty scared and intimidated. So I think that was received with a little more concern, how the kids may have been exploited."[19]

Despite the controversy, the bears—and their young messengers—were just the beginning. On February 14, 2012, one year after beginning their initial legislative push with balloons, the heartbeat ban proponents switched deliveries, with Porter and her cohorts sending two thousand roses to the senate—one dozen roses to senate leaders and eight dozen to each member of the committee that would need to pass the bill before it could go to the full body. "This is the largest rose delivery in statehouse history," Porter told reporters. "Last year we had the largest balloon delivery in statehouse history, but helium balloons aren't allowed in the senate as it turns out, so we had a delivery of red roses."[20]

A follow-up push to force the senate to vote on the bill came in April, when Willke took out a full-page ad in the *Columbus Dispatch* attacking senate leaders and others he accused of blocking the bill. The ad, which took the form of an open letter from Willke, demanded Ohioans put pressure on their elected representatives, calling it his "dying wish":

> Republican Senators who ran on a pro-life platform have been sitting on the Heartbeat Bill since it passed the Ohio House of Representatives in June of 2011. They will tell you that they have passed several pro-life bills this session; that is true, and we commend them for their regulatory bills. But make no mistake, when I founded the pro-life movement it wasn't to regulate how abortions would be done, it was to bring the abortion killing

to an END. . . . Tell the Ohio GOP Senate to pass the strongest Heartbeat Bill now—or we will work to replace them with people who will.[21]

Fed up with the pressure tactics, senate president Tom Niehaus sent an "open letter to pro-life supporters" the following month, making it clear he was no longer going to allow Faith2Action and their followers to badger the senate over not bringing the bill up for a vote:

> Unfortunately, the leaders of an organization called Faith2Action have made exaggerated and inflammatory statements about the status of Substitute House Bill 125 without offering a full explanation of the debate that has emerged within the pro-life community. Their claim that we "lose more than a school bus full of children every day" due to a lack of Senate action on the bill is simply false, and I will not continue to allow the organization to question the commitment of my colleagues to ending the scourge of abortion. Ohio Senate Republicans have done more in the past 16 months to advance the protection of unborn children than any previous General Assembly in our state's history.[22]

Neihaus explicitly stated there would be no vote unless advocates could come up with a compromise that would allow the ban to go into effect without a court battle. That announcement should have been the death knell of the heartbeat ban, but it wasn't, as Porter responded to Niehaus's open letter with one of her own:

> Make no mistake: this bill was crafted with the Supreme Court in mind. Those who say the bill is "unconstitutional," fail to realize that it is *Roe v. Wade* that is un-

constitutional and the only way to reverse it is with a challenge. If the few who stand against the Heartbeat bill want a gutted, "informed consent only" bill, the best thing the Ohio Senate can do is to pass the strongest Heartbeat Bill now. If the naysayers are right and the courts say "no" to legal protection, the severability clause will ensure that they still get everything they say they want: Informed Consent. Meanwhile, the "trigger clause" in the bill will restore legal protection to babies with a favorable High Court ruling in the future. There simply is no downside. As a former President of Ohio Right to Life, Jane Grimm said, "The Heartbeat Bill is a win-win for everyone. Let the judges decide what's Constitutional and let the Senate do what we elected them to do: Protect human life."[23]

Porter's ceaseless campaigning wasn't just an attempt to pass a groundbreaking abortion ban; it was an effort to build her group's profile and raise money as well. "There's no question that she's been fundraising and building organizations," said Kellie Copeland. "They've done quite a bit of fundraising throughout their advocacy. So definitely I think there's that component. I also think that there's a bit of an ego thing here for her as well. It's been interesting watching her and President Niehaus communicate with each other through the press. It's clearly two egos."[24]

While it might have been easy to write off Porter's bravado as a symptom of her staunchly anti-abortion politics, the truth is that anti-abortion advocates had every reason to feel comfortable litigating controversial abortion issues like this in the state of Ohio, a jurisdiction in which they've often met with significant success. As an example, in June 2004, Ohio passed HB 126, a law that banned the off-label use of mifepristone, an abortion-inducing medication. On the surface, this would seem to have little to do with the heartbeat ban, aside from the fact that both laws restrict abortion rights and access. However, the litigation success surrounding the mifepristone ban helps explain why Ohio anti-abortion advocates have pushed so hard for the heartbeat ban, despite strong opposition.

HB 126 regulates and restricts the use of mifepristone by mandating that it can be administered only in the exact dosage approved by the Food and Drug Administration back in 2000. This is a specific and intentional prohibition of off-label use of the drug, a common medical practice by which doctors alter the dosage of a medication based on current medical knowledge and individual patient needs. The law also imposes criminal and administrative penalties on doctors who prescribe mifepristone more than forty-nine days after a woman's last menstrual period (LMP). For abortion-seeking women with gestational ages through forty-nine days LMP, HB 126 requires an oral dose of 600 mg of mifepristone followed by an oral administration of a lesser dose of misoprostol two days later, as dictated by the FDA's original approval in 2000. However, over the past dozen years, medical practitioners have learned that this dosage is approximately three times the amount of mifepristone needed to induce an abortion in many cases. While ingesting 600 mg of mifepristone is considered safe, there is no advantage, or medical need, to take three times that amount. The increased dosage also adds $200 to the price of an abortion, often leaving surgical abortion as a cheaper option. Yet this is the law in Ohio.

The state's decision to force doctors to ignore their own experience and best practices to adhere to an out-of-date FDA protocol means that not only are legislators purposely driving up the cost and inconvenience of a medication abortion, but they have also managed to coerce a large number of doctors to refuse to provide them all together. "I think it's definitely true that doctors are not offering medical abortions because of the restrictions," says Dr. Lisa Perriera. "I know personally, when it came to my institution, I intended to get medical abortion on the formulary for the hospital or at least in my private office. I couldn't get it in the formulary."[25]

The outdated protocol also requires women to make four separate clinic visits when taking mifepristone, including one for a follow-up ultrasound to confirm termination of the pregnancy. HB 126 mandates this as the legal course of medical treatment for women, allowing no exceptions of any kind. It is, in effect, a medical protocol frozen in time. "As an evidence-based medical practitioner it is appalling to me that I can't provide medical abortions the way that it's most effective and most cost-effective for patients," says Perriera. "We do offer medical abortion at Preterm, but we have to give them the FDA regimen, which costs more money and doesn't work, and it makes me angry every time I have to give it to patients when I know they only need one pill instead of three and where I know that they can do it in a manner that's more convenient for them so that they don't have to come in for separate visits."

Almost immediately after HB 126 was passed in 2004, Planned Parenthood, on behalf of three affiliates in Ohio and Preterm in Cleveland, filed suit, seeking a preliminary injunction and challenging the bill as unconstitutionally vague, unduly burdensome to abortion rights and violating a woman's right to privacy and bodily integrity. On September 22, 2004, U.S. District Court Judge Susan Dlott sided with the plaintiffs, issuing a preliminary injunction preventing the law from going into effect. Abortion opponents then appealed the decision to the U.S. Sixth Circuit Court of Appeals; the appeal resulted in the injunction being remanded back to the District Court for further proceedings. The plaintiffs renewed their motion to have the bill blocked permanently, and in September 2006, the District Court agreed. Following this, the state of Ohio appealed to the Sixth Circuit to have the injunction overturned and challenged the District Court's finding that the law was unconstitutional because it contained no exception for the health of the mother.

Desiring guidance on how to proceed, the Sixth Circuit certified two questions to the Ohio Supreme Court, asking if HB 126 required that physicians who perform abortions using mifepristone do so in compliance with the forty-nine-day gestational limit described in the FDA approval letter, and if doctors using mifepristone must do so in compliance with the treatment protocols and dosage indications described in the drug's final printed labeling. On July 1, 2009, the Ohio Supreme Court handed anti-abortion activists a decisive victory by answering "yes" to both questions, stating that "provisions of [HB 126] are not ambiguous. It allows physicians to provide or prescribe mifepristone to a patient to induce an abortion only if 'the physician provides the RU-486 (mifepristone) . . . in accordance with all provisions of federal law that govern the use of RU-486 (mifepristone) for inducing abortions.'" Based on this decision, the U.S. Sixth Circuit Court of Appeals remanded the case back to the District Court, vacating the 2006 permanent injunction but leaving the 2004 preliminary injunction in effect. In May 2011, the District Court again sided with the plaintiffs, ruling that the law was unconstitutional. That order was appealed to the Sixth Circuit, and in October a divided court upheld the law and in doing so created yet another dangerous restriction on abortion access based on faulty medical evidence and spurious political motives.[26] As a result, most medical providers in Ohio have stopped using mifepristone altogether because of the possible criminal liability attached, effectively making abortions by medication unavailable in the state.

It is thus no surprise that Faith2Action would aggressively pursue a wide-ranging and controversial abortion restriction like the heartbeat ban, as they now have years of judicial signals that the high courts of the state are on their side. They no longer need to worry about precise legislative language since they can get the desired result without it. If the bill is vague and tied up in litigation, it will spook providers from offering the challenged service, and if it is not, the case law is increasingly shifting rightward away from women's liberty interests and toward the state's interest in protecting potential life.

Since the battle of the open letters, Porter's tactics have changed. Gone are the cookies, balloons, roses, children and stuffed animals. Now, she and her fellow heartbeat ban proponents are digging in their heels even harder, targeting lawmakers with newspaper ads, phone calls, emails and mailings. "This is a warning shot across the bow," Porter said in a press conference, holding up a copy of a newspaper ad. "You see this? Do you like this? Well it's only going to get more hard-hitting. It's going to get more frequent. And as I said before, we're just getting started."[27]

The legislative session ended on June 15, 2012, without the heartbeat ban ever coming up for a vote. Porter may have just been getting started, but Neihaus appeared to be done. At the time, Kellie Copeland predicted that as an outright abortion ban, the bill was not likely to make it to the floor while Neihaus was controlling the chamber. "Janet has tangled with the wrong guy when it comes to senate president. He is definitely unmovable with regards to the heartbeat ban the way it stands," said Copeland. She suggested that the bill might morph into a different restriction, such as an informed consent bill or a mandatory ultrasound bill. "There's a chance they could move something during lame duck in November or December before they finally adjourn for the session or into next year."

In November 2012, as the lame duck session of the Ohio legislature opened with a house panel vote to revamp state funding payments to family planning agencies in order to reduce or altogether eliminate funds to Planned Parenthood clinics, rumors swirled that a compromise had been reached on the heartbeat ban.[28] However, a term-limited Niehaus made blocking both bills from a full senate vote his last act, telling his caucus he would not put either issue up for a vote and asking them to respect his decision.[29] This action is only a temporary solution, though, as Republican Keith Faber will be taking over leadership of the senate for the 2013 session and has already stated that if the ban ever does make it to the floor for a vote, he would be in favor of it.[30]

In the end, despite their disagreements, Copeland expects that the anti-abortion forces will find a way to work together and pass the bill, as well as reach their true goal—eliminating a woman's right to control her reproductive health. "I think the thing that sometimes gets lost in all this is that they don't disagree about the goal, which is outlawing all abortions. It's just how to best do it. That's still a unifying thing."

3. WISCONSIN: THE END OF MEDICATION ABORTION

On April 5, 2012, the day before Good Friday, with lawmakers, reporters and policy trackers getting ready for the coming Easter weekend, embattled governor Scott Walker quietly signed into law a piece of legislation that would end medication abortion in the state of Wisconsin.

The Republican governor wasn't normally this shy about his political actions. Within a matter of weeks after being sworn into office in 2011, for example, he began an outright assault on the state's unions, trying to end their power to bargain collectively. Walker's previous efforts to overturn legislation that provided access to reproductive health care and affordable contraceptive coverage had also been made with gusto. The governor, who had been endorsed when he was running for office by both Wisconsin Right to Life and their more rigid, anti-birth control compatriots Pro-Life Wisconsin, was quite open about his desire to deliver major financial blows to programs that assisted women with birth control coverage. His 2011 budget had eliminated a law that required insurance companies to include birth control in their coverage, declaring it an "unacceptable government mandate on employers with moral objections to these services" that "increases the cost of health insurance for all payers."[1] In the same budget, Walker also eliminated most of the family planning and preventative health care funds in the BadgerCare program, which offered assistance to low-income and uninsured Wisconsinites. The cuts, which left more than fifty thousand Wisconsin residents without access to health screenings and preventative care, were projected to save the state $140 million a year in additional medical costs. Walker considered this a necessary tradeoff in order to prevent money from going to Planned Parenthood clinics in Wisconsin.[2]

However, when it came to 2011 Wisconsin Act 217, the Coercive and Webcam Abortion Prevention Act, Walker couldn't have been more secretive if he had signed the bill into law on Good Friday itself. In fact, that was the day he announced to the public that he had signed the act—along with fifty other bills that he had signed in the previous two days. His spokesperson claimed this wasn't an attempt to hide the legislation, but that it was "simpler" to announce all of the bills at the same time.[3] Many didn't buy that line, however. "Perhaps he thought that in doing this behind closed doors, with no public notice, before a holiday weekend for many families, his actions would go unnoticed. He was wrong," one Democratic representative said in a public statement. "We will not be silent—these issues are too important to ignore."[4]

The goal of the Coercive and Webcam Abortion Prevention Act, which was authored by Wisconsin senator Mary Lazich and representative Michelle Litjens and backed heavily by Wisconsin Right to Life, was to ban "telemed" abortions, a new type of medical access to abortion that was being tried out in states across the country. As the ability to access abortion providers was being cut off due to the closing of clinics, long wait periods, regulation of who was allowed to perform procedures and "informed consent" processes such as ultrasounds and counseling, it was becoming more difficult for women, especially those in rural areas, to obtain a legal termination. First introduced in Iowa in 2008 by Planned Parenthood of the Heartland, telemed abortions allowed a woman to go to any clinic in the state—even if her doctor didn't work there—to speak with a physician and obtain RU-486, the main drug used in medication abortions.[5] Dr. Vanessa Cullins, vice president for medical affairs of the Planned Parenthood Federation of America, explained the process on NPR:

A woman who generally is in a rural setting or setting where there is very limited physician access will visit a health care center and meet with a Planned Parenthood of Heartland nurse practitioner. That nurse practitioner, who is highly skilled and qualified to provide reproductive and sexual health care, will perform both the history, a sonogram will be done and the physical exam. The physician will meet the woman through secure Internet-based video conferencing, two-way live conferencing. And it is through this modality that the woman is able to have any questions that she has about the process answered. She can inquire of possible side effects and what to expect as it relates to the medication abortion process. And at the same time, the physician is able to confirm that this woman is indeed a candidate for medication abortion. . . . She is receiving high-quality, expert care. There's absolutely no evidence that provision of medication abortion through telemedicine is any way dangerous. In fact, the record of Planned Parenthood of Heartland is not only that it is highly safe and effective, but women are highly satisfied with abortion being provided through telemedicine services.[6]

Abortion opponents were appalled once they recognized the potential the program had to expand women's access to services. Troy Newman, the president of Operation Rescue, one of the country's most adamant and vitriolic anti-abortion organizations, filed a complaint in 2010 with the Iowa State Board of Medicine alleging that telemed abortions were unlawful because the woman didn't meet with a doctor in person, so there wasn't a "licensed physician" providing the abortion. "This is a prescription for disaster," Newman told the *New York Times*. "You are removing the doctor-patient relationship from this process. And think about it: with this scheme, one abortionist sitting in his pajamas at home could literally do thousands of abortions a week. This is about expanding their abortion base. . . .One way or another, we're going to shut this scheme down," he promised. "Health care just isn't a one-size-fits-all package of pills. And yet there it is— prearranged, prepackaged, out pops that package of pills—pop!"[7]

While Operation Rescue and other anti-abortion organizations tried to stop telemed abortions by going to the State Board of Medicine, lawmakers in Iowa who opposed the practice took a different approach—a funding ban. Though Planned Parenthood insisted that no federal money had been used for telemed abortions, abortion opponents refused to believe them. During the 2011 debate over HR 2112, the agriculture appropriations bill, Iowa Republican congressman Steve King tacked on an amendment that would have banned Planned Parenthood from receiving any sort of federal funding for telemedicine programs in general, even if the funding was to support its own infrastructure to perform other medical practices remotely. According to King, those funds could be inadvertently used for "robo-skype" abortions. "Smoe [*sic*] of us signed a letter—70 of us—to [Health and Human Services Secretary] Kathleen Sebelius and asked if they had distributed grants for telemedicine to any of the abortion providers including Planned Parenthood," King told *Lifenews*. "There [*sic*] response came back in the affirmative that they had issued several grants to Planned Parenthood. And these funds, as near as we can determine, are being used to provide telemedicine for the robo-abortions, the robo-Skype abrotions [*sic*] as I've described."[8] Despite the support for the amendment in the U.S. Senate by then Republican minority leader Jim DeMint, the proposal did not pass.

Undeterred, King tried again in May 2012, this time soliciting co-sponsors for what he called the Telemedicine Safety Act, a bill that was supposed to ensure that no federal money was used to support telemed abortion services. This was in essence a stand-alone version of the amendment that had been tacked on to the agriculture bill the year before, but without any pressing matter attached to it this time, the bill stalled out in committee. By this time, though, it was no longer necessary for anti-abortion activists to try to defund telemed abortions, as the process had actually become more helpful to the movement as a way to push for new restrictions on RU-486.

Along with misoprostol, mifepristone (RU-486) is the most common drug used in medication abortions. Mifepristone blocks the body's production of progesterone, a necessary hormone for continuing a pregnancy, allowing the lining of the uterus to thin and the cervix to soften. Misoprostol, which is given later on in the process, causes contractions, which allow the body to release the contents of the uterus, including the lining, embryo or fetus, placenta and any other products of conception that remain. There are a number of advantages to a medication abortion over a surgical one, ranging from the smaller amount of time spent in the doctor's office, the ability to abort in private, the less invasive nature of the procedure, and the shorter recovery time.

In a typical medication abortion in Wisconsin, a woman seeking a termination meets with a doctor who discusses the procedure with her. After a twenty-four-hour waiting period, the woman can return to the clinic, where she will be able to take mifepristone. She will also be given misoprostol to take later on but is allowed to leave the clinic so that she can be at home or wherever she chooses as the abortion actually occurs. The woman is encouraged to schedule a follow-up appointment after the abortion, either at the clinic or with a doctor of her choosing, to confirm that all is well. Under Act 217, however, a woman has to meet in person with the same doctor multiple times throughout the course of the abortion process, starting with the intake, then again when she obtains the mifepristone and then again for follow-up twelve to eighteen days after the drug is taken.

For doctors, a major difficulty of complying with Act 217 is the responsibility to follow up with the patient when it comes to post-procedure appointments. Based on the legislation, though the patient is allowed to refuse a follow-up appointment, the doctor can still be held responsible for not seeing her, which can result in professional discipline and even a potential loss of his or her medical license. The doctor is also held responsible for screening a patient for potential "coercion," a sign that the decision to abort was not one she came to of her own free will. Overall, Act 217 creates a new level of legislative interference in medical protocol, with potentially severe consequences, as doctors who break the law can be charged with a Class I felony, resulting in a $10,000 fine, a three-and-a-half-year prison sentence, or both.[9] In addition, any doctor charged with breaking the law would be unable to defend him or herself in court without assuming enormous legal bills. Although doctors have insurance that pays for their defense in a malpractice suit, there is no such coverage when it comes to defending from a felony since most professional liability policies contain "crime/fraud" exceptions. "What we do would be 'defensible,'" said Dr. Fredrik Broekhuizen, a Wisconsin member of the board of Physicians for Reproductive Health and Choice. "But we'd have to pay to defend it."[10]

As a result of these potentially heavy penalties, medical practitioners in the state nearly unanimously called on Governor Walker to veto Act 217. The Medical College of Wisconsin, Wisconsin Medical Society and the Wisconsin Academy of Family Physicians all opposed the bill, an unprecedented move from organizations that normally try to stay as far as possible from endorsing or opposing legislation.[11] (Dr. Broekhuizen said it was the first time that the Wisconsin Medical Society had taken a stand on any abortion law.)[12] Multiple advocacy groups also argued that the law was too vaguely written to be certain what would and wouldn't be enforced. Dr. Broekhuizen believed the bill was meant to present a set of "minimum safety standards" for patient care that would go mostly under the radar, allowing an "overzealous prosecutor" to later charge a doctor based on one of the vague, legally ambiguous points in the law, putting medical abortion availability for the entire state at risk.

Legislating medication abortions isn't a totally new concept, as Ohio passed a bill in 2004 that mandated how to provide RU-486 based on FDA regulations versus medical best practices. But that lone restriction was the only one, until anti-abortion politicians started embracing the idea of legislating nonsurgical abortions out of existence. "Medication abortion was approved in 2000 and for the most part, we didn't see anything on that method until 2011 and, all of a sudden, we see these bills, and they become law, whether it be a telemedicine ban or an FDA protocol bill," said Elizabeth Nash of the Guttmacher Institute, which conducts research on reproductive health. "These things essentially stop providers from administering medication abortion, either because you're using an outdated protocol that nobody would use . . . or you're doing this telemedicine ban which you wouldn't think would shut down clinics but it shut down every clinic or it shut down the use of medication abortion completely in Wisconsin. I just think you adopt those kinds of restrictions and you are not chipping away at Roe, you are hacking away at Roe without ever entering a courtroom."[13]

Wisconsin Right to Life put the full force of its lobbying arm behind Act 217, encouraging supporters to sign petitions, contact legislators, and fill the hearing room when the bill was introduced in the house committee. The group also promoted a video of a "Dramatized RU-486 Chemical Abortion Interview" meant to explain why a woman needed to meet multiple times with the same doctor prior to termination. In the video, a doctor tells a woman who is uncertain as to whether or not she should have an abortion that once it is clear she doesn't have an ectopic pregnancy, she can begin the procedure. "After all, it's just tissue," the woman tells the doctor, obviously trying to convince herself that she is justified in ending the pregnancy. "Well, we are all 'just tissue,'" the doctor replies, as the camera goes shaky and the picture flickers in and out. The doctor then begins to describe the procedure, including "cutting off nutrient to the embryo" to kill it, as well as the physical and emotional pain the woman will experience in the "several weeks" it could take to complete the abortion. "The pain while you are waiting for it to happen may be hard. Cleaning up afterwards may be harder," the doctor says dispassionately. "Participating in your own abortion may be the hardest part of all. Are you prepared for what you are going to see and experience?" The woman responds that she "hadn't really thought about that," as she looks away from the camera, near tears. The video ends with her sitting in her car, watching a mother carry a toddler to a nearby vehicle.[14]

Whether the over-the-top advocacy worked or the bill was already a sure thing in the Republican-dominated assembly, Act 217 passed during a knock-down, drag-out legislative session that went far into the night. (The debate lasted nearly three hours and included a Democratic attempt to add an amendment forcing men to have rectal exams prior to receiving erectile dysfunction drugs.[15]) Having previously passed the state senate, the bill went straight to the governor for signature on March 16, 2012. Despite the vast support of the legislature and his outspoken opposition to a woman's right to choose, Walker waited several weeks before signing Act 217 into law. Why would a man who had made restricting access to abortion, subsidized birth control, family planning and even emergency contraception the center point of his election campaign in 2010 try to hide one of the most sweeping abortion restriction bills the state of Wisconsin had ever seen? It could have been an attempt to rehabilitate his image as he drew closer to the June 5 recall election that could have evicted him from office before he had even finished his first term. No governor had ever successfully weathered a recall effort, and Walker might have felt that the last thing he needed was to appear to be doing a victory lap in another battle in the war against women.

Still, there was a more likely reason for his silence: it gave his opponents less time to marshal their resources against the bill. As news of Act 217 being signed into law began to trickle out into the media, many of those who opposed the bill had already left for the long holiday weekend, planning to resume their push the following week to call on the governor to veto the legislation. By the time medical personnel and advocates were back in their offices the following week, several days had passed since Walker had signed the law, which was scheduled to go into effect on April 20. That provided a much smaller window of time for these groups to talk to their legal counsels and come up with a strategy to continue providing services under the new law.

Because of the nebulous legal terrain that Act 217 created, Planned Parenthood of Wisconsin announced on April 21, 2012, that until its lawyers could better determine the ramifications of the bill, medication abortions at all their clinics would be suspended. Nicole Safar, the group's public policy director, noted that with Governor Walker signing the bill into law over a holiday weekend, Planned Parenthood's lawyers simply had not had enough time to fully analyze the impact of the new law, and how, or even if, their providers could comply without endangering their careers. "We have not even had two weeks to look at this," explained Safar. "The legislature is actually dictating patient care, and we are working with our lawyers to see how this effects [*sic*] medical best practices and procedures." She said it was "too risky" to perform the procedure in the state until Planned Parenthood was confident it understood the law.[16]

The news was shocking for pro-choice advocates, as Planned Parenthood was the major provider of abortions in the state, and roughly 25 percent of women who came in for the procedure opted for a medication abortion. Abortion opponents, on the other hand, were overjoyed, as they had found a way to restrict abortion access further in Wisconsin. Barbara Lyons, executive director of Wisconsin Right to Life, called the news a "true victory for Wisconsin women." "Because chemical abortions comprise 26 percent of Wisconsin abortions," she said, "their suspension will result in another decline in Wisconsin abortions which is great news for mothers and babies."[17] Pro-Life Wisconsin was more cautious, concerned that the Planned Parenthood move was just a ploy to convince anti-abortion activists to let down their guard. While they told a local news station, "Any day Planned Parenthood is not performing an RU-486 abortion is a good one," on their website they added this caveat: "However, we remain suspicious of their plans."[18]

On May 11, 2012, three weeks after the Planned Parenthood announcement, Affiliated Medical Services, the last provider of medication abortions in the state of Wisconsin, announced on its website that it would no longer offer the service either. Less than a month after Walker had signed Act 217 into law, access to medication abortions in Wisconsin was over. NARAL Pro-Choice Wisconsin lamented the loss of access. "It is unacceptable that women are losing health care options because Walker has put his extreme social agenda ahead of what is best for women's health," Lisa Subeck, the group's executive director, told reporters. "Women lose out when out-of-control politicians like Scott Walker practice medicine without a license and interfere in the relationship between doctors and their patients."[19]

With Act 217, anti-abortion advocates in Wisconsin were able to build on the lessons they had learned from their colleagues in Ohio, showing how a purposely vague anti-abortion statute could successfully eradicate access while simultaneously creating fodder for a legal challenge to *Roe v. Wade*. Several aspects of Act 217 are designed to make specific inroads against *Roe* and further segregate out the delivery of women's health care. First is the idea of "coercion" in the context of informed consent. Historically, dictating medical procedures or patient disclosures under the guise of "empowering" women with information—supposedly so they can properly consent to the procedure—has been the most successful means of restricting abortion access. However, informed consent as a prerequisite for medical treatment is a legal concept grounded in notions of fundamental human rights, a fact Act 217 and other similar bills that attempt to tackle the idea of "coerced abortions" blithely overlook. Built into the idea of informed consent is the presumption that such consent is given voluntarily. Coercion bills turn that idea on its head, shifting the legal burden of establishing voluntary consent to physicians. For example, the language of Wisconsin Section 253.10(3)(b), the state's "coercion" bill, reads in part:

> Consent under this section to an abortion is voluntary only if the consent is given freely and without coercion by any person. The physician who is to perform or induce the abortion shall determine whether the woman's consent is, in fact, voluntary. . . . The physician shall make the determination by speaking to the woman in person, out of the presence of anyone other than a person working for or with the physician. If the physician has reason to suspect that the woman is in danger of being physically harmed by anyone who is coercing the woman to consent to an abortion against her will, the physician shall inform the woman of services for victims or individuals at risk of domestic abuse and provide her with private access to a telephone.

Other than requiring the physician to speak to the woman alone and ask her if she is being coerced into terminating her pregnancy, the law gives zero guidance on how doctors are to make such a determination, let alone prove they followed these guidelines should they ever be challenged. Furthermore, doctors are already mandatory reporters, so should a woman present with evidence of assault or domestic violence, standard-of-care protocols dictate that they make a reasonable inquiry into that suspicion. It's unclear how Act 217 supplements, complements or conflicts with that common law standard of care. And since malpractice standards are governed by violations of the standard of care, there's also an open question as to the impact Act 217 would have on medical malpractice liability.

In addition, any informed consent requirement in the context of abortion regulation must also consider the doctor's constitutional speech rights. In Casey, the Supreme Court held that "a requirement that a doctor give a woman certain information as part of obtaining her consent to an abortion" implicates a physician's First Amendment right not to speak, "but only as part of the practice of medicine, subject to reasonable licensing and regulation by the State."[20] Normally, the government's ability to regulate speech is limited, but in the context of abortion disclosures, that is not quite the case. Because states regulate the practice of medicine, and do so to provide a common good, the court held in Casey that doctors' First Amendment rights could be restricted and, as it turns out, even circumscribed. So the question remains, is it reasonable for the state of Wisconsin to mandate an additional, nebulous procedure in the course of treatment of a woman seeking an abortion and attach criminal penalties for failing to comply?

The other issue waiting to surface in the wake of Act 217 is the manner in which it restricts the use of RU-486. According to Gonzalez v. Carhart, states are free to regulate specific medical practices, even if those regulations are not grounded in medical consensus. The requirements that women follow up multiple times with the prescribing doctors fly in the face of the scientific evidence that RU-486 is as safe and effective as a surgical abortion when done within the first nine weeks of pregnancy.[21] Furthermore, in a state as rural as Wisconsin, telemed abortions represent a real benefit for many women who are isolated from urban health clinics or hospitals where alternative abortion care could be available if needed. For these women, Act 217 cuts off access to the safest, cheapest and most immediate abortion care and instead exposes them to greater risk and expense. Even with a legal challenge, it is unlikely this would change.

On December 11, 2012, almost eight months after announcing it would no longer provide medication abortions in the state, Planned Parenthood of Wisconsin filed suit against the enforcement of Act 217, claiming that the bill violated due process by being too vague in explaining what doctors must do to satisfy the components of the law. Lawyers for the group said that the organization had waited months to file suit in order to determine if there was any way that they could potentially comply with the new law. "Planned Parenthood wanted to comply. They did not take the decision to litigate lightly," lawyer Susan Crawford told reporters during a conference call announcing the suit. "The process takes time, it is a huge use of resources. It was not brought about lightly and only after great consideration."[22] Added Planned Parenthood of Wisconsin president and CEO Teri Huyck, "We are in court to make sure that once again pregnancy decisions reside with the woman, her family and her faith, with the counsel of her doctor."[23]

4. IDAHO: WILL A FETUS IN A SHOE BOX TURN A SINGLE MOTHER INTO THE NEXT ROE?

Jennie Linn McCormack believed that having an abortion was the best decision she could make for the sake of her children. Like a vast percentage of the one in three women who get an abortion, McCormack already was a mother. Her three children, one of whom was still a toddler, already stretched her thin both financially and emotionally. The man who had gotten her pregnant was in jail. Adding another child to the family simply wasn't something she could do without neglecting the children she had already dedicated her life to.

McCormack knew that getting an abortion was not going to be easy. She lived in Bannock County, a rural, heavily Mormon part of Idaho, and finding a local provider who would do a termination was impossible, as was traveling more than two hours by car to Salt Lake City, Utah, the site of the closest abortion clinic. McCormack didn't have a car of her own, and with a twenty-four-hour mandatory waiting period in Utah (this was in 2010; currently the waiting period is three days), she would either need to make the trip twice or stay overnight and pay for the cost of a hotel. This was on top of paying for the actual abortion, which was no small expense, since McCormack believed she was in her second trimester, a point at which the cost of an abortion escalates significantly.

In desperation, McCormack spoke to her sister, who ordered RU-486 off the Internet and had the pills shipped to her. Mc-

Cormack just wanted to end her pregnancy quickly and privately and move on with trying to make the best life she could for her children with the meager resources she had. However, her private abortion never happened. Instead, when McCormack miscarried after taking RU-486, she realized that she had been quite wrong about how far along she was, and that the fetus was more developed than would be the case in a fourteen-week pregnancy. In a panic, she wrapped up the body and placed it in a shoe box. A few days later she moved the box to a covered grill on her front porch as she tried to decide what to do next. She confided her dilemma to a close friend, not expecting that he would tell his sister what had happened. The man's sister informed the police, who went to McCormack's house and arrested her for "unlawful abortion." "There's other things she could have done," the informant, Brenda Carnahan, told the *Associated Press*. "She could have asked for some type of help."[1] Carnahan believed that it was her responsibility to speak for the baby. "I'm a grandmother myself. And the love and the compassion I have for my grandkids? They're my life. And I felt that if somebody didn't speak up for this baby, who would? It doesn't have a voice anymore."[2]

McCormack was arrested under a 1972 statute that made it illegal in the state of Idaho for anyone other than a physician to terminate a pregnancy and prohibited abortions past the first trimester from being performed outside of a hospital setting. Since the law was nearly forty years old at the time of McCormack's abortion in December 2010, it was difficult to be certain if the statute applied to procuring drugs off the Internet. However, Bannock County prosecuting attorney Mark L. Hiedeman decided that any abortion initiated by a non–Idaho practicing doctor fell under the terms of the unlawful abortion statute, and as a result, McCormack was charged with a felony for ending the pregnancy on her own, outside of a hospital. "It just felt like it fit the statute," Hiedeman said. "[And] this wasn't the first time this has happened. She's had abortions before, and miscarriages.

I mean, she was obviously getting pregnant time and time again and not protecting the unborn fetus."[3] Hiedeman's comments made it seem as if he was looking for a way to punish McCormack for her personal life and what he saw as a woman using abortion as a form of birth control.

Ultimately, the county's attempt to convict McCormack failed. With Idaho attorney (and licensed physician) Richard Hearn acting as her defense lawyer, the case against McCormack was dismissed due to lack of corroborating evidence that a crime had been committed.[4] There was no packaging from the abortion drug lying around her house, no sign of RU-486 in the fetus, and nothing that could prove that McCormack did in fact take the medication or that it resulted in her miscarriage. Despite this, the judge left the case open so the prosecution could re-file, should new evidence be found. McCormack, unwilling to live her life with the specter of prison looming over her, decided with the help of her lawyer to sue the state instead, challenging several abortion restrictions, including the fetal pain and "illegal abortion" statutes, seeking to have them declared unconstitutional. This would be the first challenge to the so-called fetal pain bans that have spread across the country since Nebraska's successful passage of the first one in 2010.

McCormack and Hearn initially succeeded in obtaining an injunction that prohibited any future criminal prosecutions under the state's illegal abortion law. Challenging the twenty-week abortion ban wasn't as simple. McCormack's alleged abortion had happened on December 24, 2010, but the twenty-week fetal pain ban in the state of Idaho didn't go into effect until January 1, 2011. Since McCormack wasn't pregnant when the law went into effect, she technically didn't have standing to challenge it, the state argued, regardless of the fact that she had been arrested and charged under the law. The court agreed but would not dismiss McCormack's suit until the standing issue was resolved on appeal. This left the immediate challenge tied up in appellate review before the constitutionality of the law would even begin to be addressed. If there was no other plaintiff to challenge the law, the likelihood of the original injunction being lifted and the law being implemented dramatically increased. In effect, this meant that Idaho's twenty-week fetal pain ban and illegal abortion statute would remain law in the state.

While McCormack may have lacked standing to challenge the abortion laws according to the lower court, Richard Hearn didn't have that problem. In an unprecedented move, he filed a motion to intervene in the case, making him a party to the same lawsuit he was pursuing on behalf of McCormack. His argument was that, as a licensed physician, he might have need at some future date to perform an abortion past the arbitrary pre-viability timeline established by the state. "The judge on two occasions had found Jennie lacked the standing to bring her case challenging the laws that burdened doctors in performing abortions," Hearn said, explaining why he inserted himself into what was originally a suit meant to protect women from being arrested for obtaining abortions. "The court had found that Jennie did have standing for any laws that she would be punished under or would be put in jail for, but declined to find that she had standing and therefore it had jurisdiction to reach issues under those same laws as applied to the providers."[5]

The Supreme Court had given doctors standing to file suit against abortion regulations in 1976, in *Singleton v. Wulff*.[6] In that case, two Missouri abortion doctors filed suit against the state's welfare statute because it would not grant benefits for abortions that were not considered medically necessary. The case turned on the question of who could best represent the interests of women seeking an abortion when those women could not represent their interests themselves.[7] Based on the decision in the *Wulff* case, the answer was physicians. According to the ruling, "a woman cannot safely secure an abortion without the aid of a physician, and an impecunious woman cannot easily secure an abortion without the physician being paid by the State."[8] Therefore, the court concluded, a woman could exercise her right to choose an abortion only with the aid of a doctor—which meant that doctors had standing to challenge any abortion restrictions themselves.[9]

As a practitioner in Idaho, Richard Hearn had an immediate interest in challenging the strict abortion laws of the state, as he was potentially the only provider some women would have access to. "As a physician I am obviously such a provider, and so I was able to correct that problem by intervening to challenge the laws because those laws can be used to punish me," Hearn said. "The court did find that I had standing to do that." Hearn had standing for a second reason as well. "While I have to be injured by the threat of being prosecuted," he said, "it is not my right to perform abortions. I don't have any constitutional right to practice medicine, much less to perform an abortion. So I will not be asserting any rights that I have. And the courts have already found that doctors can assert the rights of their patients in the abortion context. So a doctor, or a group of doctors and providers, does have standing to represent the rights of their patient."

Although Hearn hadn't practiced medicine in several years, his motion to intervene was granted, making him a plaintiff in the lawsuit he had started on McCormack's behalf.[10] Yet while Hearn was able to represent her interests to some degree, in reality the court had largely removed McCormack from the proceedings and placed her interests in the hands of surrogates. In a sense, the court had determined that everyone but McCormack had an interest in challenging abortion laws in the state of Idaho. Hearn summed it up like this: "It appears to me to be paternalistic to say that women must depend upon primarily male doctors to get into court to assert their rights." In some ways, this is a logical extension of women's historical legal status under common law, according to which they used to be considered akin to juveniles or other wards of the state. This lack of legal capacity has helped foster the belief that the state has an obligation to protect women, especially in the case of abortion.[11]

By recognizing abortion rights in *Roe v. Wade*, the Supreme Court also recognized the legal interests of third parties to have a say in the termination of a pregnancy. In some instances, such as with Hearn, the interests of these third-party advocates align with those of the woman seeking an abortion, but more often than not the situation is murkier. Adding an additional layer of consent has long been a ploy abortion opponents have used to limit a woman's right to an abortion, with varying levels of success. Consent issues first came up in 1976 in *Planned Parenthood v. Danforth*, which challenged a pair of abortion requirements in the state of Missouri: one, that a married woman seeking an abortion had to get her husband's written consent first, and two, that a girl who was under the age of eighteen and not an emancipated minor had to have the written consent of one of her parents before being able to terminate her pregnancy.[12] In both instances, the state's inference was clear: a pregnant woman or teen was not considered capable of making a decision on her own and needed to confer with and gain permission from someone else in either a direct or implied paternal sense of the word.

Though both requirements for consent were ultimately found unconstitutional in *Danforth*, that didn't stop abortion foes from continuing to use consent as a means of coercing pregnant women, and in particular teens, into giving birth. Indeed, if the state had an interest in protecting potential life according to *Casey*, then, according to anti-abortion activists, that interest only increased when it came to juvenile pregnancy. For example, in July 2011, the Pennsylvania Pastors Network lent its support to a pregnant fourteen-year-old who was being pressured by her mother to have an abortion. The girl eventually won an injunction against her mother with assistance from the Independence Law Center in Pennsylvania, which argued that it was illegal to coerce a minor into having an abortion.[13] The Pastors Network applauded the girl's decision to make a choice independent of her parent's wishes, saying, "This is a hard road ahead for this young girl, but we applaud her and the future paternal grandparents of the child for standing up for life. Although this girl is in a difficult situation today, it is a blessing that she has chosen not to make a mistake that would end a child's life."[14] Ironically, the same Independence Law Center had earlier argued for judges to be given wider latitude in investigating the maturity of minors seeking abortions before granting parental consent bypasses, saying judges needed to do more to "respect parental authority."[15]

Much like physician intervention rights, parental consent and judicial bypass rest largely on the argument that the decision to terminate a pregnancy impacts the interests of other parties, who should therefore have a say in the matter.[16] In no other area of the law does such an intimate issue get decided by committee. As of August 2012, thirty-seven states required some form of parental consent or notification in order for a pregnant minor to obtain an abortion, all with varying availability for judicial bypass. And, like access to abortion itself, judicial bypass is also being targeted by abortion opponents, who want stricter rules on which judges can offer a bypass, or want judges to take their time making a decision, adding days or longer on top of specific waiting periods in clinics prior to the procedure.

Unlike parental consent, spousal consent laws have been a less effective means of limiting a woman's right to choose. The proposition of spousal consent was one of the issues that brought about the challenge that became *Planned Parenthood v. Casey*, and following that decision, no one on the anti-abortion side seemed anxious to push those restrictions again. (Ohio state representative John Adams proposed a bill in 2007, but it went nowhere.[17]) For the most part, spousal consent as a "gatekeeper" against abortion has mostly faded as an issue. Nevertheless, the paternalistic assumption that a woman doesn't have enough autonomy to make her own decision on abortion has manifested in the proliferation of "informed consent" paperwork and prepared scripts that doctors in many states must offer women seeking abortions, which are ironically dubbed "A Woman's Right to Know."

But things are beginning to change. In 2012, the Pain-Capable Unborn Child Protection Act stated, "A qualified plaintiff may in a civil action obtain injunctive relief to prevent an abortion provider from performing or attempting further abortion." According to the law, a "qualified plaintiff" is defined as "a woman upon whom an abortion is performed" or "any person who is the spouse, parent, sibling or guardian of, or a current or former licensed health care provider of, that woman."[18] Whereas originally only doctors were allowed to challenge laws on the behalf of women who were or could be their patients, this new law allows a multitude of people to have a say in the process, including physicians who may or may not represent the interests of the woman seeking an abortion. In essence, laws that were designed to protect women and girls, regardless of their inherent chauvinism, are now being used to massively expand the number of interested parties who can make a claim on behalf of the pregnant woman or girl's best interest, even if it is contrary to her own wishes.

For Jennie Linn McCormack, what was supposed to be a private, personal decision to do what was best for her family instead turned into a very public nightmare. Word traveled quickly through her small town, and the vast majority of people turned against her. After her arrest, her mug shot ran in the local paper, a community version of the scarlet letter the prosecutor appeared determined to pin on her. McCormack also lost her job working at the local dry cleaner's because neighbors claimed they didn't want her touching their laundry. She was ostracized and reached a point where she barely left her home. "My neighbors gave me nasty looks when I'd go out in public. They'd get all whispery: 'That's her,'" McCormack told the *Los Angeles Times*. "My kids, they have friends that say stuff to them, and my older two, I feel that they're a little bit ashamed. And that's hard."[19]

While McCormack may not have had much support in her small town, the situation is different nationally, where women's rights groups have filed friend-of-the-court briefs in her favor. Among these groups are the Center for Reproductive Rights, a reproductive rights legal organization that is often involved in challenging state abortion restrictions, and the National Advocates for Pregnant Women. Also filing on McCormack's behalf was Legal Voice, a women's advocacy legal group that argues that if the viability standard presented by *Roe v. Wade* isn't upheld, women's access to abortion will disappear.

The crux of the argument in the Idaho "unlawful abortion" law debate is who should be allowed to perform an abortion—doctors, any medical professional, or the patient herself? It's a question that, depending on how it is resolved, could change the face of access for women across the country. In some ways, the McCormack suit can be seen as the antithesis of the medication abortion laws that have been proposed in several states. For example, as we saw in Wisconsin, an attempt to regulate who is allowed to provide RU-486, as well as the protocol needed to administer the medication properly, can take a method meant to expand abortion access in rural areas and instead eliminate access by making the law so confusing that no one knows how to provide care legally. In McCormack's case, medication abortion has been taken to the other extreme: a drug that is safe for early-term abortions under a medical professional's guidance (although not necessarily physical presence) is instead obtained and used with no oversight or follow-up. Can there be such a thing as "too much access," and if so, could McCormack's suit be an example of that?

The situation is a complex one for both advocates of reproductive choice and those who want to restrict abortion access. On one hand, by obtaining medication and undertaking her own abortion, McCormack showed that the medical concern expressed by abortion opponents who claim that drugs like RU-486 are dangerous and cannot be handled without direct physical supervision is merely a ploy to hamper the abilities of the provider. On the other hand, the case demonstrates why a woman should have medical guidance when terminating a pregnancy. Visiting a clinic would have allowed McCormack to know she was far beyond the gestational cut-off for an optimal experience with RU-486. In fact, even at her assumed fourteen weeks gestation, she would not have been approved for the drug. "If we succeed, and we expand reproductive rights, that will be a good thing. And we're hopeful that would happen," Richard Hearn says. "What is interesting is that neither I nor Jennie prior to this case were abortion advocates. We weren't riding a horse to change laws on reproductive rights. The state, in its prosecution, prompted us to respond and we've been responding ever since. This case could open up access to abortion inexpensively—and in control of the women—to 85 to 90 percent of the women living in counties with no abortion providers. That would be a very good thing."

Not only is Hearn correct that a victory in the McCormack case would expand reproductive rights, a victory would also take out of the equation the numerous points of consent that the government has recently layered into the process of obtaining an abortion. Gone would be the mandatory "informed consent" as well as the potential for a "current or former licensed health care provider" to block access. Parental consent and the need for judicial bypass could be reduced or eliminated as well. In fact, a win for McCormack and Hearn could virtually eliminate all gatekeeping prior to an abortion. The question that must be asked then is whether this idea is appealing or dangerous. The answer would be dependent on whether the risks of open abortion availability outweigh the dangers of almost no availability at all. A woman who cannot legally access an abortion isn't likely simply to have the baby, as the McCormack case shows. Quite the opposite: she is likely to go out of her way to terminate the pregnancy—legally, safely or otherwise. Even if the termination is managed without incident, it is apparent from the McCormack case that the law can then be applied at whim to charge women for obtaining an abortion illegally.

To date, the McCormack case remains the outlier in the abortion debate. In September 2012, the Ninth Circuit Court of Appeals forcefully and unequivocally held that prosecuting McCormack for failing to abide by the state's "unlawful abortion" statute by obtaining medication online to terminate her pregnancy was a step too far, in part because it requires women to "police their providers" to ensure they are complying with the law themselves.[20] Judge Harry Pregerson, writing for the majority, noted, "Under this Idaho statute, a pregnant woman in McCormack's position has three options: (1) carefully read the Idaho abortion statutes to ensure that she and her provider are in compliance with the Idaho laws to avoid felony prosecution; (2) violate the law either knowingly or unknowingly in an attempt to obtain an abortion; or (3) refrain altogether from exercising her right to choose an abortion."[21]

The decision is remarkable because, for the first time since the Hyde Act, the court took great pains to acknowledge the barriers that women—especially low-income women—face in obtaining abortion services, including lack of providers, financial obstacles, and harassment at clinics. "This Idaho statute heaps yet another substantial obstacle in the already overburdened path that McCormack and pregnant women like her face when deciding whether to obtain an abortion," the court held.

Because of the importance of her case, *Newsweek's* Nancy Hass referred to McCormack as "the next Roe." In the end, though, McCormack never wanted to become a poster child for the abortion movement. She just wanted to make the decision that was best for her family. "My mind just kept going back to my kids, how there was no way I could do that to them, no way I could make their lives even worse."[22]

5. INDIANA: WHEN A SUICIDE ATTEMPT BECOMES MURDER

Bei Bei Shuai never believed she would find herself on her knees, sobbing and begging her lover not to leave her. A recent Chinese immigrant to this country, Shuai was eight months pregnant when her boyfriend, Zhiliang Guan, informed her that he wasn't actually planning to get a divorce and marry her as he had promised, but was instead returning to his wife. Shuai was heartbroken and believed there was nothing left for her. On December 23, 2010, she left a suicide note saying that she would "take this baby with me to Hades" and ingested rat poison, intending to end her own life.

Luckily, friends discovered Shuai and convinced her to go to a hospital, where doctors worked quickly to save her life. While Shuai was physically unharmed, sadly, the same could not be said for her baby. The infant girl Shuai would call Angel was monitored in utero for over a week, but on December 31, doctors became concerned for her condition and performed a Caesarean section. Angel came into the world on New Year's Eve at thirty-three weeks gestation. Two days later, she was discovered to have a massive bleed in her brain and was removed from life support.

If Shuai had been brokenhearted after her lover left her, it was nothing compared to how she felt after the death of her child. After Angel was removed from life support, Shuai cradled the baby in her arms for the five hours the tiny infant held on, offering in prayer to give up her own life if her daughter could be spared and demanding that the baby not be taken from her.[1]

When Angel died on January 3, 2011, Shuai was immediately transferred to the mental health wing of the hospital, grief stricken and under heavy sedation. She remained there until March, undergoing treatment. Upon her release, she was charged with murder and thrown in jail.

When Angel died, the coroner indicated the cause of death as the rat poison taken by Shuai, despite the fact that cerebral bleeding is a common condition in babies born before thirty-four weeks gestation.[2] In addition, Child Protection Services had immediately been alerted when Shuai entered the hospital. Based on these actions, the Indianapolis police arrived at the hospital shortly after Angel's death to conduct interviews to determine whether they would charge Shuai with murder or feticide.[3] In 2009, in response to a robbery that caused a pregnant woman to lose the twins she was carrying, the Indiana house had voted unanimously to strengthen the state's "feticide" law to include any action that causes an unborn child to die, excluding abortion.[4] The law was meant to add additional punishment to crimes that involved pregnant women, with a sentence of up to twenty years in prison if a pregnancy ended as the result of an illegal act. No one had considered that the law could also be used on a pregnant woman herself, especially not one who had committed her own "crime" as a result of mental illness.

At first, the police believed that Shuai had taken the poison in an attempt not to kill herself but to terminate her pregnancy. Initial news reports made no mention of suicide or of her sudden breakup with Guan. The police didn't even seem sure about a motive behind the act. "It is a very unfortunate situation, very rare circumstances that someone would take rat poison in an attempt to either harm themselves or their unborn baby," said Kendale Adams, public information officer for the Indianapolis Police Department, when discussing the case on the local ABC affiliate a few hours after the investigation had begun.[5] "The fact that there was no licensed physician supervising in a particular case means that the act of abortion is a criminal offense," former Marion County judge Gary Miller told ABC.[6]

What is most puzzling, however, was why, once it became clear that Shuai was indeed trying to end her own life and that the death of Angel was not her intent, prosecutors refused to drop the charges. In fact, the longer the investigation went on, and the more people and groups who came to Shuai's defense, the more the state seemed to dig in its heels. Prosecutors claimed they'd thought long and hard about the circumstances before deciding to charge the mourning mother. "This is a very unique case," David Rimstidt, Marion County chief trial deputy, told WRTV Indianapolis. "Every charging decision is very difficult and goes through a process where we consider all the facts, all the circumstances, and under this situation, we believe we've charged the two charges we can prove."[7]

In April, Shuai's lawyer, Linda Pence, asked a judge to set bond, a request that was denied. The judge said that no one in the state who had been charged with murder had ever been offered bond, and Shuai's case shouldn't be any different. Pence appealed the ruling in June, but bail was again denied. The judge also denied a motion to dismiss the case, despite a friend-of-the-court brief filed by more than eighty pregnancy, women's and civil rights groups—including the American College of Obstetricians and Gynecologists—in support of Shuai. "This was a depressed, seriously depressed woman who acted out of an irrational despair and tried to kill herself and, unfortunately, the fetus was harmed," Dr. David Orentlicher, a law professor at the Indiana University School of Law and an adjunct professor of medicine at Indiana University School of Medicine, told the local ABC news affiliate. "She had no intent to harm her fetus. That was not the reason she did this."[8]

The basic argument of the prosecution was that the murder and feticide charges were appropriate because the same laws were being applied to Shuai as a pregnant woman that would be applied to anyone else who had caused the death of a fetus past viability. Shuai's attorneys and supporters, on the other hand, countered with the claim that the law was being applied to her differently as a pregnant woman, as her actions couldn't be separated from the events that may or may not have caused the death of her baby. Was Shuai in fact being held to a different standard by virtue of being pregnant? After all, if she had not been pregnant, the state would not have charged her with attempted murder for trying to kill herself, as suicide is not a crime in Indiana. If the fetus had died in utero, as opposed to surviving birth, Shuai at the very least would not have been looking at a murder charge and probably would have been granted bail while she awaited trial for feticide. Even if she had sought an abortion so late in her pregnancy, while those performing the procedure would have been charged with a crime, Shuai herself wouldn't have been. But prosecutors were using the suicide as the "crime" on which they were pinning the feticide charge. However, it was because she had done everything in her power to save both herself and Angel that Shuai was facing so much time in prison. Emma Ketteringham, the director of legal advocacy for the National Association for Pregnant Women, said that Shuai had been a model patient and mother: "[Shuai] consented to everything the hospital suggested. She agreed to have a C-section and to let the hospital do whatever tests they wanted to do."[9]

In refusing to dismiss the charges against Shuai, the state of Indiana was in essence saying that unborn children had rights and that those rights outweighed those of the mother. "Prosecuting women based on the outcomes of their pregnancies violates their constitutional rights and is cruel and unusual punishment. And yet, this is what is happening," wrote author Soraya Chemaly, who followed the Shuai case closely. "In this environment, and with no confidence that their rights will be respected and protected, pregnant women will continue to be jailed, in ever increasing numbers, in unexpected ways that violate their rights.

Fear of imprisonment will result in women compromising their health and the health of their fetuses by avoiding pre-natal care, treatment for addiction and medical help if they fear they are miscarrying. They will have more abortions to avoid penalization."[10]

This is why Shuai had no choice but to fight the charges. Constitutional guarantees of due process ensure that no one "may be required at peril of life, liberty or property to speculate as to the meaning of penal statutes. All are entitled to be informed as to what the State commands or forbids."[11] Yet Shuai was denied notice of what the law forbade, as she couldn't have known that attempting suicide would subject her to criminal liability; not even the Indiana legislature had contemplated such an outcome when writing and passing the state's "feticide" law. As her attorneys noted, there was not one single case in Indiana in which a woman had been charged with murder or feticide based solely on allegations that she did or did not do something during pregnancy.[12] Nor had the homicide laws of the state ever been applied to the substantial number of pregnant women who experienced a stillbirth or miscarriage each year, or to other pregnant women in Indiana who had attempted suicide.

Shuai's lawyer, Linda Pence, has accused Marion County prosecutor Terry Curry of attempting to enforce his own version of the feticide law in order to criminalize the failure to protect a fetus while pregnant. Looking specifically at Shuai's situation, it seems clear that prosecutors were seeking out a "test case" for such a charge. Alerting Child Protective Services when Shuai arrived at the hospital, despite the fact that no child had been born yet, was in itself unusual. That police arrived soon after Angel's death and began interviewing hospital staff is another clue. Curry has been accused of building his case solely on an inaccurate, unscientific and discredited autopsy report by a pathologist employed by a private entity named Biblical Dogs. According to a briefing filed by Shuai's attorneys, the pathologist who performed the autopsy offered only a simple inferential analysis of the cause of the baby's hemorrhage based upon nothing more than temporal events and non-medical hearsay statements. In other words, merely because Ms. Shuai ingested poison, that must have caused and thus was the cause of the death of her child. Significantly, the pathologist was not aware that Ms. Shuai had received indomethacin prior to caesarean surgery which has direct side effects upon the fetus alone, including hemorrhaging, and never reviewed Ms. Shuai's medical records, thus precluding her from identifying other issues that could have caused fetal demise, such as a lack of oxygen to the brain. The prosecutor's chief witness did not rule out, nor did she even consider other possible causes of death, never performed research or scientific studies relating to newborn brain bleeds, the effects of blood thinners on persons, pregnant women, or fetuses, nor did she review the medical research in these fields.[13]

Ultimately, Shuai's case leaves pregnant women exposed to the subjective, scientifically unsound opinions of law enforcement and the state. It raises severe equal protection concerns as well, since prosecutors have effectively made suicide a crime that applies only to pregnant women. Furthermore, a state engages in gender discrimination when it places additional restrictions on women from which men are exempt, which is unconstitutional under both state and federal law. Shuai did not become pregnant by herself, and, in fact, the father of her child, who promised to care for her and their baby and instead abandoned them, was the catalyst of her emotional breakdown. Yet he was not prosecuted despite the fact that "a person who intentionally causes another human being, by force, duress, or deception, to commit suicide commits causing suicide," a Class B felony in the state of Indiana.[14] The inescapable conclusion of the Shuai case was that in Indiana, a pregnant woman now had a fundamentally different relationship to the criminal justice system than did the father of the child.

The right to procreational privacy includes the right to carry a pregnancy to term. Indeed, this is the fundamental truth to women's liberty interests: the ability to be free from state-determined procreation. What the state of Indiana was saying with the Shuai prosecution was that women with histories of mental health issues, addictions and other health conditions that might prevent them from being able to ensure a healthy birth outcome, as well as women who could not afford comprehensive prenatal care, drug treatment and mental health services, could now face prison time if they experienced a miscarriage, stillbirth, or neonatal death. And what happens to those women the state determines are a risk for endangering future pregnancies? In the past, the United States has forcibly sterilized entire generations and categories of women. How can we be sure this country will not go to a similarly dark place again?

In the end, the most frightening development to come out of the Shuai case was that a judge or jury would be allowed to decide what Shuai's true motive was in trying to end her life— as well as the true motives of women in similar circumstance in the future—and put her in jail for up to forty-five years if they sided with the prosecution. The Shuai prosecution represented the logical, real-world conclusion of Justice Kennedy's insistence that the state's primary duty is to protect the rights of potential but unborn life over the rights of the mother.

Bei Bei Shuai is far from the only woman over the past few years to fall victim to an overzealous state intent on punishing her for endangering her pregnancy. In March 2010, Iowa mother Christine Taylor fell down a flight of stairs in her home. Taylor, who was pregnant at the time, went to the emergency room to make sure her fetus was unharmed. While she was in the ER, she spoke with a nurse about her family, including her tumultuous relationship with her husband, the children she already had at home, and the new one on the way. "I never said I didn't want my baby, but I admitted that I had been considering adoption or abortion," Taylor told the *Des Moines Register*. "I admit that I said I wasn't sure I wanted to continue the pregnancy. My husband sends me money, but money doesn't make a parent. I don't have anybody else to turn to."[15] The nurse told a doctor about the conversation, and the doctor in turn called the police, who charged Taylor with "attempted feticide." The charges were later dropped, but only because the feticide law in Iowa applies to the third trimester and Taylor was still in her second.

Taylor was lucky. Not so lucky was Rennie Gibbs. In 2006, the sixteen-year-old African American girl gave birth to a stillborn child at thirty-six weeks. Soon after, it was discovered that Gibbs had used cocaine during her pregnancy. Although there was no proof to tie her drug use to her baby being born dead, Mississippi prosecutors charged the teen as an adult, accusing her of the "depraved-heart murder" of her child, which has a mandatory sentence of life in prison. A friend-of-the-court briefing filed in May 2010 on behalf of Gibbs by Tamar Todd of the Drug Policy Alliance and Poonam Juneja of Mississippi Youth Justice Project asked for the dismissal of the charges, claiming the "expanded version of the state's homicide statute violates fundamental tenets of common sense and public policy":

> The policy of prosecuting pregnant women and girls with drug dependency or other health problems is contrary to law, scientific research, and the consensus judgment of medical practitioners and their professional organizations. Furthermore, given the paucity of treatment available in Mississippi, low income women and children would be particularly vulnerable to punishment

if unable to access drug treatment or prenatal care due to barriers of poverty. . . . This prosecution jeopardizes the well-being of women and their children. Interpreting Mississippi's depraved heart murder statute to apply to the context of pregnancy will lead to absurd and dangerous public health consequences. Such prosecutions deter pregnant women from seeking prenatal care and drug and alcohol treatment. And they create a disincentive for pregnant women who do seek medical care from disclosing important information about drug use to health care providers out of fear that the disclosure will lead to possible criminal sanctions. Prosecuting women and girls for continuing to term despite a drug addiction encourages them to terminate wanted pregnancies to avoid criminal penalties.[16]

Gibbs wasn't the first woman to be charged in such a way. National Advocates for Pregnant Women defended more than forty women in Texas who were arrested and jailed after a district attorney decided that under the state's 2003 Prenatal Protection Act, (which declared unborn children individuals from the moment of fertilization) these women could be charged with delivering drugs to "minors" because they abused drugs while pregnant. "While the prenatal protection act was supposed to protect pregnant women, the DA insisted her reading of the statute was justified. Although we were eventually able to overturn the convictions, women spent years in jail while the cases worked their way through the court system," said Lynn Paltrow, NAPW executive director.[17]

There's little doubt at this point that a small but growing segment of society is intent on distorting what started out as an interest in protecting the mother and fetus by making the mother into a potential aggressor/criminal. But is this new focus an offshoot of the attacks on a woman's right to bodily autonomy? It is too soon to tell. One shift that has become apparent in the last few years is that the anti-abortion movement has begun to stray from the basic premise that there are two victims in every abortion—the mother and the child—and toward the concept of turning the mother into a villain who should be punished for what she has supposedly done to her child. From Jennie Linn McCormack's "unlawful abortion" charge to the cases of Bei Bei Shuai, Christine Taylor and Rennie Gibbs, as well as the 2011 case of a New York woman named Yaribely Almonte who was discovered having disposed of a twenty-four-week-old fetus in a dumpster after taking a tea that "may have" caused her to miscarry, leading the police to charge her with "self-abortion," prosecutors are becoming more willing and comfortable with prosecuting women for failure to produce a live pregnancy.[18] Charging women who "didn't protect the fetus," as the prosecutor in McCormack's case put it, may in fact be a way to test public opinion to see how open the country is to the idea of criminalizing women who seek abortions, should Roe ever be overturned. At the very least, these cases are checking the public's feelings about the potential injuries and even deaths that could occur if women are forced to turn to unsafe abortion tactics to end their pregnancies. If the general population cannot develop any outrage over a woman being jailed for allegedly "killing" her fetus, whether or not the fetus was wanted, whether or not its death was intentional, surely there won't be any backlash over a woman who is harmed seeking out illegal abortion procedures.

Based on all this, it's perhaps unsurprising that the majority of women so far targeted for prosecution of crimes against their fetus are poor, immigrants, or women of color. "Overall as a society, we love to beat up on poor people," explained Pamela Merritt, a reproductive justice activist who often works with communities of color. "Regardless of the fact that we have individual lives and that we are all unique people with experiences, we are a very convenient target. What I see the anti-choice movement doing is they like to co-opt the language. We are only tolerated as victims and so when we're making our reproductive health care choices the only way that the abortion is tolerated for black women is if we are some poor, downtrodden victim who doesn't know any better."[19]

Anti-abortion forces are now taking the next step and testing out laws that make women into criminals in the context of their child-birth decisions. In Massachusetts, for example, prosecutors charged a woman with involuntary manslaughter based on her decision not to seek medical support in during an unassisted childbirth. She was convicted and jailed until the Massachusetts Supreme Court reversed the lower court's ruling, finding insufficient evidence that the woman's choice not to seek medical assistance was the legal cause of the baby's death. The court warned that the prosecutor's declaration of an ill-defined "duty" purportedly owed by a pregnant woman to her fetus raised "grave constitutional concerns."[20]

The trend is clear and it is alarming: under the pretense of "protecting life," more and more states are subjecting women to criminal liabilities for pregnancies gone wrong. Much like the push for fetal personhood, feticide prosecutions targeting pregnant women effectively strip women of full legal status and instead place their rights and interests subordinate to those of the fetus. The effect isn't to challenge directly or overturn the right to privacy conferred in Roe v. Wade—it's to nullify it. "Efforts to re-criminalize abortion and the effort to establish personhood for fertilized eggs, embryos, and fetuses threaten much more than women's reproductive rights," says Lynn Paltrow. "These efforts, if successful, will ensure a second-class status for all pregnant women and deprive them of their status as persons in the constitutional community. . . . It is important to understand that the attack on 'abortion' and efforts to establish separate legal status for eggs, embryos, and fetuses do not just implicate reproductive rights but virtually every right, including the right to privacy in medical information."

After an enormous outpouring of support, as well as pressure on the state, Bei Bei Shuai was finally released on $50,000 bail on May 22, 2012, 435 days after she had been arrested. She moved in with friends and wore an ankle monitor, awaiting her trial date. In July the prosecution suddenly offered Shuai a deal—plead guilty to feticide, and they wouldn't try her for murder. The offer was tempting. With a feticide plea, though Shuai could conceivably serve twenty years in prison, the sentence could be as little as six years, and, if she was highly cooperative, she could receive a suspended sentence. If she didn't take the plea and she was found guilty of murder, she could potentially spend most of the rest of her life in prison. Was the prosecution offering a nearly irresistible plea deal in the hopes that despite everything, they could still get a feticide precedent on the books? Had the murder charge always been just a threat to get Shuai, a grief-stricken immigrant still new to the country, to agree to a lesser charge? Whatever the prosecution's motives, Shuai refused the deal. According to her attorney, Shuai is ready to fight not only to prove her own innocence but to ensure that no other woman in her circumstances is ever punished for the death of her baby if something happens during her pregnancy. She may never be able to bring her Angel back, but Bei Bei Shuai can still fight for her reputation and try to free herself from the stigma of guilt.

6. OKLAHOMA: THE SOONER PROBE

To the reproductive rights advocates of Oklahoma, their attempts to fight back against a mandatory ultrasound law must have felt like a Hollywood horror movie: no matter how many times they thought they had slain the monster, it kept popping back up, ready to do battle yet again.

The ultrasound requirement first appeared as part of a 2008 omnibus anti-abortion bill that included, among other anti-abortion legislation, a script for doctors to read to their patients that explained embryonic development; a requirement that doctors have their patients listen to the fetal heartbeat, if possible; a law that protected doctors from so-called wrongful birth suits if they refused to tell a patient about potential issues with the fetus to keep her from aborting; as well as a mandate forcing clinics to post signs regarding the dangers of abortion. Governor Brad Henry vetoed the bill, but the state legislature overrode his veto. The courts then blocked the bill prior to enforcement and struck it down altogether in August 2009, saying it "violated constitutional requirements that legislative measures deal only with one subject."[1]

That's when the legislature decided to hack the monster into pieces so that it could rise again, as anti-choice lawmakers reintroduced the omnibus bill as separate bills in 2010. As with the omnibus bill, the smaller bills were vetoed by Henry, whose veto was overridden by the legislature. "Year after year the legislature has passed these really restrictive laws and then the Oklahoma Supreme Court says, 'You are violating the state constitution, knock it off,'" remarked Michelle Movahed of the Center for Reproductive Rights, which sued to block the state's ultrasound law.

"What they do is they go back into session and they pass the same thing," said Movahed, who calls the legislature's actions a "sheer disregard for constitutional" in the pursuit of ending abortion access as quickly as possible. "It's really about chipping away at the various ways in which abortion care can happen in an effort to make it impossible for women to obtain it."[2]

As had been the case with the original set of bills in 2008, it was the mandatory ultrasound bill that received the most attention. The current slate of model legislation requiring mandatory ultrasounds prior to an abortion started in South Carolina in 2007, with a requirement that procedure must be performed (almost always vaginally, since in the first trimester that would provide the more detailed information) and that the woman be offered a chance to look at the results.[3] Within a few years a dozen states passed similar bills, all using the same "given the opportunity to view the ultrasound" requirement in their respective legislation, which according to the Sunlight Foundation was based off of an Americans United for Life model bill.[4] States passing the bill implied it was another version of informed consent: a woman can't be fully aware of what pregnancy is, that abortion ends it, and that there really is a life involved unless she can see it for herself, they argued. "Ultrasound gives a mother a window to her womb. It helps to prevent her from making a decision she may regret for the rest of her life and it empowers her with the most accurate information about her pregnancy so that she can make a truly informed 'choice,'" said Mary Spaulding Balch of National Right to Life, whose group helped find sponsors for mandatory ultrasound model legislation.[5]

Dr. Curtis Boyd, a longtime abortion provider from even before the passage of *Roe*, was less impressed by the anti-abortion faction's claim to help save women from potential "regret." "The state says, 'We are going to protect you.' And you look where this goes and you see Justice Kennedy said that he felt the state should be allowed to do these things because the woman might regret her decision. Now, whose decision is she going to be allowed to regret?" asked Boyd. "We all may have regrets about decisions we've made, but because you have some regrets doesn't mean that you've made the right or wrong decision. Somehow this woman shouldn't be allowed to make this decision? What if she regrets Justice Kennedy's decision? So he's saying, 'She's not allowed to regret her own decision but she can regret the decision I'm making for her.' That's what it philosophically gets down to."[6]

It was the state of Oklahoma that decided to take the law a step farther and force patients to view the ultrasound pictures whether they wanted to or not, as well as compel doctors to read a script regarding fetal development and force patients to listen to the baby's heartbeat. The Oklahoma law allowed no exception for women or girls who had been victims of sexual assault, who were told they could just "avert their eyes."[7]

Forcing women to view an ultrasound is a strategy that has evolved over time. Earlier versions of "women's right to know" ultrasound laws were meant primarily to increase the costs of an abortion to pregnant women as well as to limit the number of providers by running up the expense of owning a reproductive health care clinic. A majority of the early bills applied only if an ultrasound was used prior to an abortion and made viewing the image optional for the patient.[8] Alabama then took the additional step in 2002 of requiring that ultrasounds be performed on all patients and that clinics offering referrals for abortions have an ultrasound machine on-site.[9]

Ultrasound machines are expensive, however, and crisis pregnancy centers, which often offer ultrasounds to women or girls who are pregnant in the hopes that the sight of the fetus will convince them not to go through with having an abortion, spend considerable effort on fundraising to be able obtain the equipment. Groups like the Knights of Columbus and Focus on the Family gather funds and donations to cover the tens of thousands of dollars necessary to purchase just one machine, putting together charities like Option Ultrasound and Project Ultrasound for that very purpose.

For Option Ultrasound, Focus on the Family offers to cover 80 percent of the expense of a new machine for crisis pregnancy centers in "high abortion" communities.[10] The Christian conservative organization announced in October 2011 that it had given away more than "528 grants for ultrasound machines or sonography training . . . in 49 states," resulting in "approximately 100,000 women who've seen their baby's ultrasound hav[ing] chosen life."[11] In Project Ultrasound, the national Knights of Columbus offers to match any funds that a state program can raise to purchase machines.[12] One such ultrasound machine was purchased for North Side Life Care Center in Minneapolis. Executive Director Robbie Dircks told the *Minnesota Christian Examiner*, "I call the ultrasound 'our secret weapon.' That's because once a woman sees her baby and hears the heartbeat, sees it move, I think that there is some bonding that is starting. So instead of wanting to get rid of this thing, now they know that it's just not a blob of flesh—that there really is a baby there. Once a woman has an ultrasound, over 90 percent of them choose life."[13]

Do 90 percent of women indeed choose to have their baby after they've seen an ultrasound? The statistic is cited repeatedly by a myriad of anti-abortion groups, yet the specific talking point is traceable back to a Family Research Council one-page summary on mandatory ultrasound laws, which refers to "an executive director of an Iowa pregnancy resource center" who said that "90 percent of women who see their baby by ultrasound choose life."[14] The FRC summary also refers to a variety of other self-reported statistics, all from crisis pregnancy centers, stating that clients are anywhere from "30 percent more likely" to "60 percent more likely" to continue pregnancies, with one pregnancy center stating that "ninety-eight percent of women who have ultrasounds chose to carry to term."

However, those who visit crisis pregnancy centers are a fairly self-selected batch of patients to begin with. Women who go willingly to these places know that the centers do not perform abortions and are generally seeking a means to continue their pregnancies. The women who show up by mistake, assuming that they are at a full services reproductive health clinic, are likely to leave before they ever get to the ultrasound portion of the appointment. That the vast majority of women who go to pregnancy centers and see ultrasounds choose not to get an abortion shouldn't be surprising at all, but those numbers aren't replicated among women who go to reproductive health clinics to procure a termination. Although no studies have been done in the United States, a 2010 *New York Times* article stated that clinics in British Columbia reported that no patient changed her mind about terminating a pregnancy after viewing an ultrasound, and anecdotal evidence from providers in the United States tells of the same experience.[15]

In the wake of the passage of mandatory ultrasound laws, workers at crisis pregnancy clinics are being trained to do whatever it takes to get pregnant women in the door, even if it means telling them that they will need an ultrasound before an abortion and that the ones they offer are free. What they don't mention, however, is that the ultrasound required by law has to be performed by the woman's own provider prior to termination, and that the one from the pregnancy center doesn't count. In a workshop called Competing with the Abortion Industry, former Planned Parenthood employee turned anti-abortion spokeswoman Abby Johnson explained to owners and volunteers at pregnancy centers how best to get women into their clinics. "Who's your demographic? Abortion-minded clients, right?" Johnson said during the training. "We want to look professional, we want to look business-like, and yeah, we do kind of want to look medical. We want to appear neutral on the outside. The best call, the best client you ever get is one who thinks they are walking into an abortion clinic." Johnson went on to describe how to get women who mistakenly believe they are walking into an abortion clinic to submit to an ultrasound. "What I would encourage you to do is say something like this: 'No, we do not provide abortion services, but we do provide ultrasounds, and you are going to need an ultrasound before you have your abortion.' And that's true. You want them in your center that day. You want to say, 'Well, no, we don't actually provide abortion procedures here, but we do provide ultrasounds and that's one of the steps of having an abortion, so you can come in here and you can get your ultrasound done for free. Because you're going to have to do it anyway when you have an abortion.' The goal is to get them into your center as quickly as possible."[16]

As Johnson's training session reveals, for those who oppose abortion, mandatory ultrasounds are an opportunity. For those who hold women's health as a priority, however, mandatory ultrasounds actually harm women who want to terminate a pregnancy by taking away their feelings of autonomy. Dr. Tracy Weitz, associate director for public policy at the UCSF National Center of Excellence in Women's Health, writes:

> By mandating that they view the image and hear a script in accordance with the desires of the state legislature, women's own preferences are ignored. Removing women's ability to decide whether to have an ultrasound before an abortion and dictating the manner in which the ultrasound is administered is likely to reduce women's perceptions of decisional control regarding abortion, and thus may have negative psychological and physical health outcomes, impede adjustment, and increase the risk of decisional regret in all women seeking abortions under such conditions.[17]

Over the governor's objections, Oklahoma's mandatory ultrasound bill became law on April 27, 2010. The law was active for only a few days before the state's attorney general and the Center for Reproductive Rights, which was challenging the law as unconstitutional, reached an agreement by which a temporary restraining order was enacted, allowing clinics to stop complying with the law while the legal challenges were brought.

In those few days during which the law was in effect, however, something became very clear—namely that the "90 percent" of women who "choose life" were to be found only at crisis pregnancy centers. For example, one clinic in Tulsa, which also had an adoption center on-site, reported that not a single patient who saw an ultrasound changed her mind about having an abortion. Executive Director Linda Meeks of Reproductive Services told NewsOK that some women closed their eyes, turned their heads away, or even cried after seeing the picture, but none chose not to terminate. "It's like [lawmakers] don't think women have given serious thought and consideration before they walk through our doors."[18]

With the restraining order in place, the courts continued to bat the mandatory ultrasound law around until Judge Bryan Dixon ruled that it should be permanently blocked, calling it unconstitutional, since it applied only to abortion and no other medical procedures. Dixon said the law "improperly is addressed only to patients, physicians and sonographers concerning abortions and does not address all patients, physicians and sonographers concerning other medical care where a general law could clearly be made applicable."[19]

That should have been the end of it, but it wasn't. Unable to let the monster rest, Oklahoma attorney general Scott Pruitt filed an appeal to the Oklahoma Supreme Court asking that it invalidate Dixon's ruling. "Understood in its most basic terms, the trial court—in error—ruled that the Oklahoma Constitution forbids legislation ensuring women receive meaningful medical information obtained through ultrasounds that the clinics are currently requiring," Pruitt wrote.[20] Why would the state of Oklahoma be so unwilling to let the bill go away? One obvious answer is that abortion opponents need the federal courts to disagree on the issue, as splitting the circuit courts would prompt the Supreme Court to step in and settle the dispute.

While the Oklahoma challenge works its way through the state court system, rulings out of Texas and North Carolina are helping to grease the wheels. In Texas, forcing women to undergo and view an ultrasound prior to having an abortion wasn't just a mission, it was an emergency. The Texas senate introduced its own mandatory ultrasound bill in February 2011, and Republican governor Rick Perry (who would announce plans to run for the GOP presidential nomination six months later) fast-tracked it as an "emergency priority bill." "Considering the magnitude of the decision to have an abortion, it is crucial that Texans understand what is truly at stake," Perry said in a released statement.[21]

Although Perry considered the bill a priority, Judge Sam Sparks of the U.S. District Court for the Western District of Texas considered it a serious violation of the First Amendment. After rejecting numerous friend-of-the-court briefs from anti-abortion groups and chastising lawyers for wasting his time ("The Court has already turned down two extremely tempting offers to transform this case from a boring old federal lawsuit into an exciting, politically charged media circus," he wrote. "As any competent attorney could have predicted, the Court declines this latest invitation as well"), Sparks struck down the law.[22] The judge said the bill "compels physicians to advance an ideological agenda with which they may not agree, regardless of any medical necessity, and irrespective of whether the pregnant women wish to listen," constituting state-sanctioned speech and a clear violation of the First Amendment.[23]

Just as Oklahoma did, the state of Texas appealed the ruling. Unlike Oklahoma, however, the state of Texas received a far different result when a three-judge panel on the Fifth Circuit overturned Sparks's ruling, with Chief Justice Edith Jones ruling that opponents of the law "failed to demonstrate constitutional flaws" in the bill. The Fifth Circuit Court of Appeals, which hears cases from Texas, Mississippi and Louisiana, is known to be among the most conservative appellate districts in the country, and this is in large part thanks to Chief Justice Jones. Under her leadership, the Fifth Circuit has taken a very harsh line with regard to women's issues. This is a court that, for example, sanctioned a cheerleader for suing her school district after she was forced to cheer for a student who had sexually assaulted her. Much like her ideological counterpart on the Supreme Court, Justice Antonin Scalia, Jones is known for blistering dissents, particularly when it comes to women's rights. One of her dissents stated that a woman needed to be raped to claim actual sexual harassment, while in another she told a molestation victim that there was no legal benefit in recognizing "a constitutional right not to have her bodily integrity compromised by a teacher's sexual abuse."[24] Female bodily autonomy is clearly not a priority for Justice Jones, and this makes her the perfect appellate judge for the anti-choice movement's challenge to the ultrasound law.

In the ruling, Jones said that if states can require abortion providers to give women illustrated pamphlets showing the development of the fetus, then, as long as the information is "truthful and non-misleading," they should be able to "empower" women with even better, more specific and technologically advanced imaging. Jones held that a sonogram image was the "epitome" of truthful information, even if it is more graphic than the pamphlets showing the development of fetuses that *Casey* approved. "Only if one assumes the conclusion of Appellees' argument, that pregnancy is a condition to be terminated, can one assume that such information about the fetus is medically irrelevant," Jones held. "The point of informed consent laws is to allow the patient to evaluate her condition and render her best decision under difficult circumstances. Denying her up to date medical information is more of an abuse to her ability to decide than providing the information."[25]

While Jones considered the ultrasound "empowering" for women, the Center for Reproductive Rights disagreed. "The Texas law was addressing a problem that didn't exist because women always had the option to view an ultrasound before obtaining their abortions if they wanted to," said Michelle Movahed. "What the Texas law did was remove the agency from the women and put it in the hands of the state. So it says, 'You are not smart enough to make the choice yourself about whether you should see the ultrasound. We've decided for you.' If it was about empowering women, you would support all sorts of choices."[26] While Jones and her colleagues on the three-judge panel may have ruled mandatory ultrasounds as "reasonable" and "empowering" to women, for providers it was a clear violation of medical best practices. Dr. Curtis Boyd, who has been providing abortions under the new mandatory ultrasound law, describes the dilemma abortion providers now face in caring for patients. "The state-mandated information is part of informing the patient. Well, some of this information is erroneous. Some of it is exaggerated or inaccurate and some of it is just out-and-out wrong but we're required to give it," he said, speaking to warnings that abortion will increase the risk for suicide, breast cancer, cause future fertility issues, or a myriad of other medical issues that have been alleged by abortion opponents.[27] "You have the state intervening and mandating to doctors that they give specific information to their patient, which the doctor of medicine in general may not agree with and may in fact clearly disagree with. Yet the state says, 'If you don't do this, you're subject to losing your medical license.' So I have to do it. Well, you say don't do it if it's unethical. But if I don't and I provide the service, I'm subject to having my license revoked and having a felony filed against me. In fact, I am coerced just as a woman is."[28]

As the Texas challenge was snaking its way through the Fifth Circuit, one from North Carolina was simultaneously working through the Fourth Circuit Court of Appeals. Under North

Carolina's ultrasound law, a doctor must perform an ultrasound on a woman seeking an abortion and then display the images to her, noting "the presence, location, and dimensions of the unborn child" and describing "external members and internal organs, if present and viewable." Several North Carolina doctors and health care providers challenged the constitutionality of the law in *Stuart v. Huff*.

Judge Catherine Eagles of the U.S. District Court for the Middle District of North Carolina preliminarily enjoined the "speech-and-display requirements" of the law, as she called them. "The First Amendment," she wrote, "generally includes the right to refuse to engage in speech compelled by the government." The North Carolina ultrasound law required speech via words and imagery, "even when the provider does not want to deliver the message and even when the patients affirmatively do not wish to see it or hear it," Eagles said. She also found "no medical purpose" in the speech-and-display requirements. While some procedural issues are under appeal, a trial challenging the merits of the law is set for 2013. If the Fourth Circuit breaks with the Fifth and agrees with Judge Eagles that the law infringes on doctors' speech rights, it's very likely the Supreme Court will step in and settle the dispute.

If it comes to that, it won't be the first time the Supreme Court has weighed in on the balance of rights between state restrictions on abortions and a doctor's speech rights in the practice of medicine. In *Bigelow v. Virginia* (1975), the court ruled that the First Amendment protects abortion advertisements and that states can't prevent publishers from running ads for abortion services. Jeffrey Bigelow, editor of *The Virginia Weekly*, had published an ad for a New York agency offering to connect women in Virginia (where at the time abortion law was more restrictive) with doctors in New York (where abortion law was more permissive). He was convicted under a Virginia law that made it a crime to "encourage or prompt the procuring of abortion." Bigelow filed suit claiming the law violated his First Amendment right to free speech. The Supreme Court overturned his conviction, noting that the First Amendment gives some protection even to commercial speech, concluding that the abortion ad was entitled to protection because it promoted services that were legal in New York and contained information of "constitutional interest" to the general public.[29]

The court later took up the specific issue of regulating doctors' speech and First Amendment rights in *Casey*, finding that legislatures can mandate doctors to provide "truthful, nonmisleading information about the nature of the procedure, the attendant health risks and those of childbirth, and the 'probable gestational age' of the fetus" in a way that prevents the compelling of speech.[30] But while it dealt with the issue generally, the Supreme Court did not address what level of scrutiny courts must employ when analyzing speech claims such as these, therefore leaving open the question of just how specifically legislatures can script medical disclosures in the name of restricting access to abortion.

Compelled speech or not, some doctors are still searching for a way to balance the rights of patients to get accurate information with the state's decision to press a script on doctors. Dr. Boyd has his own way of reconciling the two—he provides the state script, then adds his own thoughts at the end of it. "Sometimes I wonder what would happen if the state wanted to make an issue of it," Boyd mused. "You know: 'We've already told you what you must say; now you can't say. . . .' I don't know. They can't rule that I can't have an opinion. They have sort of ruled what my opinion must be to the patient but it doesn't say clearly you can't tell the patient you think something differently. So I do it. I think, 'Well, they'll just have to take me to court.' There's just a limit to how far they can go. I have to salvage my integrity somehow. So I say, 'This is what the state wants me to tell you, and my own belief is that abortion does not cause breast cancer,' and so forth—and that you are quite ethically competent to make this decision. I respect your decision-making process. I've given you the decision-making process the state wants you to follow."

For abortion opponents trying either to coerce pregnant women into continuing their pregnancies or to provoke a Supreme Court challenge that could overturn *Roe*, the Texas and Oklahoma situations couldn't have turned out much better. But for those who have actually had to undergo the mandatory ultrasound, it's a far different story. Reporter Carolyn Jones wrote about her own brush with the ultrasound bill in Texas, after learning that the baby she had carried for twenty weeks had a terminal anomaly and was unlikely to survive past birth. Although she technically should have been exempt from the verbal description and waiting period portion of the bill, providers were so confused at that point as to what was and wasn't legally necessary that she became subject to it anyway.

In an article in the *Texas Observer*, Jones explained the horror of being forced to listen to a description of the fetus, while her doctor apologized for his part in her suffering. He didn't want to give her this information, but his hands were tied. It was the law.

> "I'm so sorry that I have to do this," the doctor told us, "but if I don't, I can lose my license." Before he could even start to describe our baby, I began to sob until I could barely breathe. Somewhere, a nurse cranked up the volume on a radio, allowing the inane pronouncements of a DJ to dull the doctor's voice. Still, despite the noise, I heard him. His unwelcome words echoed off sterile walls while I, trapped on a bed, my feet in stirrups, twisted away from his voice. "Here I see a well-developed diaphragm and here I see four healthy chambers of the heart . . ." I closed my eyes and waited for it to end, as one waits for the car to stop rolling at the end of a terrible accident.[31]

Her ultrasound ended, and like nearly all women forced into mandatory ultrasounds, Jones had her termination. No matter how many times this monster comes back to life, pro-choice forces will have to do battle against it, until they finally kill it off once and for all.

7. SOUTH DAKOTA: COME FOR THE ABORTION, STAY FOR THE CONVERSION TO CHRISTIANITY

As the spokeswoman for Abstinence Clearinghouse, a South Dakota–based organization that "promotes the appreciation for and practice of sexual abstinence through distribution of age-appropriate, factual and medically accurate materials," Leslee Unruh believed it was her crusade to spread the gospel of abstinence until marriage, as well as to tell the world that pornography, homosexuality and masturbation were harmful to the person engaging in these activities.

But if Abstinence Clearinghouse and abstinence-only education were Unruh's crusade, it was her pregnancy center, the Alpha Center, that was her kingdom. Opened in 1984, the Alpha Center was where Unruh tended to women who had unexpectedly become pregnant, allowing her access to potential souls to save, babies to bring into the world, and financial profit, too. However, in 1987, the Alpha Center was accused of offering potential mothers money to continue their pregnancies and then give their babies up for adoption after they were born. The center was charged with twenty-four counts of unlicensed adoption and foster care practice as well as false advertising, although most of the charges were dismissed after Unruh pled no contest to five counts and paid a $500 fine.[1]

Despite this, the Alpha Center lived on, providing support for women who wanted to give birth to their unplanned babies while also trying to coax and in some cases trick women who believed they had entered a place where they could obtain an abortion into not terminating their pregnancies. Business was good, as the organization received $2 million in taxpayer dollars between 2004 and 2009 for their abstinence-only sex education programs.[2] Unruh had turned abstinence into a profitable enterprise. And while she had long been highly involved in lobbying for abortion restrictions in the state of South Dakota, once the state attempted to ban abortion altogether, she became even more engrossed in legislative efforts.

Though a total ban on abortion in South Dakota had failed in 2006, pro-life activists in the state tried once again in 2008, with Unruh spearheading the "Vote Yes for Life" campaign, which aimed to ban almost all abortions, though it allowed narrow exceptions for pregnancies resulting from rape or incest or that threatened the life of the mother. When asked why she was pushing a ban two just two years after the voters had rejected one, Unruh explained, "I don't think they gave their final word."[3] The voters disagreed with her again, as the ban was voted down, and abortion opponents were forced to look for a new restriction that would be more palatable to the general public.

To the rescue came state representative Roger Hunt. In 2011, Hunt proposed HB 1217, a bill he said would ensure that a woman's choice to terminate a pregnancy was "voluntary, uncoerced, and informed."[4] The "coerced abortion" idea was a favorite of Hunt's, a rabid opponent of women's right to choose. For example, he had been very vocal in explaining why exceptions for rape, incest and health were left out of the 2006 total abortion ban: women lie. In an interview with *Time* magazine, Hunt explained that if a woman really was raped, she could go to the hospital and take emergency contraception the night of the attack. In that instance, using emergency contraception (which he seemed to believe caused an abortion, too) would be justified. But if the state allowed a general exception for rape, how could it know a woman wasn't just claiming to have been raped in order to obtain a pregnancy termination?

So why not have an exemption for all rape victims, including the ones who are too shattered to report an assault right away? Hunt calls it "a fine line that we're walking, but some of this is just to show that we're being fair and reasonable. In cases where we cannot determine if there's an unborn child or not, we're trying to be sympathetic to a woman who alleges she's been raped." But the sympathy expires after about a week. Very honestly, Hunt adds, "We don't want to have a lot of abortion clinics questioning a woman and having the woman say 'well, I was raped four months ago, I need an abortion.' We're trying to be sensitive to women who are legitimate rape victims—and not give abortion clinics a chance to commit fraud on the system.[5]

As for coercion, Hunt believed that almost every woman considering abortion was being pressured by someone. "She may be dealing with a lot of pressure, from family, boyfriend, husband. We have a situation in which the woman may be getting so much pressure she's not thinking clearly," Hunt told *Time*.[6]

Hunt's proposed bill would stretch the state's mandatory twenty-four-hour waiting period between the woman's meeting with a doctor and the abortion to three days. It would also compel a face-to-face meeting with a doctor, which would add an additional in-person visit for women to the state's only clinic, located in Sioux Falls. On its own, changing the waiting period from one to three days was a huge issue for a state that had exactly one abortion clinic. According to Alisha Sedor, executive director of NARAL Pro-Choice South Dakota, the Sioux Falls clinic is convenient for the large number of state residents who live in the area, but for the rest of South Dakotans, it's often easier to leave the state altogether. "While this is the largest metropolis in the state, there are women that live in Rapid City, which is five hours away. If they were interested in accessing abortion services in South Dakota they'd have to drive ten hours round trip, and if this law goes into effect they would have to do that potentially three times. So that's quite a bit of road time. There are certainly a number of women who leave the state just because it's easier, less travel, and less hoops to jump through in order to obtain services."[7]

Though forcing women to travel as much as ten hours to access abortion care was obviously fine with South Dakota legislators like Roger Hunt, it would be a great hardship for the rural poor of the state. "Obviously women who are low income and live in rural areas, they have to travel further and spend more," said Sedor. "If you don't have the resources to do that, then you don't have access to services at all, if you can't access the funds to travel to Sioux Falls or out of state." The most likely group to be impacted by an extended waiting period would be women who lived on South Dakota's Indian reservations, where health care access was already difficult to obtain. "Anecdotally, I think that women on the reservation, Native women, are impacted more so than others because the reservations are located in some of the poorest counties in the country," Sedor added. "Not only do they lack resources but also information and there's very little access to services on the reservation. That is extremely problematic from our point of view because you're impacting minority and low-income women more than anyone else."

Lakota reproductive rights activist Sunny Clifford was well aware of the problems the Native American community in the state already had in accessing family planning and women's health care. "Women on the Pine Ridge Reservation face great distances between their homes and clinics," said Clifford, a Pine Ridge resident and board member for NARAL Pro-Choice South Dakota. "Some women are fortunate enough to live near the hospital or clinics, but there are some who must find a way to travel up to sixty miles, one way. Not everybody on the reservation owns a vehicle and if there is vehicular access then they must find the gas money, which isn't always there. We do have a public transit system and a lot of people utilize that, but access is only on weekdays. Also, clinics and access to the women's health clinic is only available on certain days of the week."[8] Add in a seventy-two-hour waiting period and accessing abortion would become nearly impossible for the women of the community. "Let's say a woman from the reservation is seeking an abortion. If the woman is from Pine Ridge Reservation she has to find a way to get to Sioux Falls, which is a five-hour trip. She's already on a time limit. Then, when she gets there, she must go through mandatory counseling and then wait seventy-two hours and in the meantime provide herself lodging when she probably barely had enough money just to make it to Sioux Falls. The seventy-two-hour wait places unnecessary struggles on Native American women with little money and little time. What if by trying to get enough money she was then running up against the legal limit to have an abortion? Those additional seventy-two hours could very well make her ineligible."

While the extended wait time and additional travel expenses were a problem, it was the bill's other requirement that really got women's and civil rights supporters up in arms. Under HB 1217, as part of the new standard for pre-abortion care, a woman would be forced to enter a crisis pregnancy center and allow the volunteers there to try to talk her out of terminating her pregnancy. According to the bill:

> Prior to the day of any scheduled abortion the pregnant mother must have a consultation at a pregnancy help center at which the pregnancy help center shall inform her about what education, counseling, and other assistance is available to help the pregnant mother keep and care for her child, and have a private interview to discuss her circumstances that may subject her decision to coercion. That prior to signing a consent to an abortion, the physician shall first obtain from the pregnant mother, a written statement that she obtained a consultation with

a pregnancy help center, which sets forth the name and address of the pregnancy help center, the date and time of the consultation, and the name of the counselor at the pregnancy help center with whom she consulted.[9]

If there was any doubt that the intent of the bill was to ensure that women were talked out of their decision to have an abortion, it was dispelled by the bill's definition of a "pregnancy help center":

> The pregnancy help center has a facility or office in the state of South Dakota in which it routinely consults with women for the purpose of helping them keep their relationship with their unborn children; that one of its principal missions is to educate, counsel, and otherwise assist women to help them maintain their relationship with their unborn children; that they do not perform abortions at their facility, and have no affiliation with any organization or physician which performs abortions; that they do not now refer pregnant women for abortions, and have not referred any pregnant women for an abortion at any time in the three years immediately preceding July 1, 2011.[10]

The greatest concern for activists in South Dakota was that under the guise of making sure a woman wasn't being coerced into having an abortion, pregnancy centers would instead be acting to coerce her out of one. "Often crisis pregnancy centers are religiously affiliated, they are explicitly anti-choice and their sole goal is to talk women out of seeking services," said Sedor. "In some cases it's abortions and in others it's abortion and birth control and anything else that has to do with healthy sexuality. In this case, I think that this legislation was brought with hope that, if women are forced to walk in the door of these places, that they will be able to inundate them with anti-choice rhetoric and talk them out of seeking the services that they are looking to find. It also left these crisis pregnancy centers relatively unregulated in what they can and can't say to women. So there's nothing to say that they just can't out and out lie. Our fear is that, while this legislation talks about women who are coerced into abortions, that their goal is to actually coerce women out of having them even if that's a decision that's right for them and their family."

By mandating that the pregnancy center "counselors" could discuss religion with a client only if she first signed a form in agreement, the bill did make it clear that the counselors wouldn't be conducting religious conversions while doing their evaluations. Still, there was no doubt that under the bill, women seeking terminations would be forced into dealing with faith-based organizations. As Allen Unruh, Leslee Unruh's husband and co-founder of the Alpha Center, explained, the "entire Alpha Center story was inspired by God, and the rising up of godly people with courage to be salt and light; to take action against the most evil act in this generation—the killing of innocent unborn babies and the deliberate deception of millions of women."[11]

Planned Parenthood condemned HB 1217 as a bill designed to force women to discuss basic medical care with a person who had no medical background. "This bill, the first of its kind in the nation, would require women in some of the most difficult circumstances, including victims of rape and incest and mothers facing serious complications, to get permission for a legal medical procedure from an unregulated agency staffed by untrained volunteers," stated Sarah Stoesz, CEO of Planned Parenthood Minnesota, North Dakota, South Dakota. "It's outrageous that the state would mandate that a woman must seek permission from so-called crisis pregnancy centers, which are not legitimate medical facilities, before she could access safe, legal abortion care from her doctor."[12]

The crisis pregnancy centers wouldn't just be granting permission, either, as Alisha Sedor explained. The centers would also keep personal and contact information on every woman in the state seeking an abortion. Although an updated version of HB 1217 required that such information be kept confidential, it still provided no penalties if the center did not. "There is nothing that can be done if, let's say, that information was released," said Sedor. "It also just says that they can't release the information; it doesn't say what they can't do with it themselves. So they certainly can continue to reach out to these women and you can just imagine a slew of ways in which they harass and shame these women out of receiving services. It's certainly scary, an explicitly anti-choice organization in the middle of a woman and her physician as she's trying to obtain these completely legal services."

The bill angered not just the standard reproductive rights advocates but civil rights groups as well. Americans United, a group committed to the separation of church and state, was concerned that the state might in fact be legislating religion on top of violating the right to medical privacy. "There has been some talk about challenging this provision of South Dakota's law in court," wrote Rob Boston of Americans United. "I hope that happens. I also hope it is struck down as a violation of the fundamental right of conscience."[13] The South Dakota chapter of the American Civil Liberties Union vowed to fight the bill in court if it was ever signed into law, joining Planned Parenthood.

If the opposition from these two groups was to be expected, opposition from another corner was much more surprising: many pregnancy centers were also against the bill. Some worried that providing a woman with verification that she had met with them would make them complicit in the abortion itself. "We are not here to talk women into or out of anything. We are here to make it possible for women to carry to term if that's what they want to do in their heart of hearts," Bella Pregnancy Center executive director Roxanne Johnson told the *Rapid City Journal*. "Because I have seen firsthand the devastation that abortion has caused many women and families, I would have a difficult time providing any statement that would assist or facilitate an abortion."[14] Leslee Unruh seemed less concerned, saying that the centers weren't complicit since the patient could always lie. "The woman can walk in the door and walk out without talking to anybody and say she was there. It's an honor system."[15]

Anti-abortion activists like Unruh may have been ready to move on the bill, but South Dakota's Republican governor, Dennis Daugaard, wasn't quite so anxious. The state had already incurred hundreds of thousands of dollars in legal fees from defending other abortion restrictions that had been passed and then blocked by the courts, and if it lost the fight over HB 1217, it would again be responsible for paying the plaintiff's legal bills. South Dakota had already paid about $500,000 to Planned Parenthood for legal fees in prior years, and Daugaard didn't want to run up another tab. As a result, nearly two weeks went by after the passage of the bill before he finally signed it into law. The governor gave no interviews but said in a statement, "I hope that women who are considering an abortion will use this three-day period to make good choices."[16]

The reason for the lag between the bill's passage and Daugaard's signature was that the governor was unwilling to sign until he knew who was going to pay for the litigation that would inevitably come. Once again, Representative Roger Hunt came to the rescue. If Daugaard signed the bill, Hunt promised, he would solicit donations to a legal fund the state could use to pay for the expected litigation. "They want to put their money where their mouth is in the sense of protecting unborn children," Hunt said of the donations his group received.[17] Lawmakers, even Republican ones, however, were less excited by the prospect of anonymous or outside donors paying for the state's legal expenditures. "Either the state of South Dakota believes as a matter of policy that this is what we do and we pay for it or we don't," said Senator Joni Cutler, a Republican from Minnehaha County. "When we open the door for outsiders to come in and pay for it, that's just bad. When we're using the state's resources to litigate private matters just because someone claims someone else is going to drop a coin into a bucket, that's just bad government."[18]

Ultimately, some money flowed into the fund, but not a great amount. In the week between Hunt's pledge to solicit donors and Daugaard's signing of the bill on March 28, 2011, the fund gained about $15,000. Most of the money came from small pledges, though a few bigger donations came from people who were actively involved with Leslee Unruh's "Vote Yes" campaign. A donation of $2,500 came from the Gerard Health Foundation, best known for funding Lila Rose's Live Action and their inaccurate attack videos attempting to discredit, defund and otherwise shut down Planned Parenthood.[19] Most interesting were two small donations. One, a twenty-dollar anonymous donation, was a reminder that there was no requirement to disclose where the money came from, as is the case with campaign donations. Another hundred dollars came from Allen Unruh, Leslee's husband and co-founder of the Alpha Center.[20]

Planned Parenthood Minnesota, North Dakota, South Dakota and the ACLU both followed through on their promise to challenge HB 1217. There are two ways to challenge abortion laws like these: on their face, or as they are applied. Facial challenges usually carry a more difficult burden because the plaintiffs have to show that in a "large fraction" of the cases in which the relevant law would be applied, a substantial obstacle to a woman's decision to undergo an abortion would be present. However, to challenge as applied would mean waiting until after the law had gone into effect.

Not wanting women to be forced to violate their privacy and civil rights in order to terminate a pregnancy, Planned Parenthood and the ACLU had no choice but to challenge the law on its face. The two groups filed suit on May 27, 2011, blocking the bill well before its scheduled start date of July 1. "The act has both the purpose and the effect of severely restricting access to health care, and violates patients' and physicians' First Amendment rights against compelled speech and patients' right to privacy in their personal and medical information," said Planned Parenthood attorney Mimi Liu when announcing the suit.[21]

For his part, Roger Hunt couldn't comprehend what all the fuss was about. "I don't understand why [they are suing], because it just seeks to give women more information and it seeks to remove coercion, seeks to deal with a number of coercion elements where you have possible rapes and problems within families and whatnot, and we're trying to help those women deal with that coercion," he told the Associated Press. "All of that seems to me to be in support of women, but for some reason Planned Parenthood sees their money supply and the abortions being dried up so obviously they're going to fight."[22]

Hunt may not have understood the lawsuit, but U.S. District Court Chief Judge Karen Schreier certainly did. She ruled that the law would remain blocked, and that compelling women to visit pregnancy centers was likely unconstitutional: "Forcing a woman to divulge to a stranger at a pregnancy help center the fact that she has chosen to undergo an abortion humiliates and degrades her as a human being. The woman will feel degraded by the compulsive nature of the Pregnancy Help Center requirements, which suggest that she has made the 'wrong' decision, has not really 'thought' about her decision to undergo an abortion, or is 'not intelligent enough' to make the decision with the advice of a physician. Furthermore, these women are forced into a hostile environment."[23]

Following Schreier's ruling, the Alpha Center and another South Dakota pregnancy center successfully sued to intervene in the case. Their reasoning was that because there were approximately 700 abortions performed yearly in South Dakota, they could be denied access to that many clients by the Planned Parenthood suit.[24] Much as Jennie Linn McCormack's lawyer, Richard Hearn, had intervened on her behalf in Idaho as a physician who could potentially provide care and be affected by the abortion ban he was challenging, the pregnancy centers had decided to step in as a new type of "provider" that could intervene on behalf of pregnant women as potential patients. Once more, the definition of a provider and medical entity was being turned on its head.

The challenge to HB 1217 raised a series of important issues in the clash between reproductive rights and the practice of medicine. At the heart of the case was the issue of informed consent. According to *Planned Parenthood v. Casey*, because an informed consent requirement must "facilitate the wise exercise" of a woman's right to abortion, such a requirement presents an undue burden unless it provides "truthful and not misleading" information.[25] The legal principle seems simple and straightforward: if government is going to mandate that doctors disclose certain information to women in the course of rendering medical treatment, that information must be truthful. But since *Gonzales v. Carhart* declared that legislatures can craft law in areas where there is no medical consensus, then what does it mean to have a "truthful" disclosure? This question would presumably coalesce with medical standards of care in treating pregnant women. But that hasn't been the case, in large part because of the impact of the *Gonzales* decision and a shift in the courts to deferring to legislators over doctors when dictating what information a woman needs to know prior to making the decision to abort.

The legal battle over the contours of "informed consent" and "truth" as determined by anti-choice legislatures dates back to 2005 and initial legal challenges to a previous South Dakota informed consent law that stated that physicians, before performing an abortion, were required to read to their patients various state-mandated disclosures that included medically inaccurate information about the risk factors of the procedure.[26] After several challenges at the district court level, in 2009 the Eighth Circuit Court of Appeals ruled that the portion of the informed consent law that required doctors to disclose a link between abortion and an increased risk of suicide—a link rejected by nearly the entire medical community—was unconstitutional because it unduly burdened a woman's right to choose abortion, in addition to violating doctors' First Amendment right to be free from state-compelled speech.[27] When rendering its decision, the court addressed this tension between mandated disclosures and medical standards of care, noting that common law duties of care that doctors owe patients already dictate what should and should not be disclosed in the course of treatment. Therefore, the specific requirement of the law that doctors disclose a heightened risk of suicide or suicide ideation was unnecessary.

But if medical standards of care made these specific state-mandated disclosures unnecessary, the fact that the medical community did not generally recognize a causal connection between suicide and abortion made the risk of misleading women out of getting an abortion very real. "Legislatures have 'wide discretion to pass legislation in areas where there is medical and scientific uncertainty,'" the court held, "but the suicide advisory asserts certainty on the issue of medical and scientific knowledge where none exists."[28] The court didn't stop there: "The required suicide advisory would significantly constrain doctors' exercise of their professional judgment. South Dakota common law already requires doctors to inform patients of all the known material or significant risks of a medical procedure. Thus, if a doctor considers suicide a known material risk of abortion, there is a common law duty to warn patients."

It is the focus on whether the content of the statement is truthful that is important here. According to the state of South Dakota and the proponents of this mandated disclosure, the connection between abortion and suicide ideation and risk was the truth, despite the fact that the professional medical community disagreed. In the battle of medical testimony, anti-abortion advocates came up short, according to the court:

> The record does not demonstrate a generally recognized causal connection between abortion and suicide. In fact, it reveals vigorous debate over whether an apparent statistical correlation results from common cofactors rather than a showing that one causes the other. In the course of evaluating relevant peer reviewed literature, the American Psychological Association concluded that there is no evidence that risk of mental health problems among women who abort unwanted pregnancies is any greater than that of women who miscarry or deliver such pregnancies.

It was on this point that pro-choice advocates thought they had scored a major victory. Despite the latitude an abortion-hostile Supreme Court had granted state legislatures in crafting anti-abortion regulations, they did not have license to lie to women. Or they didn't until July 24, 2012, when the Eighth Circuit Court of Appeals, in the case of *Planned Parenthood v. Rounds*, ruled that they did. In a ruling that fully reversed the earlier decision, a panel of conservative justices all appointed by Ronald Reagan held that the suicide disclosure was, in effect, not a lie, and that doctors must tell women they run an increased risk of suicide after having an abortion because that information will "help" women make an informed decision regarding their medical care.[29]

The *Rounds* decision over informed consent and compelled disclosure illustrates the very damaging effect of the *Gonzales* decision. When there is a battle over scientific evidence to support a proposed medical regulation like disclosure of an abortion-suicide link, state legislatures are free to choose which evidence they believe and courts must defer to that choice, even if there is a mountain of evidence to the contrary. "Based on the record, the studies submitted by the State are sufficiently reliable to support the truth of the proposition that the relative risk of suicide and suicide ideation is higher for women who abort their pregnancies compared to women who give birth or have not become pregnant," the *Rounds* ruling declared.[30] It didn't matter that the journal articles cited as evidence to support the alleged causation between abortion and suicide had been discredited by further research, or that no one had been able to replicate the original study's findings. In fact, the article was believed to be so fatally flawed that the journal that had published it was considering retracting it altogether.[31] The Supreme Court in *Gonzales* had given the Eighth Circuit the cover it needed when it ruled that nothing prevented legislatures like South Dakota's from coming up with new, stricter definitions of medical risk in the context of restricting access to abortion. Basically, the court ruled that in order to render the suicide advisory unconstitutionally misleading or irrelevant, Planned Parenthood would have had to show that abortion had been ruled out, to a degree of scientifically accepted certainty, as a statistically significant causal factor in post-abortion suicides. And Planned Parenthood would have had to make this showing of "scientifically accepted certainty" despite the fact that such a degree of certainty is not required to justify the disclosure in the first place. Simply put, in South Dakota, when legislating against reproductive rights, abortion restrictions didn't need to be supported to a medical degree of certainty, but challenges to those restrictions did.

Even before becoming the law of the land in South Dakota, HB 1217 had an effect on the laws of other states. In May 2012, the state of Utah decided to pass a similar bill. The only difference was that Utah left out the requirement that a woman first visit a crisis pregnancy center for an evaluation. Apparently that one change made all the difference, as the bill was approved by the Utah house and senate and received the governor's signature. Reproductive health centers decided that rather than go straight to a court challenge, they would evaluate the effects of the three-day wait and decide whether it was worth the risk of initiating a court case that could easily turn in the state's favor and set a precedent that would encourage other anti-abortion states to enact the same restriction.

Within a few months of Utah's new three-day waiting period going into effect, it became clear that if the bill was meant to deter women from having abortions, it wasn't working, as the rate of women seeking terminations was basically unchanged. Other than eliciting resignation that the state had placed another hurdle to accessing abortion and provoking anger that the government was intruding on women's personal medical decisions, the law had little practical effect. According to Heather Stringfellow, vice president of public policy for the Planned Parenthood Action Council of Utah, doctors stated that "the law really hasn't changed anything. We are still providing abortions in a similar number to what we were prior to the law. We don't see people not returning more often. Women still make their decisions before they come in for the consultation before the abortion. Most people just kind of take it in stride," said Stringfellow. "There have been a handful of women and partners who have been very dismayed and upset by having to wait for three days. There have been a handful of people who have been pretty traumatized by the affair. But few people are surprised that there are all these hoops they have to jump through."[32]

Could the fact that the extended wait period has no power to change a woman's mind potentially support the state of South Dakota's stance that HB 1217 does not represent an undue burden under *Casey*? That concern may have been behind Planned Parenthood's decision to discontinue their full challenge of the bill. In December 2012, Sarah Stoesz, President and CEO of Planned Parenthood Minnesota, North Dakota, South Dakota announced that the organization would request that their challenge to the seventy-two-hour waiting period associated with the bill be dropped, with resources to be redirected to the mandatory crisis pregnancy center visit portion of the bill. "Currently, we are focusing our energy and resources on fighting the most egregious part of this law—the Crisis Pregnancy Center requirement," Stoesz said in a statement. "We still believe the 72-hour waiting period provision of this law is unconstitutional and an example of politicians interfering in the medical care of women. However, we have found a way to implement this provision while minimizing the negative effects for our patients."[33] Planned Parenthood asked for the challenge to be dropped "with prejudice," meaning that it would reserve the right to challenge again down the road if circumstances changed. Either way, the mandatory crisis pregnancy center visit would continue to be litigated—and blocked.

By dropping the challenge to the waiting period, however, Planned Parenthood provided abortion opponents with just the precedent they needed to consider passing similar super-size waits in other low-access states. There was little doubt that another state would follow South Dakota and Utah's lead. The only question was which state would do it first.

8. WASHINGTON, DC: TUG OF WAR, MEDICAID-STYLE

As a quirk of being the nation's capitol, Washington, DC, has little control over its own budget and laws, and what control it does have is granted by the U.S. Congress. However, when James Madison decided that Congress should have ultimate decision-making power when it came to legislating on the city's behalf, he likely never realized what a coup it would become for those who want to limit a woman's access to a full spectrum of reproductive health care services.

The fight over a woman's right to choose reached a fever pitch in Washington, DC, in 2012, when the U.S. House of Representatives proposed numerous bills that would directly affect abortion laws in the city. In essence, conservative legislators had decided to treat the city as a microcosm of what abortion opponents wanted to do across the country, if provided with enough freedom. The most controversial bill was Arizona representative Trent Franks's attempt to block the city from allowing any abortions after the fetus reached twenty weeks—a version of the 2010 "fetal pain" bill that had been passed in Nebraska. Since no one had challenged the Nebraska law, and it had passed in other states as well, Franks stated in a press release that it was a constitutionally sound law that should also be passed in DC.[1]

Women's rights advocates and medical professionals disagreed. DC's congressional delegate, Eleanor Holmes Norton, argued that if the bill were so sound, Franks and his cohorts would pass a federal version instead. "Why wouldn't they put this bill in for the entire country if they feel so deeply about it?" Norton asked the *Huffington Post*. "The reason is that they're bullies, so they know that you pick on the district whose member cannot vote on the House floor, you pick on the member who does not have any senators to protect her, and maybe you can get somewhere."[2]

It seemed Holmes had a point, as Franks had proposed the same restrictions when he was in the Arizona House of Representatives in the mid-1980s and they had failed to pass. Gloria Feldt, the former president of Planned Parenthood, recalled that it was the constant pressure from women's rights activists in the state that had kept Franks's attempts to limit a woman's right to choose in check. "In Arizona we had done things like defeating a ballot initiative that would have outlawed most abortions, all except rape and incest, by the largest percentage that has ever happened to defeat a ballot initiative in the state," Feldt recalled. "We had gotten rid of Trent Franks, who is now back in Congress proposing the same legislation that he tried to get passed in Arizona that he couldn't."[3] Abortion activists were just as anxious to keep Franks in check in DC, but without the ability to vote him out of office, it was hard to have much impact.

The right to an abortion has been a tug-of-war issue ever since *Roe v. Wade* was passed in 1973, especially for women who are poor and lack health insurance. In many ways, Washington, DC, is an ideal barometer of this back-and-forth. For the past four decades, for example, whenever the Republican Party has had control of the U.S. House of Representatives, it has voted to ban Washington, DC, from using Medicaid funds to pay for abortions for women in poverty. Whenever Democrats have regained control of the House, the ban has been repealed and Medicaid abortions allowed again. This pattern has continued into the Obama administration. In July 2009, because Democrats controlled the White House, Senate and House, Washington, DC, was allowed to use its own Medicaid funding to assist low-income women in obtaining abortions.

Marcia D. Greenberger, co-president of the National Women's Law Center, explained that allowing DC to fund abortions for the poor is a matter of social justice and equality. "Restrictions on public funding for abortion disproportionately affect women of color, a quarter of whom in DC are living in poverty and are more likely to rely on public funding for basic medical services," Greenberger said. "The time needed to save money, if indeed they even can, often results in poor women experiencing delays in obtaining an abortion. The greater the delay in obtaining an abortion, the less safe the procedure becomes. Those women who are unable to secure the funds can be denied affordable services altogether."[4]

Following the 2010 midterm elections, Democrats lost their majority in the House and the DC Medicaid abortion funding ban returned.* This time the ban was reinstated as a condition in last-minute negotiations to prevent a potential government shutdown caused by a congressional impasse over a new budget. House Republicans, feeling emboldened by their transition from minority to majority, as well as a wave of victories across the country that had turned multiple legislative bodies and even entire states to Republican control, roadblocked the passage of a continuing resolution that would have provided additional funding for the daily operations of the government. Their original asking price to keep the government afloat was the complete elimination of all Title X family planning funding. In this case, the Democrats held strong and refused to allow money for contraceptives, health screenings and treatment for sexually transmitted infections to be eliminated, as this would have left the poor without quality care. The House Republicans then modified their request: they would leave in place family planning for the

---

*The ban is not automatic but enacting it is usually one of the first things Republicans do when they take over the House, either by introducing it as a standalone bill or tacking it on to some other bill.

poor in the rest of the country, but in exchange, Washington, DC, would once again have to give up their local funding of abortion for women who lacked financial means.

Congresswoman Norton tried to stop the ban before it could be enacted. Prior to the final deliberations, she sent a letter to President Obama urging him not to let the poor women of Washington, DC, be used as pawns. "It would be unacceptable to use the District's low income women as a bargaining chip at a time when women's rights advocates and the District have been particularly focused on protecting the city from a return to this restriction," she wrote.

"District residents, women's rights advocates and the entire civil rights community worked too hard to remove all D.C. riders while Democrats controlled Congress to have their efforts immediately turned around at the insistence of House Republicans."[5] However, the president and congressional Democrats yielded to the Republicans and the ban was put back in place as part of the final continuing resolution budget deal passed on April 8, 2011. Norton was livid. "It looks to me that we were easy enough to throw under a bus, and that's where we landed," she told the *New York Times*. "The district becomes a sitting duck."[6]

The last-minute rider left women who already had Medicaid abortions scheduled in a dire situation. The clinics that had previously scheduled procedures were surprised to learn that the ban was going into effect immediately and that as of Wednesday, April 13, at midnight, Medicaid would no longer cover terminations. "Tonight we received an urgent call from a partner clinic to notify us that DC Medicaid is ending its coverage of abortions at MIDNIGHT TONIGHT," the DC Abortion Fund (DCAF) wrote on its webpage. "The clinic had to call 28 women who are scheduled tomorrow and bringing their DC Medicaid as payment that they need to fundraise for the total cost of their procedure by their appointment tomorrow because Medicaid will no longer cover the cost of their abortion. These women are devastated."

Val Vilott, board president of DCAF, vividly remembers the panicked call she received from the clinic once it learned that insurance would no longer cover the remaining payments for the more than two dozen women who would be having second-trimester terminations the following morning. The total cost was likely to run $1500 per woman. "The clinic was trying to find out if they needed to tell these women to reschedule or if they could raise the money," recalled Vilott. "Postponing the procedure would mean that the cost would go up. The cost was already a barrier for these women, and now it was about to become an increasingly tall one."[7]

The DCAF board took an emergency vote and agreed to cover the difference between the cost of the abortions and what the women could afford to pay. As a result, DCAF had to fundraise to try to regain all of the emergency funding it had provided. "We needed to combat the hit to our own finances," explained Vilott. "To fund twenty-eight patients in one day is not something that is typically a part of our process. Normally we have a very strict and regimented budget that we work with and per-patient caps based on the term of the pregnancy. This broke away from our system altogether." With the help of its email and social networks, DCAF was able to raise the money it needed to recoup the costs of the last-minute blow to its already stretched budget. But although those twenty-eight women were able to have their procedures, other women who had intended to use Medicaid to pay for their abortions were left on their own financially.

Only fifteen states in the country currently allow Medicaid to pay for abortions in most instances, rather than just in cases of rape, incest, or medical necessity. For those states, allowing terminations to be covered by Medicaid is a civil rights issue. In Minnesota, for example, the State Supreme Court ruled in 1995 in the case of *Doe v. Gomez* that since a woman had a legal right to an abortion, abortion services must be paid for via Medicaid in situations where the woman didn't have the money to pay for the termination herself. The *Doe* ruling stated that a woman does not lose access to abortion simply because she doesn't have the ability to pay for one. Otherwise, abortion is a right only for those who aren't poor. Megan Peterson of the National Network of Abortion Funds explained the problems many women have obtaining enough money to have an abortion in states with a funding ban. "As we know from other states where Medicaid doesn't cover abortions, it basically means that women don't get the abortions they need or want, or they go to great lengths and endure significant hardship in order to come up with the money."[8]

The average first-trimester abortion, be it medication or surgical, costs about $500 out of pocket. Add on to that the expenses associated with receiving an abortion, such as for gas to travel back and forth to appointments and to adhere to waiting periods, lodging if the provider is too far away for the patient to do a round trip easily in one day, childcare for the 60 percent of women seeking abortions who already have children, and time away from work for those who are employed. According to the Guttmacher Institute, which tracks research and trends in reproductive health care:

> In 2008, just one-third of privately insured U.S. women having abortions used that coverage to pay for their procedures; it is not clear how many of their plans offered full or partial coverage for abortion, or how many women were deterred from using their coverage because of concerns about confidentiality. Among women having abortions that year, methods of payment included paid out of pocket (almost 60%), private insurance (12%), and Medicaid (20%; almost all of whom lived in the few states that use their own funds to cover medically necessary abortions).[9]

So how do women pay for abortions and the associated expenses, which can easily come to $1000 just for a first-trimester procedure, especially those who are struggling financially, among the primary reasons women choose not to continue their pregnancies in the first place? For the National Network of Abortion Funds, it's a question they're asked often, and one for which they have developed an extensive list of answers. "Abortion funds may be able to help you pay for your abortion and you may be able to get a discount at your clinic," the group's website says. "But abortion funds just don't have the money to cover the entire cost of your abortion, so you're going to need to come up with some money on your own. . . . Remember that these are just ideas—please don't ever do anything that makes you feel unsafe or could put your health in danger."[10] Unfortunately, most of the ideas the organization suggests will either drive a woman farther into debt or force her to accept someone else's generosity to control her own reproductive freedom. Advice includes cashing in bonds and returning recently purchased items to stores for cash, selling gift cards at less than face value, selling belongings, and borrowing money from friends, family or support groups. For those who don't want to explain to others what the funding is needed for, they suggest financing the abortion with money meant to pay other bills and then asking friends or family members for a loan to pay those bills .

Raising the money to pay for an abortion also takes time for most women, and the farther along the gestational age, the more expensive the termination becomes. After nine weeks, a medication abortion is no longer an option, while after twelve weeks, many states won't perform an abortion in a clinic, requiring women to go to hospitals or travel to other states. With each delay comes a new expense; each new expense creates another delay. For some women, the delays accumulate to the point that they can no longer have an abortion at all. "The research literature clearly shows that restricting Medicaid funding for abortion forces many poor women—already at greatest risk of unintended pregnancy—to carry an unwanted pregnancy to term," reports Stanley Henshaw, a senior fellow at the Guttmacher Institute and author of the 2009 study *Restrictions on Medicaid Funding for Abortions: A Literature Review.* "Antiabortion advocates are using these restrictions in a misguided attempt to reduce the nation's abortion rate. Instead, we should be focusing on reducing the underlying cause of abortion—unintended pregnancy—by ensuring better access to and use of contraceptives." According to Henshaw's research, poor women who do not have access to abortion coverage via Medicaid tend to delay their abortions an average of two to three weeks as they try to come up with the money to pay. In the end, approximately 25 percent of poor women seeking abortions are forced to give birth because funding for a termination is unavailable.[11]

That average is consistent with what Val Vilott sees at DCAF. "They just disappear," she said, referring to the women who start the process of trying to get an abortion but eventually give up because there are too many barriers. "There is a continual kind of drop-off as the process goes on. We have a general sense that once we have worked with a woman and had two or three conversations and make a pledge [to cover the additional funds she needs] that it will pan out. But in 2011, 515 women got to the point where we offered a pledge and sent that pledge to a clinic. Out of that, 352 of those pledges were redeemed. We never know whether something came up, whether they got called in to work, whether a partner found out and they suddenly don't feel comfortable—we have no way of knowing that. We are very conscientious about racing the clock." It's a race that many lower-income women seeking help to afford a termination lose. "Of the 515 women that we offered pledges, 380 of them were second trimester. Second trimesters tend to be the bulk of our work because the price just ticks up so dramatically. Women who are good advocates for themselves still aren't able to come up with hundreds and hundreds of dollars to help cover that procedure." For these women, there is no "equal access" to health care, and there may never be.

Following the *Roe* decision in 1973, it took the Supreme Court less than a decade to pivot from finding that a woman had a liberty interest in being free from coerced procreation, to endorsing the ability of states to regulate that interest out of existence by banning the use of Medicaid dollars to pay for abortions. The first funding challenge to reach the court came in 1977 and with it the embrace of a legal precedent for privileging state interests in "encouraging" childbirth over abortion. Title XIX of the Social Security Act had established the Medicaid program, under which participating states could provide federally funded medical assistance to persons in need. The statute required states to provide qualified individuals with financial assistance in five general categories of medical treatment, including inpatient and outpatient hospital and physicians' services.[12] Although Title XIX does not require states to provide funding for every and all medical treatment falling within the five general categories, it does require that state Medicaid plans establish "reasonable standards" in delineating care available under Medicaid programs, so long as those services are "consistent with the objectives of [Title XIX]."[13]

In the case of *Beal v. Doe*, a group of Medicaid-eligible pregnant women challenged a Pennsylvania regulation that prohibited the use of state Medicaid funds to pay for abortions for indigent women unless a physician certified in writing that the procedure was "medically necessary." The Pennsylvania regulation in effect at the time stated that an abortion was deemed "medically necessary," and therefore compensable under the state Medicaid program, if the mother's health was at risk, if the fetus would be born with an incapacitating physical or mental deficiency, or if there was documented evidence that the pregnancy was a result of forcible rape or incest. If a physician certified that one of those conditions was met, then two other physicians would have to concur in writing and the procedure would have to be performed in a hospital.[14]

Among their claims, the plaintiffs in *Beal* alleged that Title XIX of the Social Security Act required Pennsylvania to provide coverage in its Medicaid plan for all abortions, not just those deemed "medically necessary." The plaintiffs objected to the exclusion of nontherapeutic abortions, or those that would not fit the definition of "medically necessary," from the state Medicaid program on both economic and health grounds. The former objection was based on the view that abortion is generally a less expensive medical procedure than childbirth. Therefore, states that refuse to fund nontherapeutic abortions are increasing public health costs, not reducing them.[15] Furthermore, the plaintiffs argued, banning nontherapeutic abortions also increases the risk to women, since early abortion poses less of a medical risk than childbirth.[16] The Supreme Court already recognized pregnancy as a unique medical condition and therefore, the plaintiffs argued, the idea that it is reasonable for states to ban nontherapeutic— i.e., *unnecessary*—abortions should not apply.[17]

But the majority of justices on the court were not convinced by these arguments and as a result established by judicial fiat that poor women were not entitled to the same kind of access to abortion services as women with financial means. Without determining whether the plaintiffs' economic and health-related objections were accurate, the court did not agree that the exclusion of nontherapeutic abortions from Medicaid coverage was unreasonable under Title XIX. The plaintiffs, the court held, had failed to take into account the state's "valid and important interest in encouraging childbirth."[18] Although the court conceded that under *Roe*, before viability a woman's constitutionally protected privacy interest outweighs that state interest, the majority was quick to clarify that even pre-viability, the state's interest in a woman's pregnancy is "significant" and continues to be so throughout the course of her pregnancy.[19]

Writing for a six to three majority, Justice Lewis Powell concluded that the statute merely required that participating states provide financial assistance to broad categories of care, nothing more. That meant that so long as a state's plan included reasonable standards for determining eligibility, and so long as those standards were consistent with the objectives of Medicaid, states were free to place restrictions on coverage for abortion access because those restrictions would not interfere with Medicaid's goal, which was "to enable each State, as far as practicable, to furnish medical assistance to individuals whose income and resources are insufficient to meet the costs of necessary medical services."[20] And, as if sensing the looming battles ahead, the court made it clear that states that tried to exclude necessary medical treatment from their Medicaid plans would likely run afoul of Title XIX, whereas because these were "elective" abortions—what the court characterized as "unnecessary (though perhaps desirable) medical services"—excluding them was completely consistent with the Social Security Act.[21]

While Justices William J. Brennan, Thurgood Marshall and Harry Blackmun each filed separate dissents in the case, it was clear that not even five years after *Roe*, the retreat from women's reproductive rights as a matter of settled law had begun. In his dissent, Justice Brennan argued that pregnancy was a medical condition, of which live birth was only one possible outcome. Which course of treatment a woman selected to address this condition was a matter that should be left up to the "complete freedom" of the patient and her physician.[22] "Once medical treatment of some kind is necessary," he wrote, "Title XIX does not dictate what that treatment should be."[23] Brennan also stressed that Pennsylvania's policy of not paying for the cost of nontherapeutic abortions could not be justified by either cost considerations (because the medical costs associated with childbirth are higher than those associated with abortion) or by an interest in maternal health (because abortions early in pregnancy are safer than carrying the child to term).[24] Justice Marshall dissented principally on the grounds that the state's policy of not funding nontherapeutic abortions was intended to coerce poor women into continuing their pregnancies.[25] Justice Blackmun argued that the statutes, regulations and policies at issue were all designed to do indirectly what the state and municipalities could not do directly, which was to interfere with a pregnant woman's decision to obtain an abortion.[26]

Beal wasn't the only funding challenge to appear before the Supreme Court in 1977. In the case of *Maher v. Roe*, a Connecticut regulation limited state Medicaid benefits for first-trimester abortions to those that were "medically necessary," a term that was defined also to include psychiatric necessity. (The state enforced a limitation on psychiatric necessity by requiring prior authorization from the Department of Social Services before an abortion could be performed.) In order to obtain authorization for a first-trimester abortion, the hospital or clinic where the abortion was to be performed had to submit, among other things, a certificate from the patient's attending physician stating that the abortion was medically necessary. Two indigent women who were unable to obtain this certificate challenged the regulation, contending that Title XIX of the Social Security Act required the state of Connecticut to provide coverage in its Medicaid plan for all abortions, not just those that were medically necessary. The plaintiffs claimed that Connecticut had to treat abortion and childbirth equally in its regulation and couldn't show a policy preference by funding only medical expenses related to childbirth.[27] The plaintiffs also challenged the funding restrictions on equal protection grounds, arguing that it was discriminatory for the state to prefer childbirth over abortion in funding.

Again by a six to three vote, the Supreme Court held that the Constitution did not require states to pay for the costs of nontherapeutic abortions for indigent women. Writing for the majority a second time, Justice Powell pointed out that the Constitution "imposes no obligation on the States to pay the pregnancy-related medical expenses of indigent women, or indeed to pay any of the medical expenses of indigents."[28] However, he added, "when a State decides to alleviate some of the hardships of poverty by providing medical care, the manner in which it dispenses benefits is subject to constitutional limitations."[29]

For purposes of equal protection analysis, a statute, regulation or policy is subject to "strict scrutiny" if it classifies on the basis of a suspect personal characteristic (e.g., race, national origin, alienage) or if it impinges on the exercise of a fundamental constitutional right. In this case, the court determined that the Connecticut abortion funding limitation did neither. "An indigent woman desiring an abortion does not come within the limited category of disadvantaged classes so recognized by our cases," Powell wrote.[30] "Nor does the fact that the impact of the regulation falls upon those who cannot pay lead to a different conclusion," because the court "has never held that financial need alone identifies a suspect class for purposes of equal protection analysis."[31] Furthermore, the court held, a poor woman wasn't really injured by the privilege accorded to pregnancy by the Connecticut statute in that she was no worse off than she would be had the state chosen not to favor childbirth since it already prevented Medicaid funds for nontherapeutic abortions.

Having decided that the regulation limiting abortion funding did not require application of the strict scrutiny standard of review, the most rigorous legal test a court can apply when considering the constitutionality of a law regulating a personal right, the court then considered whether the limitation satisfied the more relaxed rational basis standard of review. Under that standard, the question was whether the distinction the regulation drew between childbirth and nontherapeutic abortion was "rationally related" to a "constitutionally permissible" purpose.[32] The court concluded that it was. "*Roe* itself," Justice Powell observed, "explicitly acknowledged the State's strong interest in protecting the potential life of the fetus . . . an interest honored over the centuries."[33] The Connecticut regulation "rationally furthers that interest," Justice Powell explained, because "the medical costs associated with childbirth are substantial" and "significantly greater than those normally associated with elective abortions during the first trimester."[34] Subsidizing the costs incident to childbirth "is a rational means of encouraging childbirth," he concluded.[35]

Justice Brennan, joined by Justices Marshall and Blackmun, dissented and cut right to the chase, namely that the court's decision would force poor women to carry unwanted and dangerous pregnancies to term. "As a practical matter," Brennan wrote, "many indigent women will feel they have no choice but to carry their pregnancies to term because the State will pay for the associated medical services, even though they would have chosen to have abortions if the State had also provided funds for that procedure, or indeed if the State had provided funds for neither procedure."[36]

If states are free to restrict Medicaid funding for nontherapeutic abortions, what happens if federal funding for those permitted becomes unavailable? Are states required to step in? That was the issue before the court in *Harris v. McRae*. And the answer was no.

Almost immediately following the 1976 passage of the Hyde Amendment, the act that blocked Medicaid insurance from covering abortion except in very specific cases, the law faced a legal challenge in federal court in New York. Cora McRae, a New York Medicaid recipient, pressed her case that Hyde violated her Fifth Amendment due process rights as well as the First Amendment's establishment clause. On the day the lawsuit was filed, the federal court issued a nationwide injunction preventing implementation of the Hyde Amendment while the legal challenges proceeded. Months later, the Supreme Court decisions in *Beal v. Doe* and *Maher v. Roe* establishing that states were not required to reimburse for elective abortions effectively lifted the New York district court's injunction and sent the case back for reconsideration. The game was afoot.

The legal battle over the impact the Hyde Amendment would have on the lives of poor women would not last much longer. Judge John Francis Dooling Jr., who handled the McRae matter from the beginning, issued a temporary restraining order accompanied by lengthy findings of facts and conclusions of law, thereby preventing the Department of Health, Education and Welfare from implementing the law and temporarily protecting the rights of poor women to more broadly access abortions. But, on June 30, 1980, in the case of *Harris v. McRae*, a sharply divided Supreme Court reversed Judge Dooling's order, ignoring his comprehensive findings of fact as well as the principle that the state must respect the constitutional rights of the poor in distributing or limiting welfare benefits, and held that the extreme limitations on Medicaid funding in the Hyde Amendment were constitutional. For poor women it wouldn't matter if an abortion was necessary to save their lives—anti-abortion lawmakers were free to cut off Medicaid dollars to pay for the procedure. The Supreme Court approved the elimination of abortion from publicly funded health care programs even in cases where a pregnant woman's health was gravely endangered or she was pregnant as a result of rape or incest. The decision was nothing short of an affront to the foundations of *Roe* and an endorsement of segregating health care.

Under the Medicaid program, states were not obligated to fund abortions for which no federal funds were available. The court concluded that the Medicaid statute created a cooperative funding scheme and that if the federal government declined payment, then the state did not have to provide the funds. Put another way, *Roe v. Wade* created no affirmative right to a government-funded abortion. Thus, it is permissible, the court said, for the government to use its funding powers to show a preference for childbirth over abortion.

Justice Brennan, joined by Justices Marshall and Blackmun, again led the dissent, finding that the denial of federal funding under the Hyde Amendment was tantamount to governmental coercion because it discouraged poor women from exercising their abortion rights granted by *Roe*. Justice Marshall filed a separate dissent, finding that the denial of funding for abortions for the poor was "equivalent" to a denial of legal abortion. He said in this case the governmental benefit in the form of funding is vital because, barred from accessing service, a woman would either seek an illegal abortion or carry a child to term and lose control over the direction of her life. He said the class of poor women affected by the Hyde Amendment included many minorities and that the governmental interest at issue—the protection of potential life—did not measure up to the rights of the women. Marshall predicted that decision would have a "devastating" impact on the lives and health of poor women. He couldn't have been more correct.

On the same day in 1980, the court issued a companion ruling on the funding of abortion in *Williams v. Zbaraz*. This case involved an Illinois law that prohibited the use of state medical assistance funds to pay for abortions for indigent women under the state Medicaid program (and two other medical assistance programs financed solely with state funds) unless the procedure was necessary to preserve the life of the mother. Two Illinois physicians who performed abortions, an indigent woman who alleged that she sought an abortion that was medically necessary but not necessary to save her life, and a welfare rights organization brought a lawsuit in federal district court challenging the funding restrictions.

After the case bounced back and forth several times between the district court and the court of appeals, the district court was finally directed by the court of appeals to rule on the constitutionality of the Hyde Amendment, which had not been challenged by the plaintiffs, as well as the Illinois law in question. The district court held that both the Hyde Amendment and the Illinois law denied indigent women seeking abortions equal protection under the law because each prohibited funding of "medically necessary abortions" even though all other medically necessary operations were funded.[37] Accordingly, both the state law and the Hyde Amendment were declared unconstitutional. The district court, however, enjoined enforcement only of the state law, not the Hyde Amendment. Under the law in effect at the time, the district court's judgment was appealed directly to the Supreme Court, bypassing the court of appeals.

The court divided on the issues of the case, unanimously holding that the district court lacked jurisdiction to decide the validity of the Hyde Amendment but ruling by a vote of five to four that the state of Illinois could restrict public funding of abortions to those necessary to preserve the life of the mother. In the first part of its opinion, the court held that the district court lacked jurisdiction to decide the constitutionality of the Hyde Amendment because it had not been challenged by the plaintiffs and vacated that portion of the lower court's judgment. In the second part of its opinion, the court noted that both plaintiffs' statutory claim (under Title XIX) and their constitutional claim (under the Equal Protection Clause) were foreclosed by the court's decision the same day in *Harris v. McRae*.[38] With that, the court consigned poor women to a life where reproductive health services were simply not readily available and accessible.

How large a problem is the financial burden of paying for an abortion? From 2000 to 2008, 40 percent of all abortions were obtained by women who were at or below the poverty level, according to the Guttmacher Institute.[39] While the rate of abortions in general was decreasing, thanks in part to greater access to contraception and sex education, for poor women the number continued to grow. "There is an overrepresentation of the poor, of women of color, and clearly the economic recession that was at its height at the time this data was collected and had an impact on poor women's decisions to proceed or not with a pregnancy," Carole Joffe of the Bixby Center for Global Reproductive Health at the University of California-San Francisco told *USA Today* in 2011.[40]

The stories women tell about trying to find the money to afford the procedure can be heart-wrenching. On its website, Women's Medical Fund, an organization that helps provide funding to women in Pennsylvania who need abortions, tells the stories of a few of the women they have assisted:

> WS is the young mother of two small children. She supports her family on her monthly Social Security check of $670. She was sexually assaulted by her cousin and became pregnant from the rape. When he threatened to kill her if she told anyone about it, she was too fearful to turn to family members for help paying for her abortion. She managed to set aside some money from her monthly benefit check and $122 from WMF filled the remaining gap.

> PT is the young mother of a toddler who receives $158 per month in welfare to supplement her monthly wages of $140. Unable to afford her own place, she pays $150 each month to rent a room from a friend. Although she uses Medicaid for her other health care needs, she is prohibited from using it for an abortion. She struggled to set aside $200 toward the cost of her abortion, but her drug-addicted sister stole the money from her purse. After the theft, she turned to her mother and friends to borrow money, and WMF closed the gap with $96.

> When seventeen-year-old BR's mother fell behind in the rent, the landlord evicted BR and her family from their apartment. She, her mother, and her 3 siblings moved

into a motel room while her mother tried to come up with enough money for alternative housing. BR's boyfriend stopped returning her calls when she told him that she was pregnant. She is contributing her family's savings of $260 toward her abortion. WMF closed her gap with $210.[41]

In addition to the typical cases that groups like the Women's Medical Fund try to help out with, there are also special situations like that of "Sophia," in which even the health of the mother is affected by Medicaid abortion bans. In June 2012, the New York Abortion Access Fund sent out an emergency appeal on behalf of a woman they called Sophia who was being treated with chemotherapy for cancer and had been told that because of the treatment she would not be able to get pregnant. However, she did get pregnant, but because of the chemotherapy drugs the fetus suffered severe anomalies. Sophia was already too far along in her pregnancy for doctors in most states to be able to perform a termination, and in her state, Medicaid did not pay for abortion even when the mother was ill and the fetus was deemed incompatible with life.

There was just one clinic in the country able to perform the termination, but the cost was $12,000. Donors were stepping in, and the clinic offered to absorb as much of the cost as it could, but Sophia was still short nearly $2000. "It is clear that this young woman deserves our funding, yet $1750 is ten times our average grant amount," the fund wrote in a plea for help. "We are turning to you today to request an emergency contribution to help this woman terminate this pregnancy that poses serious risk to her health."[42] Though the fund eventually received the money it needed to help Sophia, she was just one case. As more women find it impossible to afford a termination, and more states refuse to allow women and girls to use Medicaid to cover the cost of terminating a pregnancy, abortion funds have taken over the lion's share of filling in the gap, which is not a sustainable long-term solution.

By allowing Medicaid funding to be used to pay for prenatal care and birthing costs but not for terminations, the government is essentially advocating for poor women to give birth, regardless of a woman's personal choice, a fate that other women can avoid simply because they have the financial means. That was the argument behind a law in Washington State that would have required insurance plans to include coverage for abortion if they also covered maternity care. But when state Democrats tried to expand the scope of the bill to include both public and private insurance plans, Republicans killed it by tying it to the state's budget bill to block it from getting to the Senate for a vote.[43]

As frustrating as it is when anti-abortion politicians block legislation that would make it easier for women who are poor to have the same reproductive choices as women of means, at least women who live in states that deny coverage are being blocked by their own legislators. The same can't be said for those who reside in Washington, DC, where the preference of the majority of the residents is being overruled by a group of lawmakers whom the citizens have no ability to hold responsible for their votes. This is just what the House GOP relies on and is why they chose Washington, DC, as a testing ground for model legislation they wish to implement in the rest of the country.

Despite the fact that she quite literally had no voice, being both denied a vote on the legislation affecting her city and refused a chance to speak at the hearings where the laws for DC were being written, Congresswoman Eleanor Holmes Norton continued to advocate on behalf of her constituents, even if the media was her only audience. "During the past four years, I worked to carry out the will of D.C. residents and our local government by successfully removing all of the accumulated appropriations riders that eliminated the District's right to decide how to spend its local funds on behalf of its residents, including for abortion for low-income women," she said. "Not only do Republicans seek to trample on D.C.'s rights as a self-governing jurisdiction, they apparently seek to trample on my right as a Member of Congress to participate in the legislative process by giving testimony on a bill that directly affects the District." Trent Franks and his anti-abortion cohorts might be relentless, but Norton swore she would be just as vigilant. "We will not give up on our efforts to use every legitimate means to stop all anti–home rule attempts to roll back the progress the District has made over the past four years, including today's attempt to prevent D.C. from funding abortions for low-income residents."[44]

9. TEXAS: AN INACCESSIBLE MEDICAL SYSTEM FOR POOR WOMEN

"I've met too many prospective moms and dads from all across Texas who want nothing more than the chance to love a child they can call their own. I know of too many families that have been blessed and made whole by the glorious gift of adoption to ever believe there can ever be such a thing as an 'unwanted child.'"[1] When Texas governor Rick Perry spoke those words at a fundraiser for the Downtown Pregnancy Center of Dallas in 2009, he was singing the praises of organizations that support women and teens in the state who choose to carry unintended pregnancies to term. However, what the governor didn't mention was that, between his gutting of family planning funding and his ceaseless vendetta against the state's Planned Parenthood affiliates, he himself has been and continues to be the biggest factor in creating "unwanted children" by blocking access to affordable contraception, especially for women who are uninsured or rely on the state's low-income Medicaid coverage to meet their health care needs.

Texas isn't the only state to attempt to cut off Title X family planning funding to Planned Parenthood. In 2011, Shelby County in Tennessee shifted its funding to Christ Community Health Services, effectively cutting off Planned Parenthood Greater Memphis Region from Title X funds. While Christ Community Health Services did not provide access to emergency contraception or offer referrals to places that did, it did offer a lecture on God. One patient testified at a public hearing that a practitioner told her, "If only [your] relationships with people and God were right, [you] would have fewer health problems."[2]

In response to Shelby County's action, the federal government awarded Planned Parenthood Greater Memphis Region a grant so that the organization could continue to provide care to its low-income and uninsured patients. In July 2012, the health care provider announced it had received a three-year grant worth $395,000 annually for Title X family planning services from the U.S. Department of Health and Human Services Office of Grants Management. "This grant award means that Planned Parenthood will be able to resume providing essential health care services to the low-income women and teens who depend on us every day to help them plan their families," Planned Parenthood Greater Memphis Region CEO Barry Chase said when the grant was announced. "It means our patients who qualify will be able to get the confidential, unbiased care they need from the provider they prefer and trust."[3]

While Tennessee tried to defund Planned Parenthood by choosing a different provider, Ohio attempted to defund the group by creating a hierarchy of providers that could have Title X funding and putting Planned Parenthood in last place on that list. The move was meant to ensure that funding would run out before Planned Parenthood ever got to the front of the line. Under the proposed amendment, all family planning dollars in the state would first be allocated to local health departments, then "federally qualified community health centers," a definition that didn't include Planned Parenthood clinics. Anything still left would go to private care centers, and, last, Planned Parenthood. Advocating for the amendment was Ohio Right to Life president Mike Gonidakis, who told the *Cleveland Plain Dealer* that family planning funding should be going to places like Lower Lights Ministries, which also catered to low-income women. "This money should be going to them, as opposed to the abortion industry," Gonidakis said, either not knowing or not caring that the faith-based clinic he was referencing had multiple doctors who wouldn't even provide birth control.[4] The amendment to reprioritize family planning funding in Ohio was added to the 2011 midyear budget review but was stripped out because of negative feedback from constituents. It was returned during the lame duck session in 2012, but Ohio senator Tom Niehaus refused to let that bill—or the contentious heartbeat ban—out for a vote.

The Texas bid to defund Planned Parenthood wasn't any more popular with its residents. The state was already deep in a health care crisis; less than half its population had private insurance coverage, and a quarter of its citizens were completely uninsured. In 2010, Texas ranked number one in the percentage of uninsured adults in the country, with nearly five million uninsured between the ages of nineteen and sixty-four.[5] The numbers were even worse for minority groups. According to the Texas Medical Association, "37 percent of Hispanics/Latinos, 21.4 percent of African Americans, and 21.1 percent of Asians" in the state were uninsured, "compared to 13.5 percent of whites."[6] As a result, the state was suffering from an epidemic of adults who lacked primary care doctors, often skipped preventative care, and were forced to use emergency rooms as their primary health care source.

The situation was even worse for women, especially the Latina population in the state, who without access to physicians would be unable to obtain birth control or other family planning needs, increasing the rate of unintended pregnancies and continuing their cycle of poverty. "Latinas as it stands currently have the least amount of access to health insurance of any ethic group of women in the United States," explained Veronica Bayetti Flores, a policy research specialist at the National Latina Institute for Reproductive Health. "Low-income Latinas who would otherwise qualify for public assistance such as Medicaid or any other kinds of programs that are there to provide public assistance often don't qualify because, if they're immigrant Latinas, sometimes they're undocumented. So that would prevent them from qualifying for a number of different health care programs.

Latinas are already operating from a context of disproportionate poverty and lack of access to care, so when you take away the cornerstones like that, it's actually a huge impact on Latinas."[7] In fact, according to Flores, sometimes it takes getting pregnant to get any health care at all. "Those are some of the places where undocumented women are actually able to get care when they're pregnant. It's a disturbing feeling for them that that's actually one of the only times that they're able to receive any care, when they're pregnant."

It was exactly these sorts of issues that had led to the development of Title X funding as a federal program in the first place. With the federal government providing grants, women who were poor, uninsured or using Medicaid could obtain exams, contraception, prenatal care and other basic health care services without having a primary physician. Access to contraception was understood to be crucial in reducing unplanned pregnancies and cutting health expenses associated with abortion and giving birth. According to a 2012 report from the Brookings Institute, for every dollar spent on contraception, taxpayers save between two and six dollars.[8]

These were the types of arguments that led to the creation of the Texas Medicaid Women's Health Program (WHP). The program serves low-income, uninsured women in the state, allowing them to visit providers for family planning needs and health screenings for cancer as well as testing for sexually transmitted infections. The funding for the program is used entirely for these screenings and for providing contraception, and no clinic that participates—including Planned Parenthood affiliates in the program—offers abortions. Yet it was the specter of "fungible funding" that Governor Perry and his cohorts used to pass a law forbidding Planned Parenthood affiliates from being a part of WHP. "Planned Parenthoods across the country provide abortions, are affiliated with abortion providers, or refer women to abortion providers," the governor's spokesperson told the

New York Times in March 2012.[9] Republican state representative Wayne Christian agreed. "I don't think anybody is against providing health care for women. What we're opposed to are abortions. . . . Planned Parenthood is the main organization that does abortions. So we kind of blend being anti-abortion with being anti-Planned Parenthood."[10] However, when Christian was asked if this was a "war on birth control," he responded, "Of course it's a war on birth control, abortion, everything—that's what family planning is supposed to be about."[11]

To assist in the defunding process, Texas dropped its two-year budget for family planning from $111 million to $38 million.[12] The elimination of two-thirds of its family planning budget would cut services for about three hundred thousand women in the state and was projected to lead to twenty thousand unwanted pregnancies that would cost the state about $230 million.[13] Those who were familiar with Governor Perry's record knew that this wasn't a money-saving endeavor. In 2005, Perry had taken a swing at the state's family planning funding, transferring $10 million to Federally Qualified Health Centers (FQHCs), community-based clinics that provide a full range of health care services, choosing to fund those clinics instead of Planned Parenthood or reproductive health centers. According to reporter Jordan Smith, while those funds may have gone to FQHCs, that doesn't mean patients were served. Smith wrote in the Nation that in the first year, $2 million of that $10 million was returned to the state, unused. Though their costs per client were fifty dollars more than what Planned Parenthood spent, the FQHCs continued to return funds every year[14] Perry also took $5 million in family planning funding and gave it to crisis pregnancy centers, allowing them to use taxpayer funding to counsel women with unintended pregnancies to give birth rather than choose an abortion. According to a report by the *Washington Independent*, almost all of the funding to the state's pregnancy centers went to Christian-centric nonprofit agencies.[15]

It didn't take long for the federal government to make it clear that Texas's move to cut Title X funding was unacceptable. The Department of Health and Human Services warned Governor Perry that purposely ousting Planned Parenthood as a provider, and prohibiting the organization from receiving Title X funds, put the state in danger of losing all of its family planning funding. Still, Perry insisted that it was the Obama administration that was putting a political agenda over the well-being of the state's poor and uninsured women. He wrote in a March 8, 2012, op-ed:

> Why would the Obama administration take away access to health care for low-income Texas women? Because this administration puts funding for abortion provid-ers and affiliates ahead of funding for women's cancer screenings and other preventive health care. Texas, oper-ating under the direction of an overwhelming and bipar-tisan majority of legislators, prohibits abortion providers and affiliates like Planned Parenthood from receiving taxpayer money.
>
> Because Texas refuses to fund abortion providers and their affiliates, the federal government has announced that it will cancel the Women's Health Program. To me, this reflects a twisted set of values, not to mention a con-tinued disregard for the basic concept of states' rights.[16]

Perry approved the ban on Planned Parenthood affiliates be-ing used in WHP, even if it meant the loss of federal funds, and vowed to replace the lost $30 million from the state budget. "I am directing you to begin working with legislative leadership to identify state funding to continue to provide these services, in full compliance with Texas law, should the Obama Administration make good on its threat to end the health care to these 100,000-plus women," Perry wrote in a public letter to Texas Health and Human Services Commissioner Tom Suehs. "Texans send a substantial amount of our tax dollars to Washington, DC, and it is unacceptable that the Obama Administration is denying Texas taxpayers the use of those dollars to fund this program, simply because of its pro-abortion agenda."[17]

Supporting Perry in his mission was the Catholic Bishops of Texas, which argued that ousting Planned Parenthood as a provider, despite the fact that the Texas clinics in question didn't offer abortion services, actually reinforced "comprehensive" women's health care:

> There are only 44 Planned Parenthood locations in the Women's Health Program and many do not provide comprehensive health care—say, for example, mammograms or many common gynecological services—which are critical for women's health. It is the Texas bishops' position that true women's health services should be separated from services that are not health care: namely, contraception, sterilization, and abortion.
>
> By insisting that the state of Texas cannot direct funds to thousands of providers statewide who offer true, comprehensive, women's health care—and instead require Medicaid funds go to prop up 44 Planned Parenthood clinics—the federal government risks removing preventative health care from hundreds of thousands of women in Texas.[18]

That the bishops referred to contraception as "not health care" is telling. The WHP program is supposed to offer family planning services to low-income women, and those who advocate the exclusion of Planned Parenthood from the program and the use of alternative providers are admitting that they don't believe birth control should be offered at all. It's a variation of the same argument used to oppose the birth control mandate in the Affordable Care Act. "The bishops want contraception out of the Affordable

Care Act entirely," explained Jon O'Brien, president of Catholics for Choice. "That would affect all Americans. And if you think that's the whole story, again you are wrong."[19] According to O'Brien, the bishops' fight against contraception is motivated by their desire to continue to get federal funding for their charity work while still being allowed to adhere to and enforce their own set of moral rules. "They've carefully constructed a very bogus argument taken to the far extreme," O'Brien says.

In the end, the bishops got their way, when, in March 2012, the state of Texas began phasing Planned Parenthood out of the WHP. Governor Perry touted the more than 2,500 doctors in the state as a primary reason why it would be just fine to move women away from Planned Parenthood services. However, as Texas-based freelance journalist Andrea Grimes discovered in her own personal investigation, getting access to a doctor was very complicated for patients without insurance:

> Most places I telephoned did not provide reproductive health care and instead focused on providing low-income housing, job training and addiction-recovery programs. A homeless shelter on the FQHC list did tell me I could get a free pap smear if I could prove I was homeless. I then got sidetracked looking into something called Project Access, a low-cost program that helps uninsured people who don't qualify for Medicaid—but because I made more than about $20,000 last year as an unmarried woman without kids, I don't qualify for that, either. And the Texas Breast and Cervical Services, which is supposed to provide low-cost screenings for Texas women? It referred me to Planned Parenthood. So that was a no-go.[20]

The full switch to the Texas-funded program wasn't expected to be complete until November 1, 2012—conveniently a few days before the 2012 election. But concerns began to grow as women were told that as of May 1, they would no longer be able to use Planned Parenthood as their provider. Texas Planned Parenthood filed suit against the state on April 11, and on April 30, the Fifth Circuit Court of Appeals blocked the ban from going into effect, saying it was "likely unconstitutional because it bars [Planned Parenthood] from participating in the Women's Health Program based on their affiliation with legally and financially separate entities that engage in constitutionally protected conduct related to abortion."[21]

Perry and his administration appealed the ruling by reassessing how a provider for the program could be barred. Now, instead of disqualifying only groups associated with an "abortion provider," they also banned any group that so much as referred patients for or even mentioned abortion.[22] This essentially created a state gag rule that many medical providers feared would jeopardize their ability to assist patients. Collectively, the Texas Medical Association, the Texas division of the American College of Obstetricians and Gynecologists, the Texas Association of Obstetricians and Gynecologists, the Texas Academy of Family Physicians and the Texas Pediatric Society sent a letter to the Department of State Health Services expressing their concerns about the law. "The relationship between patient and physician is based on trust and creates the physician's ethical obligations to place the patient's welfare above his or her own personal politics, self-interest and above obligations to other groups," wrote the organizations, which represented more than 47,000 medical practitioners. Among other worries was the concern that doctors might leave the program because of the new regulation, making an already precarious provider situation even worse.[23]

As Perry continued to fight the federal government over funding for women's health care, an even bigger storm was brewing in 2012. The Supreme Court had just ruled that the Affordable Care Act, President Obama's signature health care reform bill, was constitutional, and that states would need to extend Medicaid eligibility or be prepared to give up their expansion funding. The expansion would be a boon to Texas, a state that relied heavily on Medicaid, by cutting the costs of the uninsured on the state health care system. On principle, however, Governor Perry had to remain as stubbornly committed to rejecting the funding as he had been to rejecting WHP funding. In a July 2012 letter to Health and Human Services Secretary Kathleen Sebelius, Perry pointedly stated his opposition to the expansion of Medicaid funding:

> I oppose both the expansion of Medicaid as provided in the Patient Protection and Affordable Care Act and the creation of a so-called "state" insurance exchange, because both represent brazen intrusions into the sovereignty of our state. I stand proudly with the growing chorus of governors who reject the PPACA power grab. Thank God and our nation's founders that we have the right to do so. Neither a "state" exchange nor the expansion of Medicaid under the Orwellian-named PPACA would result in better "patient protection" or in more "affordable care." What they would do is make Texas a mere appendage of the federal government when it comes to health care.[24]

But rather than forcing a state to become "a mere appendage of the federal government" in regards to health care, Medicaid—and Title X specifically—were designed to function as a partnership between individual states and the federal government, with both working toward the common goal of delivering health care services to those most in need. By its very design, Title X assumes cooperation between states and the federal government, cooperation that the Perry administration refused to give. Where the law envisioned a marriage of federal and state interests, the Perry administration insisted on going it alone, refusing to enter into a partnership with the Obama administration and instead moving forward with turning Texas into a health care desert for the poor and uninsured.

Title X of the Public Health Services Act authorizes the secretary of health and human services to make grants and contracts with public or private entities to help establish and operate voluntary family planning projects that offer a broad range of "acceptable and effective family planning methods and services."[25] Since its inception in 1970, the act has been the target of anti-abortion (and anti-birth control) activists, despite the fact that Section 1008 of the act specifies that none of the federal funds appropriated under Title X "shall be used in programs where abortion is a method of family planning."

Despite the specific statutory language that prevents Title X funds from going to programs that provide abortions, activists on the right have nevertheless consistently pushed challenges to the law. For example, in 1988, the Department of Health and Human Services issued regulations that, among other things, prohibited Title X family planning projects from engaging in abortion counseling or referrals and required said projects to maintain "objective integrity and independence from the prohibited abortion activities" by using separate facilities, personnel and accounting records designed to provide "clear and operational guidance" to grantees about how to "preserve the distinction between Title X programs and abortion as a means of family planning."[26] The regulations also prohibited Title X programs from "indirectly" encouraging or promoting abortion, such as by weighing a list of referrals in favor of providers who performed abortions or by excluding available providers who did not perform abortions.[27] Title X projects were also expressly prohibited from referring a pregnant woman to an abortion provider even if she directly asked for such a referral.[28] These changes created a host of new regulatory burdens on family planning programs, making accessing family planning services by poor women even more difficult than it had been previously under Medicaid.

Before these regulations went into effect, Title X grantees and physicians who supervised Title X funds filed several lawsuits in federal court. After working its way through the lower courts, one challenge made its way to the Supreme Court for review. In *Rust v. Sullivan* (1991), the court upheld the 1988 regulations, solidifying a bias against reproductive services as part and parcel of comprehensive family planning.[29] Chief Justice William Rehnquist wrote the majority opinion for the court, rejecting the plaintiffs' argument that the regulations were not authorized by Title X.[30] In addition, the court rejected the argument that the regulations violated the First Amendment because they discriminated on the basis of viewpoint, prohibiting discussion about abortion but mandating information promoting childbirth.[31] When the government appropriates public funds to establish a program, the court held, it is entitled to define the limits of that program even if that means funding some rights at the expense of others.[32]

The court also rejected the plaintiffs' alternative First Amendment claim that the regulations conditioned the receipt of Title X funding on the relinquishment of a constitutional right, namely the right to engage in abortion advocacy and counseling.[33] According to the court, this claim fell short because the government was not denying a benefit to anyone but was "simply insisting that public funds be spent for the purposes for which they were authorized."[34] Moreover, the court said, the regulations did not force a Title X grantee to relinquish any abortion-related speech. Instead, they simply required that the grantee keep such activities "separate and distinct from Title X activities."[35] The regulations, the court explained, were aimed at Title X projects, not Title X grantees, a distinction that was significant on paper but fell short in reality. According to the court, Title X grantees remained free to perform abortions, provide abortion-related services, and engage in abortion advocacy so long as those activities were conducted through programs that were separate and independent from projects that received Title X funds.[36]

Despite the court's ruling in *Rust v. Sullivan* that the federal government could place restrictions on Medicaid dollars going toward abortion services—as well as its decision in *Dalton v. Little Rock Family Planning Services*, a 1996 case that made it clear that states would be given wide berth in regulating the economics of abortion access—it wasn't until June 2012 that the balance of power between federal and state cooperative spending was upended. In *National Federation of Independent Business v. Sebelius*, the Supreme Court, for the first time ever, invalidated a condition on federal spending, in this case the Medicaid expansion under the Patient Protection and Affordable Care Act, on the grounds that it coerced the states into acting by making the conditions of receiving federal dollars essentially too good to turn down. The decision provided the perfect cover for the Perry administration and its charge against universal health care access as envisioned in the act, especially for women.

The Affordable Care Act represented an unusual expansion of access and equalizing of price that embraced a vision of women's equality and demanded that the private sector provide parity in coverage. For those who opposed expanding care for women, what better place than Texas to reinforce the isolationist states' rights approach and create a stand-off with the federal government over access to reproductive health care? After all, Texas is the only politically red state with a large enough population that, by standing alone and apart from the Medicaid program, it could cause a significant political impact across the country. If that impact happened to harm women, especially those without insurance, so be it.

Harm women it did. Within a year of the initial family planning cuts instituted by the Perry administration, sixty clinics across the state of Texas were forced to close.[37] Of those sixty clinics, only twelve were actually run by Planned Parenthood, the alleged original target of the cuts. As a consequence of the governor's actions, federally qualified health centers across the state are now refusing new clients because they lack the resources to deal with the increase in numbers, and in remote areas, thousands of women are going without services of any type due to lack of money and access. "In hoping to punish Planned Parenthood, politicians had gone too far, with devastating consequences for women's health," wrote Carolyn Jones in an article for the *Texas Observer*. "Lawmakers, they said, had thrown the 'baby out with the bath water.'"[38]

Today, with a growing list of case law that allows states broad regulation of health care spending related to abortion, and the Supreme Court's embrace of the legal theory of "coercion" related to federal-state cooperative spending, states now have the power to cut off federal spending to clinics for reproductive health care. And in Texas, that's exactly what they've done.[39] As the effects of these cuts are being felt throughout the state, with clinic closures and a lack of providers able and willing to take on new Medicaid patients, it has become clear that Texas has succeeded in creating a separate health care system for women, based on income. And as has been the case throughout our history of segregated public benefits, there's not a shred of equality in it.

10. KANSAS: ALWAYS LET YOUR CONSCIENCE BE YOUR GUIDE

In the Walt Disney version of *Pinocchio*, Jiminy Cricket tries to keep the fumbling puppet on the straight and narrow path, telling the wooden boy that he should let his "conscience" tell him what to do. "When you get in trouble and you don't know right from wrong, give a little whistle! And always let your conscience be your guide," Jiminy Cricket eagerly advises. It's a simple message that reduces the complexity of most decision-making processes, allowing the avoidance of potential gray areas and providing comfort in moral absolutism. This absolutism is taken to its extreme in the state of Kansas, where conscience trumps all when it comes to decisions involving a woman's reproductive health and autonomy, no matter how tangentially the "provider" is involved.

Conscience clauses have long played a role in medicine, primarily in Catholic hospitals and health clinics, where doctors and nurses have routinely refused to provide birth control, offer sterilizations or terminate pregnancies. Ostensibly intended primarily to protect a religious medical provider from participating in something that could be seen as a moral sin, conscience waivers in fact reflect a paternalistic attitude that has historically gone hand in hand with the belief that women aren't able to make their own medical decisions and need a man—be it a husband, father or religious advisor—to provide guidance and permission.

These clauses were originally seen as protecting the individual rights of those affiliated with religious institutions, but as anti-abortion advocates have ramped up their fight on choice over the past several decades, conscience clauses have been expanded to allow entire corporate health care systems to refuse to supply services or abide by non-discrimination policies that conflict with their religious mission. As religiously affiliated groups and Catholic hospitals in particular have taken over large portions of the country's health care system, as well as a greater share of the clinics that provide day-to-day and preventative care for those of lower income levels or who are uninsured, religious doctrine and dogma have created serious roadblocks to women's care and safety. For example, there have been many instances of Catholic hospitals refusing to allow the termination of a pregnancy endangering the mother's life, dallying over how far a woman's health must deteriorate before an abortion is no longer a mortal sin but instead a lifesaving procedure. Those in charge of approving such terminations are often at the mercy of church officials, who not only review each case but also decide whether the medical practitioner involved has earned excommunication from the church based on his or her actions.

The issue came to a head in 2009, when an Arizona nun approved a lifesaving abortion in a Catholic hospital for a mother of three who was eleven weeks pregnant. The hospital's medical board ruled that due to the woman's pulmonary hypertension, continuing the pregnancy would likely have killed her, and recommended an abortion before the fetus developed further and placed additional stress on the woman's heart. Because of this decision, Sister Margaret McBride was reassigned from serving on the ethics committee of St. Joseph's Hospital in Phoenix as well as excommunicated from the Catholic Church.

"I am gravely concerned by the fact that an abortion was performed several months ago in a Catholic hospital in this diocese," Bishop Thomas J. Olmsted told the *Arizona Republic*. "I am further concerned by the hospital's statement that the termination of a human life was necessary to treat the mother's underlying medical condition. An unborn child is not a disease. While medical professionals should certainly try to save a pregnant mother's life, the means by which they do it can never be by directly killing her unborn child. The end does not justify the means."[1] Bishop Olmsted eventually revoked St. Joseph's status as a Catholic institution when doctors at the hospital would not agree not to provide an abortion if the same situation presented itself again. The hospital refused to capitulate to the bishop's demands, saying, "Morally, ethically, and legally we simply cannot stand by and let someone die whose life we might be able to save."[2]

Bishop Olmsted, like many of the faith who work with religious institutions and their health care entities, believes that it is always better to err on the side of God than on the side of women's health and that adhering to the tenets of faith outweighs the right of the patient to receive needed care. "The equal dignity of mother and her baby were not both upheld," Olmsted said at a news conference. "The mother had a disease that needed to be treated. But instead of treating the disease, St. Joseph's medical staff and ethics committee decided that the healthy, 11-week-old baby should be directly killed."[3] However, the only "treatment" available to save the woman's life was to end her pregnancy— there was no surgery, medication or other option that could have successfully treated her condition. The incident became just the most public of the many documented in complaints that the American Civil Liberties Union has sent to the government informing them of Catholic health institutions that have denied women care due to "moral objections." "No woman should have to worry that she will not receive the care she needs based on the affiliation of the nearest hospital," wrote Brigitte Amiri of the ACLU Reproductive Freedom Project in a July 2010 report on the state of emergency reproductive care in religiously affiliated hospitals.[4]

It is the strict devotion to faith over medicine that makes the growing refusal of services under the guise of "conscience" such a threat to women's health. And with a federal judiciary that has steadily inched rightward in deciding claims based on the free exercise of religion, it's a movement that benefits from broad legal cover. For example, there are currently more than forty outstanding challenges to the contraception mandate of the 2010 Patient Protection and Affordable Care Act, which requires most employers who provide health insurance benefits to cover contraception at no additional co-pay to employees. "Resolution of these cases will likely depend on a ruling by a Supreme Court that has upheld the constitutionality of a host of statutes that it found to be "particularly burdensome" to women, including twenty-four-hour waiting periods and the inability to use Medicaid to pay for an abortion. As a result, there is every reason to believe that the court would find conscience clause legislation, or laws that permit health care professionals not to provide certain services based on their individual beliefs, acceptable despite the fact that it creates similar burdens in the form of "increased costs and potential delays."[5] In the meantime, conflicting decisions at the district court and appellate court level as to the enforceability of the contraception mandate have created a political opportunity for religious conservatives to push for additional concessions related to contraception coverage under the PPACA while arguing to the public that individual religious freedom is under assault by government overreach.[6]

Though the Supreme Court has yet to directly address the constitutionality of conscience clause statutes, some state courts have. The Supreme Courts of New Jersey and Alaska both found their state conscience clauses unconstitutional as applied to private, nonsectarian hospitals because the clauses infringed on constitutionally protected reproductive rights. In those cases, the state courts required such hospitals to provide abortion services, even though those services conflicted with the hospitals' religious beliefs.[7] In general, state constitutions tend to protect a woman's right to abortion more broadly than the U.S. Constitution does. But the real battle will be over the anti-abortion belief that life begins at conception, which leads anti-choice activists to define emergency contraceptives and even some types of hormonal birth control and intrauterine devices as a form of abortion. Whether the Supreme Court affords reproductive services like emergency contraceptives greater protection than abortion as it decides the scope of conscience clause objections will ultimately depend on the legal definition of when life begins. This is the real fight anti-abortion activists are angling for.

Kansas governor Sam Brownback has long been familiar with the idea of faith trumping science. As a senator from the state from 1996 through 2011, Brownback was as radically against abortion, contraception and family planning as any politician in Congress. He received a perfect rating from the National Right to Life Committee in 2006 and a rating of zero from NARAL Pro-Choice America in 2003.[8] Among his many anti-choice actions as a senator, Brownback fought to have the Fourteenth Amendment cover the "preborn," advocated for the government to legislate that life begins at the moment of conception, and opposed funding to reduce teen pregnancy via contraception and fact-based sex education.[9] He became even more devoted to anti–women's health policies upon his election as governor of Kansas in November 2010.

Despite the fact that the late Dr. George Tiller, famous for providing late-term abortions, had a clinic in the state, Kansas has never been known for its liberal stance on reproductive choice. In fact, the state has long been the literal center of the anti-abortion movement, with groups like Operation Rescue moving to Kansas for the sole purpose of putting pressure on Tiller to shut down his practice. While Kathleen Sebelius, a Democrat, served as governor from 2003 to 2009, anti-abortion activists tried to create as many legal obstacles to obtaining abortions in the state as they could. However, most of the legislation they were able to get passed was vetoed by Sebelius. Once she was appointed Health and Human Services Secretary by President Obama in 2009, the only thing standing between the extreme anti-abortion Kansas legislature and the decimation of women's reproductive rights in the state was gone.

"Kansas provides a perfect example of two kinds of Catholics," explained Meghan Smith of Catholics for Choice, a progressive reproductive health policy organization. "We had Governor Sebelius, who was a pro-choice Catholic and while she was governor talked about being a pro-choice Catholic, and we immediately had Governor Sam Brownback, who was an anti-choice Catholic. Both of them are Catholics, and both of them talk about their faith, and both of them approach this issue from two very different places."[10]

The age of Brownback has been one of laser-like focus on limiting abortion in any way possible. The governor signed bills restricting abortion access and removing coverage of abortion from state—as well as private—insurance plans. He also sought to eliminate family planning money from Planned Parenthood and to close the state's few remaining abortion clinics by passing legislation that would force the clinics to spend tens of thousands of dollars in upgrades or else be shut down. Still, that wasn't enough for anti-abortion activists, who then presented the governor with a set of bills that would create the most expansive protections in the nation for those who refused to provide medical services on the grounds of "conscience."

Kansas, like many other states, already had a bill on the books that allowed individuals to refuse to participate in an abortion. However, in recent years, religious leaders and their followers have begun to push the definition of "participation" to extreme forms, in the process helping to establish precedents that anti-abortion advocates are eager to extend. For example, in 2010, Edwin Graning, a bus driver in Texas, argued that he was illegally terminated from his position after he refused to drive a woman to a Planned Parenthood clinic, believing that the woman was about to undergo an abortion. Graning, an "ordained Christian minister" who was defended by evangelical leader Pat Robertson's

American Center for Law & Justice, received a $21,000 settlement from the Capital Area Rural Transportation System, since the company thought it would cost them more to fight the suit.[11] Graning actually never knew for sure that the woman he was driving was going to have an abortion; he said that he had his wife call the clinic and a recording at that number instructed that if a woman was having complications, she should go to the hospital. "I'm a Christian. . . . I love the Lord and I'm not going to be a part of something like this," Graning told *LifeSiteNews*. "I pastored years ago, and I've done a lot of things—and normally I wouldn't have made any issue out of this—but you know, I'm really getting tired of Christians getting kicked around. I mean, we see other things as going on in this country, and somebody somewhere along the line is just got to quit bending the knee to Baal and letting this government run over us."[12]

Edwin Graning wasn't the only one to take the definition of assisting in an abortion to an extreme. In 2011, a group of nurses in New Jersey sued their employer for "forcing" them to participate in abortions at the University of Medicine and Dentistry of New Jersey. Their definition of participating, however, consisted of checking women into the hospital, taking vital information like blood pressure and temperature, entering the women's names into a computer and walking them out of the hospital after the abortion was over. The lawyer for the nurses defined assisting in an abortion to be any activity, no matter how tangential, that involved interacting with a patient seeking an elective abortion procedure. "If they did that, they'd be helping to make it happen," attorney Demetrios Stratis told the *New Jersey Star Ledger*. "They're doing much more than that, obviously."[13]

At least the New Jersey nurses who objected to participating in an abortion weren't putting women's lives in danger. In 2010, a pharmacist at a Walgreens in Idaho invoked the state's Freedom of Conscience for Health Care Professionals law and refused to fill a woman's prescription for the drug Methergine, which controls bleeding, saying that she believed it was likely being used in abortion aftercare. Kristen Glundberg-Prossor of Planned Parenthood of the Great Northwest told the *Boise Weekly*, "We have heard of a lot of accounts where individuals across Idaho are being refused, but this is the first incident that we know of involving one of our own nurse practitioners. [Methergine] is neither an abortifacient or contraceptive. But the pharmacist asked our practitioner, 'Do you need this because of an abortion?' Our practitioner told the pharmacist in keeping with federal law, she couldn't disclose that. And then the pharmacist said she wouldn't fill the prescription. When our practitioner asked to speak to another pharmacist, she was hung up on."[14] Although Walgreens reprimanded the pharmacist for not passing the prescription to a colleague to be filled, the Idaho Board of Pharmacy refused to take any action on the complaint, arguing that the state's conscience clause was "not under board domain."[15]

Jon O'Brien, the president of Catholics for Choice, believes that cases like these are attempts "to prevent someone else from trying to exercise their freedom of conscience." According to O'Brien, if "what you do impedes on someone else's free exercise of will, I don't believe that is a conscience situation. That is impeding someone else from being able to do what they need to do. I think that is wrong ethically and morally. I can tell you it's wrong as a Catholic, but I can also tell you it's wrong from the point of view of respecting other people and being honest in the way we do things."[16]

The state of Kansas, however, believes that "conscience" should be open to limitless interpretation. In early 2012, two bills proposed in the state legislature sought in different ways to expand what could be designated a moral objection to "assisting abortions" as well as what was considered a "taxpayer-funded" abortion. HB 2598, the No Taxpayer Funding for Abortions Act, went beyond the scope of the Hyde Amendment, which prohibits the use of Medicaid funding for any abortion except in cases of rape or incest or to preserve the life of the woman, by seeking to eliminate the University of Kansas Medical Center's program to train doctors on how to perform abortions. The bill stated that since the center was funded with taxpayer dollars, providing abortion training was tantamount to paying for abortions. Previously, to ensure that they could be trained in abortion care without violating any potential prohibition, the university had sent students who wished to learn the procedure (common surgical abortion procedures are used in miscarriage management as well, making them a regular part of ob-gyn training) off campus to a Planned Parenthood clinic. HB 2598 sought to end that practice.

HB 2598 also defined any entity associated with the state's public schools to be taxpayer-funded, meaning that no employee, contractor or even school volunteer would be allowed to be associated with a provider of abortion. In an attempt to ensure that members of Planned Parenthood and similar groups would not have the opportunity to inform students about health issues or offer age-appropriate sex education, the bill sought to ban members of those organizations from volunteering at schools, even if their tasks were unrelated to health education. And in one of the most unusual aspects of the bill, the state proposed what amounted to a sales tax on abortion itself, a 6.5 percent tax on every medical exam and procedure associated with termination. On top of that, HB 2598 would also end tax credits for companies that did any business with abortion providers, as a disincentive to forming any sort of financial relationship.

Elizabeth Nash, state issues manager for the Guttmacher Institute, told *Raw Story*, "This is a complete turnaround in this idea of small government. Somebody spent hours, if not days, combing through the entire Kansas tax code to find every spot where you could possibly prevent abortion providers from being a nonprofit healthcare provider. It's really amazing. The bill is sixty-eight pages long. Somebody spent days trying to figure out how to manipulate the tax code to disqualify abortion providers. That is a level above and beyond what we have ever seen."[17]

Introduced during the same legislative session as HB 2598, HB 2523 made the unprecedented move of proposing that in addition to covering drugs that caused abortions (i.e., RU-486), "no person shall be required to perform, refer for, or participate in medical procedures or in the prescription or administration of any device or drug which result in the termination of a pregnancy or an effect of which the person reasonably believes may result in the termination of a pregnancy."[18] When used in legislation, language like *reasonably believe* and *may* are extremely loaded and intentionally vague terms that leave those in charge of administering medication or filling prescriptions with enormous power. Although the Kansas state legislature said that the language was meant to apply only to filling medication abortion prescriptions, doctors and women's rights advocates noted that by adding the word may, the legislature opened an avenue for pharmacists also to refuse to fill birth control pills and emergency contraception such as the so-called morning-after pill.

"When the bill went to committee, it was clear from the testimony that was given by the pro-life side that the bill was about contraception," said Holly Weatherford, program director of the ACLU of Kansas and Western Missouri. "They had pharmacists testify that they believed contraception was abortion and they didn't want to then administer or fill prescriptions for birth control. When the bill actually went to the floor in front of the full chamber in the house, the author of the bill described it simply as dealing with abortion and sterilization and unfortunately the legislators didn't know the law well enough to understand that Kansas has had longstanding conscience refusals in law in Kansas for abortion and sterilization. We did hear in some of the comments on the house floor that some of those pro-life legislators knew exactly what the bill was about and they made off-the-cuff comments about needing to protect against people having mail-order abortions, referring to emergency contraception, but in the end it passed overwhelmingly.[19]

Despite medical evidence to the contrary, the Food and Drug Administration's official literature on the morning-after pill (also known as Plan B) states that one possible way the medication works is to inhibit the implantation of a fertilized egg in the uterine lining.[20] In 2012, the *New York Times*, after doing its own scientific research and contacting medical experts, declared that the FDA's statement simply isn't true. "The notion that morning-after pills prevent eggs from implanting stems from the Food and Drug Administration's decision during the drug-approval process to mention that possibility on the label—despite lack of scientific proof, scientists say, and objections by the manufacturer of Plan B, the pill on the market the longest," reported the paper. "Leading scientists say studies since then provide strong evidence that Plan B does not prevent implantation."[21]

However, anti-abortion activists still insist on calling emergency contraception, as well as the birth control pill itself, an abortifacient, claiming that it potentially blocks a fertilized egg from implanting and growing into an embryo. For those who believe that a fertilized egg is the equivalent of a living, breathing person, the use of emergency contraception therefore seems akin to abortion. The majority of the medical profession, however, understands that a pregnancy cannot begin until after implantation (ask any woman who has undergone in vitro fertilization if she is pregnant simply because she has fertilized eggs waiting to be implanted).

Still, a very vocal batch of anti-abortion doctors, pharmacists and others have continued to claim that contraception causes abortions, spurred on by groups like Physicians for Life and Pharmacists for Life. As a result, a growing number of medical practitioners are refusing to prescribe contraception, citing their religious beliefs. Dr. Gabrielle Goodrick, a family planning and abortion practitioner in Arizona, noted the rising number of doctors refusing to prescribe contraception to their patients, citing religious issues. She told the story of one doctor who decided that for Lent, she'd stop offering tubal ligations as well as birth control.

"A drug rep came and told me this and I didn't believe it and she said, 'No, it's absolutely true.' This is what she told her staff and they had to cancel patients and patients that wanted birth control had to see someone else," Goodrick said. "I don't think it's malpractice," she continued. "I think they can do that. But I've had patients come in here with unplanned pregnancies. They had gone in and seen their doctor for their annual and said, 'Okay, I need my birth control,' and the doctor said, 'Oh, I'm sorry, I don't prescribe birth control,' and they're like, 'What am I supposed to do?' and the doctor says, 'You'll have to schedule with another provider.' They won't even get another doctor to write them the prescription and so then they end up here."[22]

Jon O'Brien of Catholics for Choice believes that the conscience decisions of individuals should be respected but that, "if you are a pharmacist or a doctor, and even if you are against contraception, it doesn't mean within Catholicism that you have to refuse it to someone else. You can be a Catholic pharmacist, you'll never use contraception, it's against my religion, but you still could prescribe it and be a good Catholic. That's the way my religion actually works." O'Brien also says that the health of the patient should never suffer because of the conscience issues of the provider. "But let's say you are a Catholic doctor and you don't want to perform the abortion or fit the IUD, or you don't want to prescribe the pill. I say okay. As a woman, I wouldn't want them performing any sort of procedure on me that they feel uncomfortable doing. So it's partly about protection of the patient or client. But the most important thing is that the end user should not have to suffer as a result of your conscience."

In addition to increasing the number of drugs covered under "conscience," HB 2523 would expand the definition of who could be considered a "provider." Although the language in the bill was assumed to refer to medical professionals such as doctors, nurses, health care providers and pharmacists, there was no guarantee that it couldn't be extended to anyone who happened to be in charge of handing out medication. As an example, in Florida, a rape victim was denied access to the second of two pills comprising a dose of emergency contraception when a prison guard refused to provide it to her, citing moral objections. The victim, who had an outstanding warrant for failure to appear in court, had been arrested and jailed when she showed up at the police station to report that she had been raped. She had already been examined and given the first dose of medication at a health clinic, but the second pill, which was confiscated when she was put in jail, was kept from her by the whim of the guard in charge.[23]

Both HB 2598 and HB 2523 were heatedly debated in the Kansas legislature, then substituted into senate bills that had already passed committee. However, HB 2598 died in the senate, mainly because of a fear that the University of Kansas Medical Center could lose accreditation if it did not allow students to learn how to perform abortions, which are considered a basic component of gynecological care. Unlike its counterpart, however, HB 2523 passed through the Kansas senate and was signed into law by Governor Brownback on May 14, 2012. The bill is designed to facilitate conscience refusals for contraception, but as the ACLU's Holly Weatherford explains, "There is a common misunderstanding of the ban, which is, 'What's the big deal if someone doesn't want to prescribe birth control or emergency contraception? They shouldn't have to.' But their follow-up is always that they should then refer patients to where they can receive those services. This bill includes a referral ban, which means that hospitals and organizations don't have to require physicians to refer for certain services. Kansas is a managed-care Medicaid system. That means women need referrals for services to be provided, so the referral ban is simply another barrier for women."

These barriers are particularly harmful to women in the western part of the state. "These are a low-income rural population that might have one pharmacist within a thirty-mile radius, which is a significant distance for someone to travel who might not have the means to travel," Weatherford explains. "And then you're also looking at affordable health care, so a lot of people will use a Planned Parenthood or a federally qualified health center, and there might not be one for four or five counties. As we see more and more restrictions to women's health being passed and implemented in Kansas, I believe we are also seeing a shift from focusing on targeting providers to targeting the patient, targeting women."

As if that were not enough, women in Kansas now have another worry when accessing reproductive care: Operation Rescue getting ahold of their names and addresses. In the spring of 2012, the anti-abortion organization made a stunning announcement: it was in possession of the records of at least eighty-six women and girls who had been treated in one month at an abortion clinic in Kansas.[24] Just exactly how Operation Rescue came into possession of this information remains a mystery. Clinic officials confirmed a break-in around the time Operation Rescue claimed it came into possession of the records, but they didn't have reason to think any patient data had been breached. Cheryl Sullenger, Operation Rescue's senior policy adviser, said that a confidential informant had provided the records and that no laws had been broken in their acquisition. "It's no secret we seek information about abortion clinics," Sullenger said. After redacting the patient names and other identifying information, Operation Rescue posted the records online. The Brownback administration then initiated an investigation against the clinic based on Operation Rescue's allegations that providers failed to report cases where a pregnancy was the result of incest or involved a minor to state health authorities. The clinic denied the allegations and challenged the charges in court.[25]

In the end, bills like HB 2598 and HB 2523, as well as the

actions of groups like Operation Rescue, reveal the strategy that is currently unfolding in the state of Kansas: regulate abortion out of existence, and whatever can't be regulated out of existence will be terrorized into submission. As Holly Weatherford explains, "Brownback's statement that he'll sign any pro-life bill that gets to his desk has empowered the pro-life community in the state in a way they had not been empowered before."

11. MISSISSIPPI: CLOSE THE CLINICS, BRING BACK THE COAT HANGER

A patient walking through the doors of the Jackson Women's Health Organization clinic in Jackson, Mississippi, needs to be prepared. As the only provider of abortions in the entire state, the clinic is rarely without at least one protester lying in wait for any woman who may be entering with the intent of terminating a pregnancy. If the patient is lucky, she'll run into Dana Chisholm, president-elect of Pro-Life Mississippi, who will sing hymns, quote Bible tracts and offer to pray with her. Less fortunate patients will encounter Roy McMillan, an elderly anti-abortion activist who takes a more aggressive approach. "Mommy, please don't kill me, mommy! I have a dream, mommy," he yells to those going in and out of the clinic.[1]

Jackson Women's Health Organization has been the sole public provider of abortions in Mississippi since 2004. As such, the clinic has become a lightning rod of controversy in a state that very much disapproves of pregnancy termination. This controversy reached a head on Election Day 2011, when Amendment 26, declaring support for "personhood"—the belief that life begins at the moment of conception and that the fertilized egg is entitled to legal rights—appeared on the ballot. The personhood movement had already failed in Colorado, where a similar ballot initiative had been voted down twice. But Mississippi, with its devout Christian population and staunchly anti-abortion leanings, was considered an ideal state for the anti-choice movement finally to get a foothold in legally redefining a person's life as beginning the moment sperm and egg meet.

Amendment 26 became the hottest topic in Mississippi's

2011 state election—even more heated than the race for governor. (Perhaps one of the reasons the governor's race was less controversial was that both the Republican and Democratic candidates came out in favor of Amendment 26.)

Despite intense advocacy by Personhood USA, a group that believes persons are "'created in the image of God' from the beginning of their biological development, without exceptions," Amendment 26 was solidly defeated, with 58 percent of the voters declaring they did not believe legal rights should be granted at the moment of conception.[2] A vigilant public relations campaign that kept voters informed about the legal ramifications of the amendment—that it could make some forms of contraception, especially IUDs and possibly even the birth control pill, illegal, that infertility treatments could be outlawed, and that women who miscarried could potentially find themselves investigated by the authorities—cooled the public's interest in granting rights to fertilized eggs, even if the amendment promised to end abortion in the state.

One of the leaders of the grassroots informational campaign was the Jackson Women's Health Organization, whose owner, Diane Derzis, formed Wake Up Mississippi as a vehicle to campaign against Amendment 26. In an open letter pleading for funds to help her new group, Derzis reiterated the need to defeat the amendment to keep abortion legal not just in Mississippi but everywhere else as well:

> Legislators and anti-choice zealots continue every year with their assaults on reproductive healthcare making MS abortion laws the most restrictive in the land. AND . . . We are still standing STRONG! However, on November 8th, the MS ballot will include the Personhood Amendment which will end abortion in MS and will more than likely take Roe-v-Wade to the Supreme Court. WE CANNOT ALLOW THIS TO HAPPEN!

And neither can you. . . . If passed, Personhood Amendment #26 will not only ban abortion BUT ALSO ban most (if not all) forms of birth control, end in-vitro fertilization, and make stem cell research illegal. In addition, women who miscarry will be subject to criminal investigation! THIS MEASURE GOES TOO FAR AND IS A THREAT TO—NOT ONLY WOMEN IN MISSISSIPPI—BUT THE ENTIRE COUNTRY![3]

The 2011 election also ushered Phil Bryant, a Republican, into the Mississippi governor's office. A co-chair of the "Yes on 26" campaign, Bryant had advocated for Amendment 26 so thoroughly that his staff passed out bumper stickers supporting the amendment during campaign events. Prior to Election Day, Bryant told *Salon* that the fight over Amendment 26 was "a battle of good or evil . . . the evil dark side that exists in this world is taking hold. And they're saying, what we want you to be able to do is continue to extinguish innocent life. You see, if we could do that, Satan wins."[4]

Nothing strikes at the heart of *Roe v. Wade* the way the concept of fetal personhood does. The entire premise of a constitutionally protected right to abortion pivots on a balance between the actual life of the pregnant woman and the developing life of a fetus and assumes the two are not always equal. Fetal personhood laws upend this balance, moving the slogan "life begins at conception" from an aspirational statement to one with legal consequences.

The first legal notions of personhood came in 1989, when the Supreme Court, in *Webster v. Reproductive Health Services*, considered a challenge to a Missouri anti-abortion law that, among other items, had in its preamble a statement that the life of each human being begins at conception and that state law could be interpreted to give unborn children the same rights enjoyed by other persons. Writing for the majority, then Chief Justice William Rhenquist noted that the preamble did not regulate abortion but merely expressed a judgment favoring childbirth over abortion, a judgment that prior case law, specifically *Maher v. Roe*, permitted. But the court added that if the state were to use the preamble to limit the conduct of the plaintiffs as abortion providers, this might present a justiciable issue at a later date. The court further observed that the preamble had applications in other aspects of state law, such as tort and probate law, and to give it full force and effect could expand it beyond the legislative intent. As to whether or not a declaration that life begins at conception is constitutional, for the time being the court did not comment.

Justice Harry Blackmun, joined by Justices William J. Brennan and Thurgood Marshall, led the dissenters. Blackmun accused the court of attempting to erode *Roe* by endorsing, even tacitly, a legislative statement that directly conflicted with precedent and women's civil rights. Blackmun would have struck down the preamble because, in his view, it would chill the exercise of a woman's right to an abortion and unconstitutionally burden the use of contraceptive devices. In a separate dissent, Justice John Paul Stevens wrote that the preamble violated the Establishment Clause because it adopted an essentially religious view. He also wrote that he believed the preamble would impact contraceptive use in violation of the court's precedent on that issue in *Griswold v. Connecticut* and similar cases.

Justices Antonin Scalia and Anthony Kennedy joined the majority in *Webster*, and Scalia has made it clear in no uncertain terms over the intervening years that he does not believe in a woman's right to control her body. In addition, the anti-abortion makeup of the court has only grown stronger since 1989 with the addition of Justices Clarence Thomas, Samuel Alito and, of course, Chief Justice John Roberts. That anti-abortion advocates see in this shift in the court and in *Webster* an opening to attack *Roe* directly is evidenced by ongoing efforts in places like Colorado and Oklahoma to push for personhood even in the face of crushing rejection by the citizens of those states. Simply put, there is an all-out war on women's right to choose underway, under the guise of personhood. And in many ways, Mississippi is the front line in this war.

In fact, the defeat of Amendment 26 was just a temporary victory for pro-choice advocates in Mississippi, as multiple abortion bans were proposed during the state's 2012 legislative session. Like Ohio, Mississippi proposed a ban on abortion after the point at which an embryonic or fetal heartbeat can be detected. Although the bill passed the house, the senate chair of the judiciary committee refused to allow a vote, saying he had no interest in passing a law that was so obviously unconstitutional. However, unlike in Ohio, anti-abortion legislators in Mississippi tried to do an end run around the committee chair, as house leaders attached the ban as an amendment to a separate bill that changed the maximum prison sentence for someone charged with child homicide. The bill once more passed the house but stalled in the senate when the chairman again refused to let it out of committee for a full vote. The senate's refusal to pass either the heartbeat ban or a second ban prohibiting RU-486 from being dispensed unless a doctor was present in the room caused abortion opponents to refer to the state senate as a "chamber of death." However, the senate won back the approval of anti-choice activists in April 2012 when it passed HB 1390, a Targeted Regulation of Abortion Providers (TRAP) bill that may wind up ending elective abortion in the state of Mississippi once and for all.[5]

Traditionally, TRAP legislation is meant to enact backdoor abortion bans by restricting access to clinics via an incremental process that usually harms a few providers at a time. A TRAP law will, for example, limit the locations of clinics in order to force providers into costly moves, or prohibit their ability to move to more accessible locations. The legislation may also limit who can provide abortions or do the pre-screening, so as to reduce the number of patients who can be seen. Some proposed TRAP bills have introduced expensive new insurance requirements in an attempt to make it too costly for doctors to continue to offer terminations. Other TRAP laws, such as one passed in Kansas, create onerous rules for buildings that house clinics, including requiring extra-wide doors for gurneys and regulating the size of "operating rooms" and even supply closets, as well as ordering that additional drugs be kept on site (and changing licensing requirements for those who dispense said drugs), even if those drugs bear no relation to the procedure being performed. (Kansas even mandated blood pressure cuffs for infants and toddlers, despite the fact that there would never be a need for those to be used in clinics.)[6] The ultimate goal of TRAP laws is to drive up costs in the hopes that clinics will be forced to close, or that doctors will refuse to do terminations because of the expensive coverage and liability (or else add the expenses to the cost of the procedure, making it unaffordable for most women).

Although they are often used to try to shut down clinics and make abortion difficult to access, TRAP laws usually do not attempt to eliminate abortion access altogether. However, Mississippi chose to go straight for the knockout blow when it came to HB 1390. Like most pieces of TRAP legislation, the bill was based on the misguided idea that abortion is a risky, dangerous medical procedure and that women need to be protected and kept safe in case something goes wrong. The bill's proponents brushed away the evidence that, especially in the first trimester, abortion is actually much safer than childbirth and that the risk of complications is quite low. Instead, they framed terminating a pregnancy as an endeavor fraught with potential life-threatening side effects, in order to mandate who should be allowed to perform the procedure and under what circumstances.

HB 1390 proposed that only board-certified ob-gyns be allowed to perform abortions and that those doctors have admitting privileges to a nearby emergency room in case of a complication requiring immediate attention. It was the second point of the law that left Jackson Women's Health Organization in a bind. While all three of its staff physicians were board-certified, only one had admitting privileges to a local hospital, and getting privileges for the other two physicians was unlikely in a state so adamantly anti-abortion. Because of threats and intimidation, two of the doctors at the clinic didn't reside in state, making it more difficult for them to get privileges from a local hospital. The only doctor associated with the clinic who did have admitting privileges was soon targeted by the state's lieutenant governor, who said that his affiliation with Jackson Women's Health Organization made him unqualified to serve on the state's Board of Health—despite the fact that he had already been serving for nearly a year and had been appointed by pro-life governor Haley Barbour. Upon blocking Dr. Carl Reddix's confirmation to the board, Lieutenant Governor Tate Reeves's spokesperson said that Reeves "had concerns about the appointment because of [Reddix's] affiliation with the abortion clinic and wanted Gov. Bryant to refer a qualified doctor to guide state health policy."[7]

Are admitting privileges for abortion providers, in particular, necessary to protect a patient's health, as the anti-abortion legislators alleged? Not according to Dr. Jen Gunter, an ob-gyn, writer, and women's health advocate, who points out that providers of other kinds of medical care are equally likely to run up against complications yet are not required to hold admitting privileges:

In the small likelihood there is a complication of a procedure it is not necessary (or sometimes even desirable) that the doctor doing the surgery correct the problem. For example, I am a gynecologist. I cannot fix every single complication of the surgeries that I perform. If I inadvertently damage the bowel during a hysterectomy I need a general surgeon to help me. If we extended HB 1390 to all surgical procedures (and we really should if it is for safety purposes) then no surgeon could do any surgery of any kind because no surgeon is trained to fix every single complication. Why single out women getting abortions? Shouldn't every patient at a surgical center benefit from the same law?[8]

Dr. Gunter's explanation shows how the very essence of a TRAP law is the direct targeting of those who provide abortions.

Mississippi is not the first state to propose that doctors must have admitting privileges if they perform abortions. Alabama, Arizona, Indiana, Kansas, Missouri, Oklahoma, South Carolina and Utah have the same requirement in place, and each of these laws has withstood court challenges. However, in these other states, the question of whether a particular provider can or cannot obtain admitting privileges doesn't determine whether access to safe, legal abortion in the state will be cut off entirely, as would be the case in Mississippi. "If the intent of the bill and the result of the bill are to shut down the only provider in the state, it may raise different constitutional questions than were raised in other cases where admitting privileges were an issue," Jordan Goldberg of the Center for Reproductive Rights told the Associated Press.[9]

Lawmakers in Mississippi were unabashed in acknowledging their desire to close the clinic and end access to legal abortion in the state. When questioned about what would happen if HB 1390 forced the only clinic in the state to close, and whether that might prompt women to pursue unsafe abortions, Senate Public Health Committee Chairman Dean Kirby said, "That's what we're trying to stop here, the coat-hanger abortions. The purpose of this bill is to stop back-room abortions."[10] State Representative Lester "Bubba" Carpenter told supporters at a GOP event that although HB 1390 could eventually end up in court, the bill would hopefully stop abortion in the state—that is, unless a woman had a coat hanger available. Caught on video, Carpenter said, "It's going to be challenged, of course, in the Supreme Court and all—but literally, we stopped abortion in the state of Mississippi, legally, without having to—*Roe vs. Wade*. So we've done that. I was proud of it. The governor signed it into law. And of course, there you have the other side. They're like, 'Well, the poor pitiful women that can't afford to go out of state are just going to start doing them at home with a coat hanger.' That's what we heard over and over and over. But hey, you have to have moral values. You have to start somewhere."[11]

Carpenter's comments were a refreshing bit of honesty from a legislature that for the most part continued to use the guise of "women's safety" as a means toward banning abortion. Diane Derzis was unmoved by their alleged concern. "These people hide behind words like 'safety,' 'women's health,' 'concern' and 'compassion,'" she told *Politico*. "This kind of legislation—they bring [it] up every year. Up to this point we've jumped through the hoop."[12] This time, however, the hoop was just out of reach, as Governor Bryant eagerly signed HB 1390 into law on April 16, 2012. "This legislation is an important step in strengthening abortion regulations and protecting the health and safety of women. As governor, I will continue to work to make Mississippi abortion-free," Bryant stated once the legislation had passed through both legislative chambers. On the day he signed the bill, he was much more forthright. "If it closes that clinic, then so be it."[13]

Bryant might have been trying to make Mississippi "abortion-free," but in reality, he and his legislative cohorts were actually making it inaccessible, expensive and unsafe. In 2010, nearly 2,300 abortions were performed in Mississippi, the vast majority at the Jackson Women's Health Organization clinic.[14] Most of these abortions were performed on women who were "nonwhite, unmarried, had a high school degree or less and already had children" and who claimed a "lack of financial and personal stability" as reasons for choosing a termination.[15] Closing the clinic would leave women in such circumstances with three options. First, they could travel out of state to obtain an abortion, increasing their costs, even though many women who seek abortions are already struggling financially. Second, they could continue their pregnancy, either adding another child they couldn't afford or putting the baby up for adoption in the hopes that someone else would be able to raise it. Finally, they could try to terminate the pregnancy on their own, an option that harks back to the dark days before abortion was legal in this country.

Under normal circumstances, the Jackson Women's Health Organization clinic would have had several months from the passage of HB 1390 to come into compliance, but the lawmakers demanded more immediate enforcement, aiming for a July 1 start date. House Public Health Committee Chairman Sam Mims sent a letter to the state health officer, Dr. Mary Currier, demanding that the department work quickly. "I am certainly aware that the Health Facilities Licensure Division is responsible for regulatory and enforcement duties on many types of facilities and does so with a limited number of employees," Mims wrote. "However, as the author of HB 1390, this legislation was one of my priorities as chairman of the Public Health and Human Services Committee, and I consider it an important accomplishment."[16] Mims requested expedited action on the bill, stating that he was looking into ways to ensure that the Jackson clinic would not be allowed any sort of grace period to come into compliance. The state representative told Reuters that he did not "want to give the facility 10 extra days to perform abortions" and was discussing with lawyers the legality of asking for immediate action against the clinic.[17]

Deciding not to wait to be officially shut down, Jackson Women's Health Organization and Willie Parker, an ob-gyn based in Washington, D.C., who traveled to Mississippi to do abortions at the clinic, filed a lawsuit demanding an injunction to bar HB 1390 from going into effect. The suit, filed on June 27, 2012, requested that a federal judge block the legislation, calling it an unconstitutional attempt to eliminate abortion in the state of Mississippi.[18] Parker and the clinic were represented by the legal team at the Center for Reproductive Rights. "For years, we have been beating back Mississippi's underhanded tactics to close the only abortion clinic in the state," said Nancy Northup, president and CEO of the Center for Reproductive Rights. "Mississippi lawmakers' hostility to women and their reproductive rights does not give them license to violate their constitutional rights. This measure would force Mississippi women who are already facing difficult circumstances to travel hundreds of miles to a neighboring state to get an abortion. That is simply not an option for many poor and working-class women, and will certainly lead some to consider unsafe and illegal alternatives that pose grave risks to their health, lives, and reproductive future."[19]

A temporary restraining order was issued late on the evening of Sunday, July 1, preventing HB 1390 from going into effect. The district court met again on July 11 to discuss a permanent injunction, with the state claiming that the clinic could pose a safety hazard and that even if the law went into effect, it would take at least ten months for the clinic to be closed down completely. The Center for Reproductive Rights and Jackson Women's Health Organization argued that without the clinic, there would be no access to abortion within the state of Mississippi for most women, a clear violation of undue burden under *Planned Parenthood v. Casey.*

Judge Daniel P. Jordan III, a Republican appointee, was stuck in an unenviable position. If he sided with the plaintiffs, he would set a precedent on what constituted undue burden. If he sided with the state, he would also set a precedent, in this case saying that the right to access a first-trimester abortion was not jeopardized by there being no clinics in a state—a ruling that would allow the rest of the country to separate into legal and illegal abortion states simply by regulating providers out of existence.

When Jordan returned his decision late on a Friday evening, the judge showed that he had found a way to avoid both these outcomes. He ruled that HB 1390 was legal and that Mississippi could put the law into effect. However, he also ruled that the doctors at the Jackson Women's Health Organization would not face any criminal or civil penalties under the new law. "The Act will be allowed to take effect, but Plaintiffs will not be subject to the risk of criminal or civil penalties at this time or in the future for operating without the relevant privileges during the administrative process," wrote Judge Jordan. "This will maintain the status quo in this litigation because the Defendants will be precluded from taking action that they do not now contemplate while Plaintiffs will be permitted to operate lawfully while continuing their efforts to obtain privileges as they said they would."[20]

"The judge sort of punted on the substance for the time being," says Michelle Movahed, staff attorney at the Center for Reproductive Rights. "He really focused on whether he felt we had shown irreparable harm. Certainly, I think he signaled that he was not looking at it that way and our challenge is not confined to specific circumstances—the two doctors providing the bulk of the abortions at the clinic right now." The ruling actually did cause harm even if the clinic remained free of criminal penalties for now, according to Movahed. "The clinic continues to try to find providers who can meet the needs of women in Mississippi, and since they've been having to look for providers outside the state, a requirement like the admitting privileges requirement or the ob-gyn requirement is going to artificially restrict the pool of providers they can draw from. By constricting the number of providers, that's going to have a serious impact on women's ability to access care."[21] In this outcome, Mississippi may represent the starkest example of the floor-to-ceiling approach anti-choice activists have taken to challenging *Roe*. With only one clinic in the entire state and a litany of restrictions on accessing abortion services, Mississippi lawmakers have succeeded in nearly making abortion legal in name only. Even if the lawmakers do nothing else, women in the state will, simply by virtue of geography, exist in a world with fewer health care options than that of their sisters to the north.

What would it mean for the women of Mississippi to live in a state that literally offers no legal access to abortion? It would be devastating for a population that already struggles with one of the highest poverty (and child poverty and infant mortality) rates in the country. The Mississippi Department of Health attributes the state's high infant mortality rate—ten deaths per every thousand live births—in part to the often unplanned nature of pregnancies as well as to a lack of quality prenatal care.[22] Jackson Women's Health Organization's Willie Parker says that, growing up in poverty in the South, he has seen these kinds of problems up close—the reason he is fighting to keep the clinic open. "For me, being from the South, having been reared in poverty, and as an African American person in the South in particular, I began to feel a sense of responsibility. Mississippi has one of the highest poverty rates in the country. The poverty rate for Mississippi in general is 20 percent and it's 48 percent for African Americans. This is the context in which African American women are experiencing unplanned, unwanted pregnancies and it meant that, if that clinic closes, a large proportion of the women affected are black and poor."[23]

Notably, the state's anti-choice policies target a population that has one of the lowest abortion rates in the country. "The abortion rate nationally is about nineteen per one thousand women," says Parker. "The abortion rate in Mississippi is six. The irony is it's an extremely low abortion rate, relatively speaking, and yet disproportionately it is made of women who are more likely to have one child or multiple kids. A woman who already has a child living in poverty, and we know that's much more likely to be an African American woman; the poverty rate is double for blacks versus whites in Mississippi. It's the perfect storm around why, if that clinic closes, disproportionately African American women are going to be affected."

If Mississippi already has one of the lowest abortion rates in the country, why are the state's politicians so aggressive when it comes to anti-abortion legislation? It could have something to do with the state's legislative makeup. According to the *Mississippi Clarion Ledger*, of all the states in the country, Mississippi has the fifth-lowest representation of women in its legislature, with females holding just 26 of 174 seats in 2011.[24] Pamela Merritt, a writer and reproductive justice activist from Missouri, says that lack of representation makes it easy for lawmakers to enforce legislative control over women's lives. "I think, as a woman who works in politics and a woman of color, I don't see a lot of me. You don't see a lot of women. We are definitely not representative of what we are in the population and you certainly don't see a lot of women of color. What you really don't see working politics or lobbying politically are your average, everyday 'sista.' The fact that we're not represented in government, we are challenged to speak truth to government, makes us an incredibly easy target."[25]

Without proper advocacy in government, the cycle of poverty that many rural and minority women are already stuck in is compounded by the virtual elimination of their reproductive rights when access to abortion is cut off. "No matter what the right-to-life movement likes to say, children cost money and making money is hard," states Merritt. "For women who are not degreed and are probably not going to get a college degree, shift jobs become the norm. They tend to not have health insurance and they tend to not be very forgiving of needing to leave because your child has an ear infection. Every child that a woman has compounds that stress on her job and makes it less likely for her to stay in a work environment and move up the ladder. So there's that factor and I can't stress enough how the reality is that unhealthy people who have unplanned pregnancies have complicated pregnancies and complicated health outcomes. In a very unforgiving world it's very easy to wake up all of a sudden and you are thirty, you've got three children and you don't have choices, you have decisions to make and you have compromises to make and very often they don't allow for the kind of risk taking that people who are more affluent have."

Despite Judge Jordan's ruling that the Jackson Women's Health Organization wouldn't be penalized for failure to follow the new law requiring admitting privileges for doctors who perform abortions, the state of Mississippi nonetheless moved ahead with its efforts to shut down the clinic. Soon after the judge's order, the state made its initial inspection of the clinic to cite it for noncompliance with HB 1390. The year 2013 began with the board informing the clinic that due to its noncompliance with the new law, its license would be revoked, a potentially multi-month process that is currently underway and will undeniably bring all parties once more before the courts before it is completed.[26] Although abortion in Mississippi technically remains a legal right, access to the procedure hangs on by a thread.

12. ARIZONA: BANNING EVERYTHING BUT THE KITCHEN SINK

When Jan Brewer, a Republican, replaced Janet Napolitano, a Democrat, as governor in 2009, the residents of Arizona were quick to learn how important a gubernatorial veto can be when it comes to protecting the reproductive rights of women in a state. Brewer, the former Arizona secretary of state, took over when Napolitano was selected by President Obama to be the new secretary of homeland security. The move may have improved the safety of Americans across the country, but women in Arizona were left vulnerable to a state legislature determined to undermine the right to safe, legal abortion, birth control, and other reproductive services.

Emboldened by the knowledge that any anti-abortion bill they passed would now automatically receive the governor's signature, conservative politicians in the Arizona legislature went to work on an anti-abortion omnibus bill that Rachel Gold and Elizabeth Nash of the Guttmacher Institute said "essentially revamp[ed] abortion policy in the state."[1] HB 2564 added a twenty-four-hour waiting period after mandatory counseling from a doctor prior to an abortion, extended the ability for providers to invoke a conscience clause, and added restrictions for teens trying to obtain an abortion.

That was only the beginning. Since that 2009 legislative session, Arizona lawmakers have proposed a myriad of laws designed to coerce women out of having abortions, via methods such as insurance coverage bans and alterations to the tax code so that donations to groups that provide, refer or even mention abortion can no longer be tax deductible.[2] In 2011, the state passed

HB 2443, the Prenatal Non-Discrimination Act (PRENDA), a "race- and gender-based abortion" ban that made it a felony for a doctor to perform an abortion on a woman choosing to terminate her pregnancy because of the race or gender of the fetus. While the ban itself was mostly toothless—how exactly would one be able to know the motive of a woman terminating a pregnancy unless she told the provider in the first place?—the idea behind the ban was to make doctors nervous about potential liabilities for abortions they performed, as well as to throw up an additional hurdle for women of color seeking an abortion. For women who already had limited access to health care, such as many Latinas, this new hurdle was the last thing they needed. "That's one piece of legislation that really affects immigrant women because it kind of creates racial profiling of women," said Veronica Bayetti Flores, policy research analyst for the National Latina Institute for Reproductive Health. "Obviously legislation like PRENDA really targets immigrant women because it puts a lot of fears at the hand of the provider and the patients and again targets women of color, particularly immigrants."[3]

In addition to PRENDA, the state also passed HB 2416 in 2011, which restricted who was allowed to provide RU-486 and banned telemed programs, a two-pronged approach that left some clinics in the state no longer able to perform abortions. Planned Parenthood Arizona challenged HB 2416 as significantly increasing hardship for women who wanted access to legal first-trimester abortions. "What we're specifically contesting are aspects of the legislation about nurse practitioners and physicians' assistants providing this care, even though they have been providing this care in Arizona for over a decade with exemplary quality and safety ratings," Bryan Howard, president and CEO of Planned Parenthood Arizona, told the *Arizona Republic*. "There is no medical evidence that they should be prohibited from providing the care. And we know that given the shortage of physicians willing to provide this care, it will have a significant impact and place a burden on patients."[4]

In early 2012, while the U.S. Senate was debating the Blunt Amendment, which would allow religious employers to refuse to add birth control and other medical coverage they found "objectionable" to their employee insurance plans, Arizona was preparing to go a step farther. The state senate approved HB 2625, which would permit employers to pick and choose whether birth control pills should be covered by insurance plans based on what the employee in question was using them for. If it was for a "legitimate" medical condition, the medication would be covered. However, if a woman was taking the pills to prevent pregnancy, coverage would be denied.

The ACLU of Arizona lashed out at what was not just a violation of a woman's right to privacy but an obvious case of gender discrimination as well. Public Policy Director Anjali Abraham argued in a statement:

> The ACLU is opposed to the bill because it allows employers to impose their religious beliefs on their female employees and deny them access to important health care in the process, eliminates an existing anti-discrimination law that prevents employers from discriminating against women who independently obtain contraception from another source, and violates women's privacy by forcing them to prove that they're using contraception to treat a "non-objectionable" medical condition, such as endometriosis, in order to get coverage. Even in those limited circumstances involving medical conditions, women would still have to pay out of pocket for their medications.[5]

Proving a "non-objectionable" condition would likely require verification from a medical practitioner, since it's doubtful an employer would just take a woman's word at face value; few women are trusted to tell the truth when it comes to trying to get reproductive health services. The "she'll lie to get what she wants" argument isn't a new one, especially in regard to pregnancy. Multiple lawmakers have asked that rape and incest exceptions be eliminated from abortion bans based on the assumption that women would start lying about being raped just to get an abortion. Best known of these politicians was Idaho senator Chuck Winder, who noted during closing speeches on behalf of the state's mandatory ultrasound bill in 2012, "I would hope that when a woman goes in to a physician with a rape issue, that physician will indeed ask her about perhaps her marriage, was this pregnancy caused by normal relations in a marriage or was it truly caused by a rape."[6] Winder later clarified that he had meant that a woman would want to learn whether she had been impregnated by her husband or the rapist based on the age of the embryo or fetus, not that he necessarily thought women were lying about being raped. By that point, however, his words had been splashed across the national media, and the backlash was believed to be part of what forced the bill to be pulled.

That a doctor's judgment could trump the views of the woman when it came to her own reproductive desires became an overarching theme in Arizona. According to Dr. Gabrielle Goodrick of the Phoenix-based Camelback Family Planning, it had already become standard practice among some doctors in the state to withhold medical information from their female patients to ensure that they didn't seek out an abortion due to a problem with their pregnancies. "I had a patient come in who was told she couldn't have an assessment of the pregnancy by ultrasound until twenty weeks," recalled Goodrick. "I don't understand, they are told they have to wait another four weeks for an evaluation or more detailed ultrasound to look for abnormalities. I think that it's already happening; a lot of the doctors here are extreme in their opinions. There are really conservative doctors here and they already aren't being forthright with their patients."[7]

If a doctor withholds relevant information in the course of diagnosis and/or treatment, and a patient relies on that incomplete information to give her informed consent, and she is later injured as a result, the doctor has committed an act of medical malpractice.[8] This was a problem for Arizona lawmakers intent on providing medical providers with every incentive possible to dissuade women from obtaining an abortion. To "solve" this problem (of their own creation), in early 2012 the state advanced HB 1359, a "wrongful birth" bill that would shield doctors from any sort of malpractice suit that developed as the result of the missed diagnosis of a fetal anomaly, especially one that might cause a woman to consider terminating her pregnancy. Sponsored by Republican senator Nancy Barto, the bill aimed to eliminate the idea that "if a child is born with a disability, someone is to blame."[9] HB 1359 would protect a doctor if he or she chose not to inform a patient that her developing fetus had a condition that could significantly impact its life.

Allowing doctors to withhold information to drive a particular medical outcome means that instead of receiving an objective inquiry into her health and advice based on what the medical profession as a whole considers competent care, a pregnant woman will instead receive treatment determined by the individual beliefs of the doctor. This shifts the woman from the primary patient to, at best, a secondary consideration. If *Casey* tilted the balance to favor potential fetal life over actual maternal life, then wrongful birth bills break the scale altogether, as women can never be sure that the medical information they are receiving is accurate and unbiased, nor can they sue in the event that the information is found to be wrong or negligent. This requires women to exercise great caution and be even stronger advocates for their own care, as what constitutes accepted medical practice will no longer be easily determinable. Wrongful birth laws essentially assign pregnant women the same legal standing as juveniles or persons under legal guardianship and conservatorship, making them devoid of the ability to consent to a full course of medical treatment on their own behalf.

Ultimately, the impact of these bills will reach far beyond abortion politics. For example, birth injury suits represent a significant portion of medical malpractice cases, in large part because the costs associated with an act of negligence during pregnancy and delivery are so great. Insurance companies typically (and usually successfully) fight coverage for those costs; as a result, for many families malpractice recoveries represent the only financial means of providing for a disabled child. Wrongful birth bills will allow these claims to go uncompensated because all a health care professional will need to do to avoid liability is justify his or her course of treatment in terms of seeking to prevent an abortion. The creation of a medical malpractice shield strips women of the ability to be compensated for substandard medical care rendered to them while pregnant.[10]

Wrongful birth laws also completely shatter the bond of trust between doctor and patient. How can a woman go through a pregnancy not knowing if she should believe her doctor when he or she says the baby is healthy? Many women may not even realize the position their doctor takes on abortion until they find themselves in a situation that involves a medically futile pregnancy. Those who do learn their doctor's views are often shocked by the news. Dr. Goodrick told the story of one patient who was warned that if anything was wrong with her baby, she would still be expected to give birth. "Before the patient even said anything the doctor came in and said, 'If you have any testing or even if it's Downs, every baby deserves a chance at life.' The patient hadn't even opened her mouth and the doctor was already telling her the rules, that she would not support her if anything was wrong with the baby because every baby deserves life."

The reason it was so important for Arizona to make sure that doctors would be shielded from potential lawsuits if a baby was born with a previously undiagnosed disability that would normally have led a family to consider abortion was because the state was about to introduce HB 2036, the Women's Health and Safety Act. HB 2036 would take the "fetal pain" abortion ban Nebraska had passed two years earlier and twist it into a bill that could entirely change how women prepared for and dealt with potential complications in wanted, but medically flawed, pregnancies.

Although fetal pain abortion bans had been spreading across the country ever since Nebraska passed theirs in 2010, they had all been based on the same cutoff point—twenty weeks post fertilization, or twenty-two weeks gestation, a standard medical concept for dating pregnancies based on the woman's last menstrual cycle. With HB 2036, Arizona decided instead to set the cutoff for obtaining an abortion at twenty weeks gestation. By choosing to begin their ban two weeks earlier—based on the argument that "abortion becomes increasingly more dangerous than childbirth by twenty weeks gestation, with ever-increasing risk beyond twenty weeks"—not only would Arizona be further eroding the rights established in *Roe v. Wade*, but the state would be taking away a woman's right to decide whether or not to carry to term a fetus that was genetically compromised or that faced major health risks.[11]

Most genetic issues or anomalies cannot be detected via ultrasound until close to twenty weeks gestation, which is why a gender scan isn't offered until close to that time in pregnancy. By creating a ban that would go into effect near or even before the time that many women would learn about such problems, the Arizona legislature was taking the decision about how to deal with such pregnancies out of the mothers' hands. Women would either have to decide immediately whether or not to terminate their pregnancies or else be forced to carry doomed fetuses simply because they waited too long. A state that believed a woman should have to wait twenty-four hours after meeting with a doctor to terminate a pregnancy she didn't want now thought that a woman should rush into terminating a wanted pregnancy, possibly before she had even received follow-up care and confirmation of any health abnormalities. These were the concerns that Dr. Paul A. Isaacson, an ob-gyn who works with high-risk pregnancies, expressed when he testified against the bill in March 2012:

> In normal prenatal care, an ultrasound to assess the fetus is done in the 18–20 week range LMP. Prior to that range, an accurate fetal survey can't be done due to the small fetal size and immaturity of the organs. If an initial fetal ultrasound assessment shows a suspected abnormality, the patient is typically referred to a perinatology practice for a more thorough ultrasound. It might take several days for that to be arranged. . . . If a severe fetal anomaly is confirmed, the woman may then need time to reach a decision about whether to terminate the pregnancy. . . . For such women, this bill would force them to carry to term, often at substantial health risks to themselves.[12]

The legislature rejected Dr. Isaacson's plea and in April 2012 passed HB 2036, which Governor Brewer signed. The law was scheduled to go into effect on August 2, 2012.

Unlike the Nebraska fetal pain bill, HB 2036 was challenged in court. On July 13, 2012, the Center for Reproductive Rights and the American Civil Liberties Union filed suit on behalf of Isaacson and two other Arizona physicians who claimed that the twenty-week gestational ban would harm their ability to meet the medical needs of their patients. "This law in Arizona displays a callous disregard for the complicated and very difficult circumstances many pregnant women face—and yet proponents of the law have the audacity to claim that it is designed to protect women," Nancy Northup, president and CEO of the Center for Reproductive Rights, said in a press release, while CRR's lawyer,

Janet Crepps, decried the bill as an example of legislators playing doctor: "When state legislatures attempt to practice medicine, they get it wrong and women pay the price. By imposing criminal penalties, coupled with extremely narrow health exceptions, this law requires physicians to endanger the lives and health of their patients."[13]

Judge James Teilborg, an appointee of President Bill Clinton, presided over the case in U.S. District Court for the District of Arizona. Janet Crepps presented a straightforward challenge to the Arizona law, arguing that states are forbidden from banning abortions prior to viability. Teilborg disagreed and asked Crepps a series of questions about which abortion procedures might be involved and the relative frequency of each. He then lectured her for what he believed was a lack of compassion for the unborn, echoing the increasing concern in the federal judiciary over fetal rights. Teilborg said he had read the plaintiffs' affidavits and had found that they "reflect profound compassion and concern for their patients, the women, and presumably the fathers." However, he added, "I didn't find anywhere in those affidavits any expression of concern by the plaintiffs' positions for the unborn child— or even a hint of concern on their part." That was when it became clear that Teilborg was ready to take on *Roe*. "Given that silence on that part," he continued, "and given the silence in your own presentation, doesn't that underscore the legitimacy of the state's regulatory action out of concern for the unborn child?"[14]

On July 30, 2012, Teilborg issued his order and refused to block HB 2036 from going into effect. Barring emergency intervention, Arizona had just successfully enacted the most restrictive abortion bill in the country. Perhaps more importantly, Teilborg's decision set up a question that seemed perfect for the anti-abortion Roberts court to grab on to: In light of the *Gonzales* decision that bans partial-birth abortions both pre- and post-viability, what other pre-viability bans can survive constitutional scrutiny? For Teilborg, HB 2036 was constitutional because it wasn't a ban but a regulation:

H.B. 2036 does not prohibit all abortions after 20 weeks gestational age. Rather, H.B. 2036 regulates abortions that take place after 20 weeks gestational age. Accordingly, H.B. 2036 does not purport to ban all abortions past 20 weeks gestational age. Further, the statute allows for abortions up to and including 20 weeks gestational age. As such, H.B. 2036 is not a ban on previability abortions, but is rather a limit on some previability abortions between 20 weeks gestational age and viability (which it is undisputed usually occurs between 23 and 24 weeks gestational age).[15]

Once Teilborg did away with the idea that viability posed any true obstacle to finding HB 2036 constitutional by calling it a regulation and not a ban, he attacked the plaintiffs' arguments that the ban would force women to carry to term fatally flawed pregnancies because most fetal anomalies are detected outside the twenty-week window:

Plaintiffs argue that a pregnant woman needs time to make the extremely difficult decision as to whether to continue the pregnancy and, in such a situation, it will take longer than twenty weeks to make such a decision. Accepting these statements as true, while H.B. 2036 will make it necessary to make an immediate decision as to whether or not to have an abortion in some cases, such a time limitation cannot be construed to be a substantial obstacle to the right to make the abortion decision itself.[16]

One of the footholds Teilborg used to justify his ruling was that HB 2036 impacted only a small number of women in the state—those seeking abortions between twenty and twenty-three weeks.[17] While the number of women potentially injured by a law shouldn't matter—a law should be no less unconstitutional because it injures the rights of a few—a 2006 Supreme Court decision found that anti-abortion bills that restrict the rights of a few women are not unconstitutional.[18] In *Ayotte v. Planned Parenthood of Northern New England*, the court refused to strike down a New Hampshire parental notice law on the grounds that it would affect only a small number of people. The law prohibited doctors from performing an abortion on a minor until forty-eight hours after written notice was provided to her parent or guardian. It also included a judicial bypass provision (allowing the minor to seek a court order permitting the abortion without her parent's knowledge) and an exception where an emergency abortion was needed to prevent the minor's death. Before the law took effect, three abortion clinics and an abortion doctor filed suit seeking to overturn it on the grounds that in a small percentage of cases, a minor's health would be threatened without a "prompt abortion." The state of New Hampshire asserted that the judicial bypass provision would in fact allow for a prompt abortion in such cases.

The Supreme Court ruled that striking down the law on its face was not necessary or justified since only a few applications would present a constitutional problem. The opinion in the case was drafted by Justice Sandra Day O'Connor. It would be the last of her career before she retired from the court, and the decision seemed to reflect this fact, as the opinion went out of its way to find a reason to support the law, or as much of it as possible, while still keeping the principle of *Roe* in place. This was to be O'Connor's final attempt to find a middle ground between the hardening anti-choice fraction of the court, her own ambivalence toward abortion rights, and the reality that *Roe* was under threat." "When confronting a constitutional flaw in a statute," she wrote, "we try to limit the solution to the problem. We prefer, for example, to enjoin only the unconstitutional applications of a statute while leaving other applications in force . . . to sever its problematic portions while leaving the remainder intact."[19] Legislatures were now essentially free to pass laws they knew were in direct conflict with *Roe*, with a promise that those laws would be allowed to go into effect while constitutional challenges played out. Furthermore, the opinion made clear, those future challenges would have to come from individual women or providers who had suffered an actual injury and who could challenge the law "as applied" to them. By clearly favoring "as applied" challenges to abortion laws, the court had erected yet another barrier for women needing abortion care. If *Gonzales* had provided anti-abortion legislators with a roadmap to follow to make sure their abortion restrictions survived constitutional review, then *Ayotte* was an example for the courts in upholding abortion restrictions that were drafted specifically in conflict with established precedent.

The Center for Reproductive Rights filed an immediate appeal of Judge Teilborg's decision. The Ninth Circuit Court of Appeals then issued an immediate emergency injunction blocking HB 2036 from taking effect while the constitutionality of the law was appealed.[20] Sadly, however, whatever decision the Ninth Circuit ultimately delivers will be largely irrelevant. A reversal of the district court ruling would all but guarantee an appeal to the Supreme Court. And since both legislators and attorneys for the state of Arizona have said publicly that HB 2036 is designed to present a direct legal challenge to *Roe*, a reversal by the Ninth Circuit would be exactly the outcome anti-abortion advocates are hoping for.[21] Letting the decision stand, on the other hand, would leave those women most at risk in Arizona with almost no reproductive health care options at all. And as we've seen with other abortion restrictions, other states will follow suit. Should abortion opponents receive a favorable opinion allowing "fetal pain" to become the new standard for creating abortion bans, they will then introduce more medically disproven "science" claiming a fetus can feel pain earlier and earlier, leaving women who live in states that don't affirmatively legislate to protect reproductive health with no access at all.[22] Without a change in course, it will no longer matter what *Roe* says: women will have been legislated and adjudicated out of full and equal citizenship.

TAKING BACK CONTROL

To end the growing segregation when it comes to women's health care and reproductive rights, several steps need to be taken. First, we need to roll back the anti-abortion and anti-contraceptive initiatives that have sprung up like weeds in several states with a conservative majority in their legislatures and a conservative governor at the helm. Along with that, we must also block new anti-women laws from being passed. But more importantly, in order to establish a truly equitable health care system that isn't limited based on gender, race, location or economic means, we need to propose laws that make abortion, family planning, pregnancy prevention and health screenings a personal right, and that also expand the number of people who can provide these services.

To do all this, we must elect individuals to Congress who will push pro-women initiatives, as well as recruit and support such candidates at the state and local levels. It took the wave election of the 2010 midterms to create the current atmosphere that has allowed anti-choice policies and laws to be passed in state legislatures all over the country. Many of the bills discussed in this book were introduced in the wake of that wave, in states that had already demonstrated hostility toward women's reproductive health and rights.

"At the state level, I really do believe that people thought that these Tea Party conservatives wanted to work on jobs and the economy," Elizabeth Nash of the Guttmacher Institute says of the 2010 election. "Instead, these folks walked into a system that was already stacked against abortion rights because there had been a number of [anti-choice] successes over the past few years. So there was already essentially a network in place for passing abortion restrictions, and these new conservative candidates came right into it." States such as Wisconsin were able to take advantage of the rare trifecta of every branch of government being under Republican control, which made it possible for them to pass numerous abortion restrictions that normally would not have made it into law.

However, we will not be successful in electing politicians who support women's rights unless we first establish an activist base from which potential candidates for office can draw resources and support. According to Gloria Feldt, the former president of Planned Parenthood, what is needed is a strong, energetic core, not unlike a feminist version of the "personhood movement" that has been popping up in a variety of states. "Just as the personhood efforts are not coming from the mainstream anti-choice groups," she says, "I'd love to see a band of feisty young feminists out there leading the charge on this, saying, 'Excuse me, we are persons and we want our personhood guaranteed.'"

Feldt herself took a "feisty" stance when she became national president of Planned Parenthood, particularly on the issue of contraceptive coverage. "Why did we choose that one?" she asks rhetorically. "Because we know that almost every single American citizen uses birth control at some point in their lives, and that cast the biggest net when it comes to bringing people to your side. The abortion issue and the birth control issue, at their core, are the same issue. Those people who oppose abortion are pretty much the same people that oppose contraception coverage or funding for family planning or anything related to it. So it gave us a way to move the agenda. Now almost every insurance plan covers contraceptive. It's not perfect. They'll do high deductibles, they'll do all kinds of things to try not to pay for it, but now contraceptive coverage is standard care."[1] Feldt's work helped pave the way for co-pay-free contraception in insurance plans under the Affordable Care Act, showing that what begins as activism can eventually make its way into governmental policy.

In addition, echoing Feldt's words on the close relationship between contraception and abortion, the Affordable Care Act has also created an opportunity for policy changes involving abortion coverage in insurance plans. Several states in the past few years have proposed bills that extend insurance coverage of abortion, make abortion an essential part of health care, expand access to terminations, or seek to make contraception more readily available. In Connecticut, the legislature declared abortion to be an "essential benefit" that had to be included when the state selected its insurance exchange program. "This issue is favorably resolved for all women now in Connecticut," Jennifer Jaff, an advisory committee member of the Insurance Exchange Health Plan, told the Connecticut Mirror in June 2012. "Stripping women of elective abortions is not a tenable option."[2]

There is also the problem of women who are covered under private insurance through their employers, who have no reason or incentive to offer abortion or contraceptive coverage. That is why more states need to push beyond the welcome but still limited options provided by the Affordable Care Act and turn to the example set in Vermont, which took the coverage the ACA offered via state exchanges a step farther, providing what many progressives in the country had hoped to see implemented: universal health care. Governor Peter Shumlin signed bill H202 into law in May 2011, saying, "We gather here today to launch the first single-payer health care system in America, to do in Vermont what has taken too long—have a health care system that is the best in the world, that treats health care as a right and not a privilege, where health care follows the individual, not the employer."[3]

Until more states agree with Vermont that health care is a right, there needs to be a concerted effort to guarantee that abortion is not limited by the policies of the federal government. Unfortunately, since the 1976 passage of the Hyde Amendment, the government has increasingly restricted poor women's rights to access abortion. Like many other abortion restrictions, the Hyde Amendment started out acknowledging a wide range of allowable circumstances that were slowly chipped away over the years. For example, the original amendment allowed Medicaid to pay for abortions in cases of rape, incest, life endangerment, and physical health damage to the woman. But two years after it went into effect, the exception for physical health was dropped. Two years after that, the rape and incest exceptions were dropped as well and were not reintroduced until 1993.[4] "There are so many low-income women and Latinas who depend on Medicaid for their primary source of health care, and for abortion services not be covered by Medicaid is a huge barrier for them," explains Veronica Bayetti Flores of the National Latina Institute for Reproductive Health. "It seems completely hypocritical that there are a few people in power who can decide for low-income young women or women of color what is best for them and they're not given the dignity to decide that themselves."[5]

If the federal government cannot ensure that women, regardless of their economic means, have access to abortion, then the Hyde Amendment should be repealed. "This is an issue we have been involved in since we were founded in 1993," says Stephanie Poggi, executive director of the National Network of Abortion Funds.[6] NNAF and several other reproductive justice organizations, including the National Latina Institute for Reproductive Health, have formed a broad-based coalition dedicated to removing the ban on abortion coverage for women enrolled in Medicaid, regardless of what state they reside in. "We see how painful it is, how many women aren't able to raise money to get an abortion," Poggi says. "We talk to so many women every day who are in need of our help in order to exercise their legal right, their constitutional right, their human rights as a woman and a person to be able to decide what's best for them and their lives. Women are going to great lengths and they are not able to come up with the money, and that is because of the Hyde Amendment."

According to the Guttmacher Institute, between 18 and 35 percent of women who want an abortion and are on Medicaid continue their pregnancy because they cannot afford to terminate.[7] One of the arguments of those who oppose abortion is that no woman has ever said later on that she regrets having her child. Couldn't it be argued, then, that cutting off a woman's financial ability to obtain an abortion is, in the long run, a positive thing? Not at all, according to Poggi. "It's never a good thing to take away someone's rights. Women who are compelled to have a child when that's not the right decision to make will do the best they can. They may face poverty, they may really struggle to even meet basic needs, but they absolutely do the best they can. But the fact that women and families do the best they can in really difficult circumstances is no argument for heaping difficult circumstances upon them." The coalition plans to engage in movement building to provide supporters with the information and tools they need to explain how the Hyde Amendment harms women. Their goal is to educate not just reproductive justice supporters but other progressive organizations and policymakers as well. "We know that this is not something we can win overnight, that is clear," Poggi says of the effort, which is already underway. "But we're ready to come together and say, 'That's it. We are through with letting the Hyde Amendment do its damage.'"

While expanding a woman's ability to pay for an abortion (or at the very least have some or all of it covered under some form of insurance or medical assistance) by eliminating the Hyde Amendment would be an important step for reproductive rights, unless the number of abortion providers is increased, women will still find themselves without access to the procedure in a timely manner. Since the longer a pregnancy progresses, the more complicated and costly a termination becomes, having enough medical professionals who are able to perform abortions is vital. This is an issue that those who want to end abortion have been focusing their efforts on in recent years. As Dr. Michael New, a fellow at the conservative think tank the Witherspoon Institute, wrote in LifeNews:

> In the years since Roe v. Wade, pro-lifers have mostly focused on what could be called "demand side" legislation. In short, legislation that was designed to make it more difficult for women to obtain abortions by either imposing legal barriers or increasing the economic costs of abortion. However, in recent years, pro-lifers have pursued what could be termed "supply side" strategies. These are strategies that are designed to make it more difficult for abortion providers to either stay open or perform abortions. . . . Overall this has been a wise strategy for pro-lifers. . . . Better yet, good research shows that fewer clinics results in fewer abortions.[8]

Even before TRAP laws began limiting the number of doctors who could provide abortions, the community of providers was already dwindling, decreasing by 38 percent between 1982 and 2005.[9] Doctors who had begun practicing in the years following the Roe ruling, and in some cases before that, were starting to retire, and many of the new doctors coming into the profession were showing less interest in providing abortions. It's little wonder that fewer were interested, as being a provider since the 1980s has meant constant harassment at clinics as well as a growing sense of danger from a volatile anti-abortion movement that, ever since the assassination of Dr. George Tiller, has carefully balanced an undercurrent of violence with the plausible deniability that allows it to claim that every incident is the work of a lone wolf unaffiliated with the movement. Add in burdensome licensing and insurance regulations; new laws that allow providers to be sued by patients, their partners or boyfriends, even extended family; and requirements that providers act as counselors to determine if a woman was coerced or might have mental issues, and it is not surprising that many doctors today are not interested in offering abortions.

On top of that, fewer doctors are being trained on how to perform abortions than ever before. According to the National Abortion Federation, "A survey in 1998 revealed that first trimester abortion techniques are a routine part of training in only 46% of America's ob-gyn residency programs. About 34% offer this training only as an elective, and 7% provide no opportunity at all for young doctors to learn to provide safe abortions."[10] Medical Students for Choice concurs, stating that "97 percent of family practice residents and 36 percent of ob-gyn residents have no experience in first trimester abortion procedures."[11] While Medical Students for Choice notes that medical schools "are simply not addressing the topic," it is difficult for many to do otherwise when states are coming up with new and creative ways to cut back on training, such as the Kansas bill that attempted to end training for abortions at the publicly funded University of Kansas Medical Center. (A federal version proposed by North Carolina congresswoman Virginia Foxx was intended to cut off federal funding to any medical training program that might teach abortion procedures, a move that caused one House colleague to object, noting, "It's really not wise to have ignorant physicians."[12] Fortunately, Foxx's bill failed.)

In early 2012, California state senator Christine Kehoe introduced Senate Bill 1501, which would have allowed nurses, nurse midwives and physician's assistants to provide first-trimester surgical abortions, a change that could have greatly expanded access for the large rural population of the state.[13] Unfortunately, the senate committee in charge of the bill balked at the proposal. Although first-trimester surgical abortions are one of the safest medical procedures, the bill was also panned by the California Nurses Association. Kehoe then tried to revamp the bill, limiting the new eligibility to nurses who had already completed a pilot program in first-trimester aspiration abortions.* However, even that was too controversial for the committee. Kehoe vowed to bring the bill back one day, saying in a statement, "The issue of access to early abortion care for women across California remains an important issue and we will continue to review our options for ensuring that all women have access to care by providers they know and trust in the communities where they live."[14] Assemblywoman Toni Atkins submitted a new bill in the 2013 legislative session, which at the time of publication has yet to be heard.[15]

Kehoe's proposal may not have succeeded (and the jury is still out on the Atkins bill), but there is no reason why similar legislation cannot be proposed in other states. It is only recently that abortion—both surgical and medication—has been limited so drastically. The lack of a consistent standard across the country should make it clear that what is required of an abortion provider has more to do with the whims of a state's legislature than with medically proven practices. Mississippi's requirement that a provider be a board-certified ob-gyn and have hospital admitting privileges, for example, is meant to reduce the number of doctors who can perform an abortion, not to protect patient safety. If a state were to propose a bill mandating who was allowed to deliver a baby, in the process prohibiting general practitioners and midwives from delivering babies and threatening felony charges for anyone assisting in a birth who wasn't a board-certified obstetrician, such a law would never pass. That the same law can be viewed as reasonable when it comes to providing a first-trimester abortion is nothing but a political double standard. If anti-choice groups such as Americans United for Life and the National Right to Life Committee can draft anti-choice, anti-reproductive-rights model legislation bills that are then farmed

---

*An aspiration abortion is a simple vacuum abortion procedure done either with a hand or machine pump that does not require surgery and can be done in less than fifteen minutes in a doctor's office or clinic environment.

out to friendly politicians in states throughout the country, then pro-choice bills can also—and should also—be written and offered to favorable lawmakers to be proposed as a counterweight.

Although a woman should have the right to terminate an unwanted pregnancy regardless of her race, income and where she lives, it is still in everyone's best interest to prevent unwanted pregnancies in the first place. To that end, ensuring that contraception is easily accessible and affordable should be a priority. Yet, as we have seen, a movement has been afoot to eliminate Title X funding, especially for Planned Parenthood affiliates, and to increase protections for those who block access to birth control because of "conscience" issues. Over forty lawsuits have been filed against the federal birth control mandate in the Affordable Care Act, mostly by religious groups who are challenging the mandate on the grounds that it erodes their religious liberties.[16] These lawsuits serve a dual purpose: in the short term, they challenge the policy of making contraception widely available and affordable, while in the long run, they reframe the conversation as one in which the very idea of contraception is seen as a "controversial" issue dividing the American public.

In California, Democratic assemblywoman Holly Mitchell introduced a bill in 2012 to expand access to contraception, proposing that registered nurses be legally allowed to administer birth control. The bill was meant to address long waits at clinics when a doctor or nurse practitioner wasn't available to fill a birth control prescription. The California Women's Law Center wrote in support of the bill, saying, "An essential component of comprehensive reproductive health care for women, hormonal contraceptives are among the safest and widely studied medications available today."[17] The bill passed and was signed into law by Governor Jerry Brown, who said, "At a time when some seek to turn back the clock and restrict women's health choices, California is expanding access to birth control and reaffirming every woman's basic constitutional rights."[18]

As reproductive rights advocates like Holly Mitchell push for greater access to contraception, religious conservatives have countered with broad conscience clause claims designed to shield individuals and institutions from having to provide insurance coverage or employment protections or dispensing medications that conflict with their moral or religious beliefs. The effect has been a renewal of First Amendment litigation around the boundaries of religious liberty as it relates to choice. However, the religious or moral beliefs of the person behind the drugstore counter filling a prescription—or a company providing health insurance for its employees—shouldn't matter under "conscience" for the simple reason that refusing to provide or cover contraception is akin to impregnating a woman against her will. So far, the courts have largely agreed, but with a flood of litigation on this issue currently clogging the federal courts, it is all but certain the Supreme Court will have the final say at some point.

Furthermore, access to contraception, just like any other health care issue, should be a right that is not contingent on a person's financial status. But just as anti-choice politicians are limiting who can have an abortion, they are also limiting who can receive birth control. Being anti–birth control isn't a popular stance, which is why anti-choice activists, and especially Republican politicians, have reframed it as an effort against Planned Parenthood rather than revealing their true intention, which is to stop government funding for contraception. That family planning actually saves the government much more than it costs by reducing the need for other medical expenses the government must cover, as well as additional social services that must be paid for with tax dollars, is irrelevant to the anti-choice movement.

A secondary strategy used by anti-choice activists who wish to eliminate Title X funding is to shift such funding to religious institutions and nonprofits that supposedly provide similar types of services. Governor Rick Perry's scheme in Texas of moving a chunk of family planning money to crisis pregnancy centers was the epitome of the crusade to, on the one hand, refuse to allow taxpayer money to pay for something that one group declares morally objectionable yet, on the other hand, use government funds to funnel money to religious groups. It is a tactic that was also used in Minnesota when then Republican governor Tim Pawlenty signed the Positive Alternatives Act into law in 2005, in essence green-lighting taxpayer dollars for religious-based crisis pregnancy centers.[19]

For pro-choice activists, a reactive counterapproach would be to try to restore lost family planning funding to its original designees as well as to forbid reallocation, such as in Ohio's attempt to place religious medical facilities ahead of Planned Parenthood clinics in the line to receive funds. A proactive approach, however, would be to ban crisis pregnancy centers and religious hospitals and clinics from receiving any form of taxpayer support and then have that funding set aside specifically to subsidize contraception. After all, if abortion and birth control funding can be restricted because of the disapproval of certain groups, shouldn't tax dollars going to religious institutes be looked at under the same lens, especially since those organizations are operating without any tax liability in the first place? Such laws would no doubt be controversial—and impossible even to propose without the right politicians in legislatures and state houses across the country.

Unfortunately, for too long abortion supporters have relied on the political party apparatuses to keep a woman's right to control her own body safe. But while the GOP has steadily whittled out most of its members who identified as pro-choice, the Democratic Party has been more than happy to embrace politicians who believe that women and men shouldn't have equal rights when it comes to controlling their bodies. In many instances, Democratic groups have lent substantial support and resources to these candidates. Of these groups, the Democratic Congressional Campaign Committee has been one of the most flagrant supporters of such candidates. Offering its vast email network and soliciting donations on behalf of groups such as the so-called Blue Dog Coalition, a band of ultraconservative Democrats who, among other issues, don't believe in a woman's right to choose, the DCCC has often viewed reproductive rights as something not worth breaking alliances over. Most egregiously, DCCC chair Chris Van Hollen called up Michigan Democrat Bart Stupak in 2010, urging Stupak to run for reelection. This plea came shortly after Stupak introduced the infamous Stupak-Pitts Amendment, which removed abortion care from the Affordable Care Act, setting the stage for elimination of coverage throughout state exchanges.[20] The Democratic National Committee hasn't been any more helpful, repeatedly putting money and support behind politicians like Nebraska senator Ben Nelson, a staunchly anti-abortion Democrat who almost singlehandedly derailed health care reform before eventually agreeing to vote with his party and the president.

With groups like the DCCC and the DNC basically unsupportive of a woman's right to control her body, it is not surprising that reproductive rights advocates are increasingly looking to nongovernmental organizations like Planned Parenthood, EMILY's List and NARAL Pro-Choice America as well as state groups like Ruth's List in Florida, womenwinning in Minnesota, the Montana Women Pipeline Project and New Jersey's Women Advocating for Good Government. "EMILY's List has worked for over twenty-seven years to elect pro-choice Democratic women to stand up to the conservative right and work towards building a progressive America," says the group's president, Stephanie Schriock. "These Democratic women are the most reliable progressive voting bloc in Congress; they are the most reliable progressive voting bloc for women's health in state legislatures; and these voters are really recognizing that if you want progressive policies across the board, but especially in women's choice, you have got to get more and more pro-choice candidates and, in particular, women."[21]

The biggest challenge for these organizations is finding candidates in the first place, particularly female ones. According to She Should Run, an advocacy group dedicated to bringing equity to political representation, "women are 50% less likely than men to seriously consider running for office, less likely than men actually to run for office, and far less likely to run for higher office."[22] This is an issue that many organizations—and politicians—are trying to address. For example, in 2011, New York senator Kirsten Gillibrand launched Off the Sidelines, a website and social media network that focuses on getting women involved politically. The project's website reads:

> From local school board, to the US Senate, good candidates are needed to run every year at all levels of government. Right now, women make up only 17% in Congress and there are only 6 women governors. If you are considering running for any office, attend a campaign school such as the Women's Campaign School at Yale (1 week in the summer), or training weekends run by the Women's Campaign Forum, Eleanor Roosevelt Legacy, Emerge, Campaign Boot Camp, EMILY'S List, and other organizations to get a sense of what it is all about.[23]

Under the Off the Sidelines umbrella, Gillibrand had endorsed and raised money for long-shot congressional candidates such as Kathy Hochul, who won a special election in a Republican congressional district in New York in 2011, and Tulsi Gabbard, who was elected to congress from the state of Hawaii in 2012, as well as numerous other state and federal candidates across the country. "Kirsten is committed to helping empower women and girls to make their voices heard and make a difference in their community," says Todd Beeton, a spokesperson for Gillibrand. "That's why she started Off the Sidelines, as a call to action to women to get more involved in the issues they care about. Running for office is one aspect of that. Kirsten believes that if more women are elected to office and get a seat at the decision-making table, the outcomes will be better."[24]

Whether or not they have prior legislative experience, it is essential that candidates who support a woman's right to abortion and equitable health care be recruited to run. As we saw in the 2010 election, a large percentage of the candidates elected as representatives of the Tea Party had no previous electoral experience, and many even used that fact as a selling point in their campaigns. After being swept into office, these same legislators were responsible for creating the most hostile state environment to a woman's right to choose this nation has ever seen.

Those Tea Party electoral victories would likely not have been possible, however, with a reasonable set of campaign finance spending and disclosure laws in place.[25] Campaign finance reform and the problem of unlimited secret money flooding our elections is an issue of immediate importance for women's rights. In 2012, states enacted 122 new provisions related to reproductive health, including 43 restrictions on abortion access.[26] The connection between big corporate election spending and anti-woman legislation is undeniable. In fact, it shares an architect: attorney James Bopp Jr.[27] Bopp has served as vice chairman of the Republican Party as well as general counsel for the National Right to Life Committee since 1978. His other high-profile anti-choice memberships include the Susan B. Anthony List and Focus on the Family. Bopp regularly testifies on anti-choice legislation, and his entire career has been built around promoting an anti-choice agenda and eradicating campaign finance reform. His goal is to shroud in secrecy the large-dollar donors behind the efforts to criminalize contraception and outlaw abortion.

And because of the persistency of the wage gap, women are not able to spend as freely in elections as are their male counterparts. According to the Center for Responsive Politics, even though women slightly outnumber men in terms of overall population, they accounted for only 29.6 percent of people making federal-level political donations in the 2010 election cycle. [28] That figure gets even smaller when you look at overall dollar amounts donated. Women contribute less money less often to political campaigns, and this is true even though the number of contributions by women is on the rise.[29] As a result of this discrepancy in political donations, women's voices and interests are often drowned out.

While focusing political efforts on electing women-friendly candidates is one way to fix the inequality riddling our system, once a law is on the books, it is much harder to reverse, even if the right candidates are put into office. It's for that reason that we need to focus also on judicial, rather than just legislative, means to effect change. As we've seen over the past few years, lawmakers in states hostile to women have no problem passing bills that may be unconstitutional, then leaving it up to the judiciary to make the final decision about whether or not the bill can actually become law. Organizations like the American Civil Liberties Union and the Center for Reproductive Rights are constantly filing suit against these bills; from 2010 through 2012, the Center for Reproductive Rights filed twenty different suits against anti-women bills that had been passed and signed by Republican legislatures and governors.

As a result, federal judicial appointments at the district court and appellate levels are just as important as the makeup of the Supreme Court when it comes to matters of women's reproductive health. As of the end of 2012 there were eighty-two vacancies on the federal district and appellate courts, or a vacancy rate of about ten percent.[30] The nonpartisan Congressional Research Service recently determined that vacancy rates in the federal judiciary are at their highest levels in thirty-five years.[31] In addition, over 40 percent of the existing vacancies are in courts so overburdened that they have been designated "judicial emergencies" by the Administrative Office of the U.S. Courts.[32] Right now, we have an overburdened court system staffed by judges who are increasingly hostile to reproductive rights.

It simply cannot be stressed enough how important the judicial branch is when it comes to ensuring an equal, fair and accessible health care system for women. In the two decades following the 1992 ruling in *Planned Parenthood v. Casey*, the courts have yet to find a single case in which any law represented an "undue burden" on women seeking an abortion. Until a judge issues an official ruling that can be seen as setting a precedent as to what really constitutes an undue burden, Casey in essence can be used to do what abortion opponents have wanted ever since Roe was decided, which is to effectively ban abortion in nearly all circumstances by making it too difficult to access.

Electing sympathetic politicians and continuing to fight unconstitutional laws in the courts are both important ways to level the playing field when it comes to women's health care. However, the most immediate step is to stop anti-abortion and anti-contraception bills from becoming law in the first place.

Once it became clear that many of the conservative politicians elected in 2010 were actively engaging in a war on a woman's right to bodily autonomy, pro-choice forces began fighting back. Perhaps the best example of this is the fight surrounding two bills, one in Virginia and one in Idaho, that would have forced women to undergo an ultrasound prior to having an abortion regardless of whether a provider deemed it medically necessary or not.

After a spate of mandatory ultrasound laws were passed in states like Oklahoma and Texas, by the time a similar bill was proposed in Virginia, women were fed up. "There was a Virginia Coalition of Women's Health that was formed," says Erin Matson, the former action vice president of the National Organization for Women (NOW). "That was made up of local groups, and our local chapter, Virginia NOW, was very supportive in that. Because we were close by, we supported some of the events that the coalition did out of our national office."[33] One of the main events was a march on the state capitol demanding that the bill be shelved.[34] Activists also began referring to the bill as "state-sanctioned rape" because it mandated that, if the abortion was to take place within the first twelve weeks of a pregnancy, a transvaginal ultrasound had to be performed in order to obtain the most accurate, detailed picture possible. Since the majority of abortions occur during the first twelve weeks, the rule would have applied to most abortions performed in the state.[35]

The "state-sanctioned rape" framing caught fire among women's rights activists. Virginia delegate David Englin, a Democrat, said that if the bill was approved, it would essentially turn the doctor who performed the ultrasound into a criminal under the definition of rape in the Virginia penal code. "[Object sexual penetration] is a new issue I plan to raise when we debate the Senate version of this bill next week," Englin told Andy Kopsa of RH Reality Check. "But surely decent people who disagree about a woman's right to choose can at least agree she shouldn't be vaginally penetrated without her consent. That's a moral outrage that every decent person should oppose, regardless of partisan politics. Worse still, it appears as if the lack of any consent requirement would turn doctors into criminals by compelling them to commit object sexual penetration, which is a heinous sex crime under Virginia law."[36]

While the bill ultimately passed in early 2012, the forced transvaginal requirement was dropped, replaced by the more traditional abdominal ultrasound, a small but not insignificant victory for pro-choice forces. Virginia governor Bob McDonnell and his fellow anti-abortion lawmakers had presented the transvaginal ultrasound as a necessary part of informed consent, arguing that if a woman didn't know the size of the fetus or embryo and wasn't certain of the exact date of conception, she somehow didn't have enough information to make an informed choice to terminate her pregnancy. By changing the transvaginal ultrasound requirement to the abdominal version, despite medical evidence that, for most women early in pregnancy, the images would hardly be recognizable, it became clear that "informed consent" was never the goal, but that the purpose of the law was to set up a roadblock to abortion access.

The fight over the bill also took its toll on McDonnell and his allies. After the bill passed, polling showed that over half the state disapproved of the mandatory ultrasound requirement.[37] McDonnell's popularity went down five points, and the state legislature's popularity went down ten points. "These lawmakers grossly underestimated the outrage their insidious attacks on women's health would provoke in Virginia and across the nation," Tarina Keene, executive director of NARAL Pro-Choice Virginia, wrote in April 2012. "In fact, their agenda awakened the sleeping giant of pro-choice Virginians—the majority of citizens who believe the government should stay out of women's private medical decisions and personal family choices. With this spring awakening will come retribution at the polls this fall and in fall 2013."[38]

Erin Matson agrees that what happened in Virginia was the sign of an awakening. "I don't agree with the idea that women took reproductive rights for granted," she says. "When you grow up having access to birth control and access to reproductive rights, you have every right to expect that it will still be there…. Now that these attacks are coming on their own terms, I think that they are being experienced on their own level. We are seeing a new awakening, but when I say awakening I don't mean people were sleeping. Women had every right to expect they wouldn't be harassed this way. That's not taking something for granted, or being unaware. We have the right to be treated as full people."

Idaho Senate Bill 1387, which was proposed by Republican senator Chuck Winder, would likewise have forced women to undergo an ultrasound prior to an abortion, regardless of whether or not doctors deemed it necessary. However, Winder also included a requirement that the state board of health create a list of "health care providers, facilities and clinics" where a woman could receive a free ultrasound, a group that would be made up almost exclusively of crisis pregnancy centers. Unfortunately, many if not all of the centers didn't have the proper equipment to provide the diagnostic images the law required. The bill also stated that the ultrasound had to be performed by the same physician, or an agent of the physician, who performed the termination, neither of whom were likely to be someone at a crisis pregnancy center.

When it was explained to Winder that the pregnancy center ultrasounds might not meet legal requirements, he seemed unconcerned, saying that the purpose of the bill was to stop women from having abortions.[39] This open, brazen admission that the bill had nothing to do with health care and was just an attempt to convince women to forgo their legal right to terminate a pregnancy angered the people of Idaho into action. The day the senate committee debated the bill, a Boise woman showed up with a petition with over 4000 signatures asking that the bill be killed.[40] People in and out of the state also used social media to put pressure on Winder, other key legislators, and even the governor, asking them to table the bill. Hannah Brass Greer of Planned Parenthood Votes Northwest recalls, "We had a number of volunteer phone banks with emails going in to targeted legislators. We had a middle-of-the-week, midday rally with over three hundred people showing up."[41]

Despite the public pressure, the senate voted the bill through. Yet even with mounting protests from anti-abortion activists, who went as far as to perform live ultrasounds in the state capitol to prove that women "love" undergoing the procedure, the bill never received a hearing in the house because of the counterpressure from pro-women activists.[42] Opponents of the bill filled the hearing room as the bill was being debated in the senate, then followed up with letters, phone calls and emails that drew the attention of the local and national media.

"This was my sixth session of the Idaho legislature, and I had never been involved in a fight against a bill that had so many people come to the legislature, make phone calls, come to vigils," recalls Brass Greer. "We don't often have a lot of victories. This is a lesson in not discounting the community you are working in and not assuming what will and won't get people fired up. There is some sort of changing of the tide; people that didn't focus on these issues before are focusing on them now, both nationally and in the state. We need to fight against all of these bills with the same intensity each time. A lot of times you might lose. But sometimes you win and you win really big."

As the examples in Virginia and Idaho demonstrate, activism can prevent anti-women legislation from passing or, at the very least, keep it from being as burdensome as it might have been in its implementation. However, even in cases where it is obvious that a bill will pass, a large public outcry can change the tone of the debate and have some effect, regardless of how little it may change the result in the end. For example, it was assumed that once Georgia representative Doug McKillip proposed a twenty-week post-fertilization fetal pain ban in 2012, the bill was a given for passage. Instead, the bill was nearly torpedoed due to fracturing within the anti-choice community when the state senate made a modification in response to pressure from pro-women's groups.

When McKillip's bill was originally introduced in the Georgia house, it provided absolutely no exceptions to the ban on all abortions after twenty weeks fertilization. Medical experts testified against the bill, noting that abortions after twenty weeks are almost exclusively due to medical issues with the fetus, a fact that McKillip repeatedly disputed without evidence. After Dr. Andrew Dott testified that in all his years of practicing medicine he had never had a patient choose to have an elective abortion after twenty weeks, McKillip called him a liar, saying the doctor was making up stories to kill the bill. Jay Bookman of the *Atlanta Journal Constitution* reported, "Contradicting Dott, [McKillip] insisted that [the] 'grand majority' of abortions performed [in] Georgia past the 20th week are abortions of convenience. But again, he cited nothing more than his own considerable moral certitude as evidence."[43]

Despite the emotional testimony, the house refused to allow an exception for "medically futile pregnancies," demanding that women carry all pregnancies to term even if doctors tell them that the baby won't survive outside the womb. In response, angry activists flooded the state capitol, where they were joined by the female Democratic delegation, all of whom opposed this intrusion into women's private lives by the mostly male state government. The senate, trying to find a way out of a situation that had morphed into a political hot potato, amended the bill to allow terminations when the fetus was found to be nonviable.[44] McKillip and his cohorts were so angry at the modification that they nearly threw out the entire law. It was only after extensive negotiations, including an explicitly minimalistic definition of what constitutes a "medically futile pregnancy," that the new bill was voted into law.[45]

Although the ban made it into law, it wasn't the version that had been initially introduced, and it passed with activists chanting, "We will remember!" outside the chamber doors. At the same time, the Democratic delegation turned their backs on McKillip as the votes were cast.[46] In the end, a nearly guaranteed victory for anti-choice politicians instead became a mixed bag of success and failure, and, more importantly, the public perception of the debate shifted drastically as a result of the actions at the state capitol. The bill was then challenged by the ACLU Foundation of Georgia and is currently blocked from being enacted.[47]

In the end, if there is a silver lining to the anti-contraception, anti-abortion, anti-women laws that have been passed or enforced since 2010, it is that they have created the beginnings of a powerful activist backlash. This backlash has in turn shown that with concerted planning and effort, the decades-long erosion in women's health care rights may yet be reversed. "I think one of the really heartening things that we've seen this year is the extent to which women are standing up and saying, 'Enough of this crap,'" says Michelle Movahed of the Center for Reproductive Rights. "We are in the middle of a new 'Anita Hill moment' when it comes to reproductive rights," adds Matson. "Just like Anita Hill used the horrific way that she was treated and it galvanized women to run for office, I sincerely hope that we will see a longer-term infusion of more women ready to stand up for reproductive rights." While Matson admits these are still "dark, dark days for reproductive rights," in this darkness, she can see rays of light. "In these dark days I actually have a lot of hope," she says. "Activism is at a different level right now. Awareness is at a different level right now. People ask, 'Where are the women?' and let me tell you they are here right now fighting back against these rightwing assholes. I don't see that going away, I only see it growing. I do feel paradoxically at this horrible time a lot of hope about activism and feminism and the reproductive justice movement."

We can use the fortieth anniversary of *Roe v. Wade* to reaffirm the principle that a woman's right to control her body supersedes the right of the state to mandate how her body is used if she is pregnant. The first four decades after *Roe* have been about slowly whittling away the rights of women that were established by that ruling. Now it's time to dedicate ourselves to making the next forty years about gaining those rights back for every woman and girl in this country.

ACKNOWLEDGEMENTS

The list of family and friends who contributed their enthusiastic support to this book is a humbling reflection of the tremendous dedication and strength within the reproductive rights community, without whom this project would not have been possible. We'd like to thank the tireless providers, advocates, activists and attorneys, many of whom are featured in the book, for their work, day-in and day-out, to keep abortion safe, legal, and accessible for as many women as they can. We'd also like to thank Janel Frisina, Lisa Needham and Tara Jenson for helping turn around a manuscript in a ridiculously short amount of time and Nimbus Theatre for generously providing a creative space for conducting interviews and putting the book together on very short notice. We promise we'll give you all more time with the next project.

Robin would like to thank her children and especially her husband for all of their patience every time she said, "I just need to finish this chapter." She knows "Mommy's working," has been hard to hear so many times these last eight months and she promises to make it up to you. The book may have occupied her mind, but her heart was and always will be filled with you. She really will buy you a puppy, and now it is in print so she can't take it back.

Jessica would like to thank her father for raising her with a deeply-developed sense of justice and equality that quickly drove her out of insurance-defense work and into advocacy work, her siblings for their unqualified love and support, and Melanie Shirley for insisting she just shut up and write something. Finally, Jessica would like to thank her children for the daily reminder to find the joy in life and her husband and partner in life Kelly for keeping her laughing every day, no matter what—not an easy task, to say the least.

We would also like to thank Ig Publishing. We never believed anyone would take a risk on two first time authors with an as of yet unwritten book, much less publish it in less than a year. We are so grateful for everything you managed to rearrange to make this book a reality.

Finally, we would like to thank Physicians for Reproductive Health (formerly Physicians for Reproductive Choice and Health) and the National Network of Abortion Funds. This book would not exist without the personal stories and insights from the providers and activists who have made helping those who need access to abortion services a reality regardless of where they live, their income level and personal economic status, or the barriers put in place to stop them. We want to especially thank Alexandra Ringe, who spent hours of her own time opening the doors so we could speak with many of the doctors in this book, setting up interviews with providers on our behalf. We also want to specifically thank Stacey Burns and Megan Peterson, who did the same, helping to identify the right people at NNAF to explain to us what it is really like to try to fund an abortions for low income women who are already spending every cent they have trying to keep themselves and their families afloat. In a world where few people want to publicly discuss the harsh realities of providing and funding abortions, we are grateful to have come into contact with so many willing to speak out for equality for abortion rights for all women, not just those who can afford to have options.

NOTES

INTRODUCTION

1. Planned Parenthood v. Casey, 505 US 833 (1992).

2. "Making History in Mississippi: State's Only Abortion Clinic May Close," LiveAction News, June 25, 2012.

3. "New G.O.P Senate Hope Wendy Long Calls Gillibrand 'Extreme,' Says No One Would Miss Roe v. Wade," *Capital New York*, February 24, 2012.

4. "What If Roe Fell? The State-by-State Consequences of Overturning *Roe v. Wade*," Center for Reproductive Rights, September 2004.

1. WHERE IT ALL BEGAN: NEBRASKA—THE GOOD 'LIFE'"

1. Interview with Senator Danielle Conrad, May 20, 2012.

2. Lena H. Sun, "Neb. Doctor Who Performs Abortions in Md. Talks About Security Concerns, Future of Clinic," *Washington Post*, July 21, 2011, http://www.washingtonpost.com/national/health-science/neb-doctor-who-performs-abortions-in-md-talks-about-security-concerns-future-of-clinic/2011/07/21/gIQAaJMSXI_story.html.

3. "If You Are Pregnant: Information on Fetal Development, Abortion and Alternatives—Women's Right to Know Act," Minnesota Department of Health, January 2009, www.health.state.mn.us/wrtk/wrtk-handbook.pdf.

4. Susan J. Lee, JD; Henry J. Peter Ralston, MD; Eleanor A. Drey, MD, EdM; John Colin Partridge, MD, MPH; Mark A. Rosen, MD, "Fetal Pain: A Systematic Multidisciplinary Review of the Evidence," *Journal of the American Medical Association*, August 24, 2005, http://jama.jamanetwork.com/article.aspx?articleid=201429.

5. "Nebraska Breaks New Ground in Abortion Law with Enactment of LB 1103, Pain Capable Unborn Child Protection Act," Nebraska Right to Life Press Release, October 15, 2010, http://www.nerighttolife.org/SiteResources/Data/Templates/t4.asp?docid=571&DocName=PRESS%20RELEASES.

6. JoAnne Young, "Nebraska Legislator Speaker Flood One of Time's '40 under 40,'" *Lincoln Star Journal*, October 14, 2010, http://journalstar.com/news/state-and-regional/govt-and-politics/article_413a86b8-d7f0-11df-88c9-001cc4c03286.html.

7. Martha Stoddard, "State Could Reshape Abortion Policy," *Omaha World Herald*, February 21, 2010, http://www.omaha.com/article/20100221/

NEWS01/702219879.

8. Stoddard, "State Could Reshape Abortion Policy."

9. Julie Rovner, "Family at Center of South Dakota Abortion Debate," NPR, October 27, 2008, http://www.npr.org/templates/story/story.php?storyId=95960702.

10. Rovner, "Family at Center of South Dakota Abortion Debate."

11. Keller Russell, "Bill to Limit Abortions After 20 Weeks Draws Testimony from Across Country," *10 11 Now TV*, February 26, 2010, http://www.1011now.com/home/headlines/85374732.html.

12. Julie Burkhart, "What You Can Do About the Nebraska Abortion Ban that Just Passed," *Huffington Post*, April 13, 2010, http://www.huffingtonpost.com/julie-burkhart/what-you-can-do-about-the_b_535662.html.

13. JoAnne Young, "Bill to Tighten Abortion Restrictions Gains First-Round Approval," *Lincoln Journal Star*, March 30, 2010, http://journalstar.com/news/local/govt-and-politics/bill-to-tighten-abortion-restrictions-gains-first-round-approval/article_f8ed5360-3b99-11df-b9df-001cc4c03286.html.

14. Robin Marty, "Nebraska's Legislative Agenda: A Study in Contradictions?" RH Reality Check, April 12, 2010.

15. "Balancing Faith, Family and Practice: Focus on the Family's Conference for Medical Professionals and Spouses—April 10–12, 2008," retrieved November 21, 2012, http://go.family.org/images/medicalConf/mcBrochure.pdf.

16. Nivedita U. Jerath, MD; Chandan Reddy, MD; Jeffrey S. Kutcher, MD, "Medical Aspects of the Persistent Vegetative State," *New England Journal of Medicine*, May 26, 1994.

17. Steven Ertelt, "Fetal Pain Abortion Law Takes Effect in Nebraska, Could Set National Trend," Lifenews, October 15, 2010, http://www.lifenews.com/2010/10/15/state-5554/.

18. Robin Marty, "Nebraska Lawmakers, Seeking to Restrict Abortion Care, Ignore Science, Evidence, and Pleas of Parents," RH Reality Check, April 2, 2010, http://www.rhrealitycheck.org/blog/2010/04/02/nebraska-legislature-seeks-restrict-abortion-care-based-faulty-science.

19. Marty, "Nebraska Lawmakers, Seeking to Restrict Abortion Care, Ignore Science, Evidence, and Pleas of Parents."

20. Lauren Barbato, "Arizona Didn't Redefine Pregnancy, but Six Other States Did," *Ms. Magazine*, April 18, 2012, http://msmagazine.com/blog/blog/2012/04/18/arizona-didnt-redefine-pregnancy-but-six-other-states-did/.

21. Jason Clayworth, "Iowa Republicans Pass Nation's Toughest Abortion Restrictions," *Des Moines Register*, June 8, 2011, http://blogs.desmoinesregister.com/dmr/index.php/2011/06/08/iowa-republicans-pass-nations-toughest-abortion-restrictions.

2. OHIO: HEARTBEAT BAN CAUSES HEARTBURN IN ANTI-ABORTION ACTIVISTS

1. Faith2Action, "Nation's Largest Valentine's Day Delivery to Ohio Statehouse, Thousands of Red-Heart Shaped Balloons to Support Heartbeat Bill!" news release, February 14, 2011.

2. Faith2Action, "Nation's Largest Valentine's Day Delivery to Ohio Statehouse."

3. "Conservative Republicans Relish their New Power in the Ohio House," *Cleveland Plain Dealer*, January 11, 2011, http://www.cleveland.com/open/index.ssf/2011/01/conservative_cavemen_relish_th.html.

4. Interested Party Testimony on Substitute HB 125 James Bopp Jr.* Ohio Senate Health, Human Services, and Aging Committee, December 13, 2011, http://www.ohiosenate.gov/senate2012/Assets/Media/Content/9314.pdf.

5. Alex Stuckey, "'Heartbeat Bill' Divides Ohio Anti-Abortion Leaders," *Columbus Dispatch*, September 27, 2011, http://www.dispatch.com/content/stories/local/2011/09/27/heartbeat-bill-divides-ohio-anti-abortion-leaders.html.

6. Julie Carr Smyth, "Abortion Foes Push Vote on Ohio 'Heartbeat Bill,'" Associated Press, March 29, 2011, http://abclocal.go.com/kfsn/story?section=news/state&id=8041312.

7. Pam Belluck, "Health Experts Dismiss Assertions on Rape," *New York Times*, August 20, 2012, http://www.nytimes.com/2012/08/21/us/politics/rape-assertions-are-dismissed-by-health-experts.html.

8. Peter J. Smith, "Unborn Babies to 'Testify' in Heading on Ohio Heartbeat Bill," LifesiteNews, March 1, 2011, http://www.lifesitenews.com/news/unborn-babies-to-testify-in-hearing-on-ohio-heartbeat-bill/.

9. Aaron Marshall, "Ultrasound Images of Two Fetuses Shown to Lawmakers During the 'Heartbeat Bill' Hearing," *Cleveland Plain Dealer,* March 2, 2011, http://www.cleveland.com/open/index.ssf/2011/03/ultrasound_images_of_two_fetus.html.

10. William Hershey, "Commentary: GOP Speaker Must Walk a Tightrope on 'Heartbeat' Bill," *Middletown Journal*, May 15, 2011, http://www.springfieldnews-sun.com/news/news/state-regional/commentary-gop-speaker-must-walk-a-tightrope-on--1/nMrWr/.

11. Janet Porter, "I Can See the End of Abortion from Here," WorldNetDaily, September 12, 2011, http://www.wnd.com/2011/09/344369/.

12. Lisa Perriera, "Doctor to Ohio Senate: I Do Not Want to Tell My Patients I Cannot Help Them," RhRealityCheck, December 12, 2011, http://www.rhrealitycheck.org/article/2011/12/14/doctor-to-ohio-senate-i-do-not-want-to-tell-my-patientes-that-i-cannot-help-them.

13. Interview with Lisa Perriera, July 23, 2012.

14. Interview with Kellie Copeland, June 12, 2012.

15. Ann Sanner, "Ohio Abortions: Leader Suspends Hearings on Ohio 'Heartbeat' Bill," Associated Press, December 14, 2011, http://www.politico.com/news/stories/1211/70448.html.

16. Marc Kovac, "Kids Want Heartbeat Abortion Bill Passed," *Dix Capital Bureau*, January 11, 2012, http://www.the-daily-record.com/local%20news/2012/01/11/kids-want-heartbeat-abortion-bill-passed.

17. Jim Seigel, "Most Senators Return Anti-Abortion Bears," *Columbus Dispatch*, January 16, 2012, http://www.dispatch.com/content/stories/local/2012/01/15/most-senators-return-anti-abortion-teddy-bears.html.

18. Laura Bassett, "Anti-Abortion Group Sends Children with Teddy Bears to Lobby Lawmakers," *Huffington Post*, January 12, 2012, http://www.huffingtonpost.com/2012/01/12/ohio-heartbeat-bill-anti-abortion-group-teddy-bears_n_1202580.html.

19. Copeland interview, June 2012.

20. Blade's Columbus Bureau, "'Heartbeat Bill' Backers Send Roses to Ohio Lawmakers," *Toledo Blade*, February 17, 2012 http://www.toledoblade.com/State/2012/02/17/Bill-s-backers-send-roses-to-Statehouse.html.

21. Newsbrief, "Abortion Foes Ready New Ohio Attack," *Associated Press*, April 17, 2012, http://www.herald-dispatch.com/news/briefs/x1817470275/AP-News-Break-Abortion-foes-ready-new-Ohio-attack.

22. "An Open Letter from Ohio Senate President Tom Niehaus," May 2, 2012, http://www.ohiosenate.gov/senate2012/Assets/Media/Content/9313.pdf.

23. Faith2Action, "Janet Porter Responds to Heartbeat Opponents Quoted in Ohio Senate President's Letter," news release, May 3, 2012, http://mediafiles.f2a.org/JanetPorterResponds-May-3-2012.pdf.

24. Copeland interview, June 2012.

25. Interview with Lisa Perriera, July 23, 2012.

26. Planned Parenthood Southwest Ohio Region v. DeWine, Decided October 2, 2012. The panel decision appealed to the full Sixth Circuit for consideration and reversal, and in December 2012 the full Sixth Circuit refused reconsideration. Thus, the October 2012 decision stands.

27. Ted Hart, "Heartbeat Bill Supporters Changing Tactics," Ohio Votes.com, June 5, 2012, http://www2.ohio-votes.com/news/2012/jun/05/3/heartbeat-bill-supporters-changing-tactics-ar-1061100/.

28. Robin Marty, "Ohio Legislature Seeks to Punish Women with Unconstitutional Bills During Lame Duck Session," RH RealityCheck, November 13, 2012, http://www.rhrealitycheck.org/article/2012/11/10/ohio-legislature-to-punish-women-with-unconstitutional-bills-during-lame-du.

29. Jim Siegel, "Heartbeat Bill Dead, Planned Parenthood Funding Alive," *Co-*

lumbus Dispatch, November 27, 2012 http://www.dispatch.com/content/stories/local/2012/11/27/controversial-sente-bills-fade-away.html.

30. "A Message from President Pro-Tempore Keith Faber on House Bill 125 ('The Heartbeat Bill') and Abortion," KeithFaber.org, retrieved November 23, 2012, http://keithfaber.org/hb125/.

3. WISCONSIN: THE END OF MEDICATION ABORTION

1. Judith Davidoff, "Walker's Budget Removes Insurance Requirement to Cover Birth Control," *Capital Times*, March 2, 2011, http://host.madison.com/news/local/govt-and-politics/walker-s-budget-removes-insurance-requirement-to-cover-birth-control/article_a2f024ee-44d3-11e0-8dc8-001cc4c03286.html.

2. Maggie Fox, "Wisconsin Cuts Funds to Planned Parenthood," *National Journal*, June 26, 2011, http://www.nationaljournal.com/healthcare/wisconsin-cuts-funds-to-planned-parenthood-20110626.

3. Associated Press, "Walker Signs Slew of Controversial Legislation, Including Anti-Abortion and Sex-Ed Bills," *Wisconsin State Journal*, April 7, 2012, http://host.madison.com/news/local/govt-and-politics/walker-signs-slew-of-controversial-legislation-including-anti-abortion-and/article_94dab5ec-8008-11e1-a873-001a4bcf887a.html.

4. Associated Press, "Walker Signs Slew of Controversial Legislation, Including Anti-Abortion and Sex-Ed Bills."

5. Monica Davey, "Abortion Drugs Given in Iowa via Video Link," *New York Times*, June 8, 2010, http://www.nytimes.com/2010/06/09/health/policy/09video.html.

6. Michel Martin (host), "Growing Controversy Surrounds 'Telemed' Abortions," NPR, January 24, 2011, http://www.npr.org/2011/01/24/133182875/Growing-Controversy-Surrounds-Telemed-Abortions.

7. Monica Davey, "Abortion Drugs Given in Iowa via Video Link."

8. Steven Ertelt, "House Votes to Defund Planned Parenthood's Telemed Abortions," Lifenews, June 6, 2011, http://www.lifenews.com/2011/06/16/house-votes-to-de-fund-planned-parenthoods-telemed-abortions/.

9. 2011 Wisconsin Act 217, Section 10. 253.105(3) http://docs.legis.wisconsin.gov/2011/related/acts/217.

10. Robin Marty, "As Wisconsin Suspends Medical Abortions, One Doctor Explains How the Bill Puts Doctors at Risk," RH Reality Check, April 23, 2012, http://www.rhrealitycheck.org/article/2012/04/23/as-wisconsin-suspends-medication-abortions-one-doctor-explains-how-bill-puts-prof.

11. Planned Parenthood Advocates of Wisconsin, "Statement from Teri Huyck, President and CEO of Planned Parenthood of Wisconsin, April 20th, 2012," news

release, April 20, 2012, http://www.ppawi.org/home/news-media/newsroom/press-releases/PR042012.cmsx.

12. Interview with Fredrik Broekhuizen, July 25, 2012.

13. Interview with Elizabeth Nash, Guttmacher Institute, July 24, 2012.

14. "Abortion Pill—Fact Not Opinion," Wisconsin Right to Life Website, http://www.youtube.com/watch?v=x542DALvFosOctober 22, 2011, http://www.youtube.com/watch?v=x542DALvFos&feature=player_embedded).

15. Todd Richmond, "Wisconsin Assembly Debate Drags On," Associated Press, March 16, 2012, http://minnesota.publicradio.org/display/web/2012/03/16/wisconsin-assembly-debate/.

16. Robin Marty, "Wisconsin Planned Parenthood to Immediately Stop Offering Medical Abortions Due to New, Medically-Unsupported, Regulations," RH Reality Check, April 20, 2012, http://www.rhrealitycheck.org/article/2012/04/20/wisconsin-planned-parenthood-to-immediately-stop-offering-medication-abortions-du.

17. Steven Ertelt, "Planned Parenthood Stops Selling Abortion Drug in Wisconsin," LifeNews.com, April 20, 2012, http://www.lifenews.com/2012/04/20/planned-parenthood-stops-selling-abortion-drug-in-wisconsin/.

18. Pro-Life Wisconsin, "Planned Parenthood of Wisconsin Suspends RU-486 Abortions," Pro-Life Wisconsin Website, April 23, 2102, http://www.prolifewisconsin.org/MONUPD_files/April2312monupd.html#article2.

19. NARAL Pro-Choice Wisconsin, "Another Wisconsin Health Provider Ceases Medication Abortion in Face of Vague New Regulations," news release, May 22, 2012, http://www.wispolitics.com/1006/052212NARAL.pdf.

20. 505 U.S. 833, 884 (1992) (plurality opinion).

21. National Abortion Federation "Safety of Abortion," National Federation of Abortion website, accessed November 23, 2012, http://www.prochoice.org/pubs_research/publications/downloads/about_abortion/safety_of_abortion.pdf.

22. Robin Marty, "Planned Parenthood of Wisconsin Sues for Legislative Clarity on Act 217, Calls for End to Practicing Medicine by Legislature," RH RealityCheck, December 12, 2012, http://www.rhrealitycheck.org/article/2012/12/12/wisconsin-planned-parenthood-suit-legislative-medicine.

23. Robin Marty, "Planned Parenthood of Wisconsin Sues for Legislative Clarity on Act 217, Calls for End to Practicing Medicine by Legislature."

4. IDAHO: WILL A FETUS IN A SHOE BOX TURN A SINGLE MOTHER INTO THE NEXT ROE?

1. Associated Press, "Idaho Woman Charged After Fetus Is Found in a Box," *Idaho Press Tribune*, June 1, 2011, http://www.idahopress.com/news/state/article_

af96d919-7f3f-5969-8c77-bc918b3cc2b5.html.

2. Brittany Borghi, "Police Find Fetus in Box," LocalNews8.com, January 11, 2011, http://www.localnews8.com/news/Police-Find-Fetus-In-Box/-/308662/1562276/-/ n4rc04z/-/index.html.

3. Kim Murphy, "Idaho Woman's Abortion Case Marks Key Legal Challenge," *L.A. Times*, June 16, 2012, http://articles.latimes.com/2012/jun/16/nation/la-na-idaho-abortion-20120617.

4. Journal Staff, "Woman Accused of Aborting Fetus Will Not Face Charges," *Idaho State Journal*, August 24, 2011.

5. Interview with Richard Hearn, July 27, 2012.

6. 428 U.S. 106 (1976).

7. Id. at 108.

8. Id. at 117.

9. Id.

10. McCormack appealed the issue of standing to the Ninth Circuit Court of Appeals. Oral arguments were heard on July 9, 2012, and a decision on the issue was expected within six months of that argument. In the meantime, Hearn continues to pursue McCormack's claims on her behalf as a third party to the litigation.

11. National Advocates for Pregnant Women advances this point in their amicus curiae in the Ninth Circuit appeal. "When laws did criminalize abortion, the laws targeted the third parties who performed unlawful abortions, not the pregnant women themselves, because a primary purpose of these laws was to protect such women from third parties providing dangerous abortions" (p.19). See also, e.g., *People v. Nixon*, 42 Mich. App. 332, 201 N.W.2d 635, 639 (1972) ("The obvious purpose [of the abortion statute enacted in 1846] was to protect the pregnant woman. When one remembers that the passing of the statute predated the advent of antiseptic surgery, the Legislature's wisdom in making criminal any invasion of the woman's person, save when necessary to preserve her life, is unchallengeable").

12. 428 US 52 (1976).

13. "A Teenager Is Protected from a Forced Abortion," Independence Law Center, Independencelaw.org, http://independencelaw.org/2012/07/a-teenager-is-protected-from-a-forced-abortion/, retrieved December 15, 2012.

14. Robin Marty, "Anti-Choice Activists Applaud 14 Year Old Giving Birth," RH RealityCheck, July 25, 2011, http://www.rhrealitycheck.org/blog/2011/07/25/ antichoice-activists-applaud-year-giving-birth.

15. "PA Supreme Court Upholds Respect for Parental Consent," Independence Law Center, Independencelaw.org, http://independencelaw.org/2012/02/pa-supreme-court-upholds-respect-for-parental-consent/ Retrieved December 15, 2012.

16. States have expanded and contracted this idea with spousal consent requirements, but so far those have not passed constitutional muster.

17. Mike Hixenbaugh, "Abortion Law Would Give Fathers a Say State Legislators Propose Change: Opponents Blast Bill as 'Extreme,'" *Record-Courier*, http://www.recordpub.com/news/article/2327981.

18. HR 3803: District of Columbia Pain-Capable Unborn Child Protection Act, 112th Congress, 2011–2012. Text as of July 31, 2012.

19. Kim Murphy, "Idaho Woman's Abortion Case Marks Key Legal Challenge," *L.A. Times*, June 16, 2012, http://articles.latimes.com/2012/jun/16/nation/la-na-idaho-abortion-20120617.

20. McCormack v. Hiedeman, Nos. 11-36010,11-36015., September 11, 2012.

21. Id.

22. Nancy Hass, "The Next Roe v. Wade? An Abortion Controversy in Idaho Inflames Debate," The Daily Beast, December 12, 2011, http://www.thedailybeast.com/newsweek/2011/12/11/the-next-roe-v-wade-jennie-mccormack-s-abortion-battle.html.

5. INDIANA: WHEN A SUICIDE BECOMES A MURDER

1. Ed Pilkington, "Indiana Prosecuting Chinese Woman for Suicide Attempt that Killed Her Foetus," *The Guardian*, May 30, 2012, http://www.guardian.co.uk/world/2012/may/30/indiana-prosecuting-chinese-woman-suicide-foetus.

2. "Premature Birth Complications," American Pregnancy Association, http://www.americanpregnancy.org/labornbirth/complicationspremature.htm (retrieved January 6, 2013).

3. Heather MacWilliams, "Police: Baby Dies After Pregnant Mother Ingests Rat Poison," Fox 59, January 4, 2011, http://www.chicagotribune.com/news/education/wxin-police-baby-dies-after-pregnan-01032011,0,3796473.story (retrieved January 6, 2013).

4. Jon Murray, "Indiana House OKs Feticide Bill 95-0," *Indy Star*, April 6, 2009, http://www.indystar.com/article/20090406/NEWS05/90406046/Indiana-House-OKs-feticide-bill-95-0 (retrieved January 6, 2013).

5. "Infant Dies Days After Pregnant Mom Drank Rat Poison," RTV6—ABC, January 3, 2011, http://www.theindychannel.com/news/infant-dies-days-after-pregnant-mom-drank-rat-poison (retrieved January 6, 2013).

6. "Infant Dies Days After Pregnant Mom Drank Rat Poison," RTV6—ABC, January 3, 2011.

7. "Attorney Rips Prosecutor in Infant Rat Poison Death," WRTV Indianapolis, March 16, 2011, http://www.theindychannel.com/news/attorney-rips-prosecutor-in-infant-rat-poison-death (retrieved January 6, 2013).

8. "Doctors Want Charges Dropped in Infant Rat Poison Death," RTV6—ABC, April 1, 2011, http://www.theindychannel.com/news/doctors-want-charges-dropped-in-infant-rat-poison-death (retrieved January 6, 2013).

9. Eleanor Bader, "Criminalizing Pregnancy: How Feticide Laws Made Common Ground for Pro- and Anti-Choice Groups," TruthOut, June 14, 2012, http://truth-out.org/news/item/9772-criminalizing-pregnancy-how-feticide-laws-made-common-ground-for-pro-and-anti-choice-groups (retrieved January 6, 2013).

10. Soraya Chemaly, "The United States: Where Pregnancy Is Probationary and Your Body Is a Crime Scene," RH Reality Check, May 16, 2012, http://www.rhrealitycheck.org/article/2012/05/16/united-states-where-pregnancy-is-probationary-and-your-body-is-crime-scene (retrieved January 6, 2013).

11. Lanzetta v. New Jersey 306 U.S. 451 (1939).

12. "Pence, a former federal prosecutor, has argued that [Marion County prosecutor Terry] Curry never should have pursued the case. She said prosecutors have discretion, and can choose not to press charges in any given case, especially one like Shuai's where there are so many controversial issues. Shuai's case is also the first of its kind in Indiana, she said, so there's no clear precedent for charging a mother with murder based on her actions during pregnancy." Carrie Ritchie, *The Indianapolis Star*, January 5, 2013, http://www.usatoday.com/story/news/2013/01/05/infants-death-raises-womens-rights-questions/1566070/ (retrieved January 6, 2013).

13. Attorney Linda Pence, "The Criminalization of Pregnancy: State of Indiana v. Bei Bei Shuai," http://www.pencehensel.com/Briefs/The-Criminalization-of-Pregnancy-State-of-Indiana-v-Bei-Bei-Shuai.pdf (retrieved January 6, 2013).

14. IC 35-42-1-2, http://www.in.gov/legislative/ic/2010/title35/ar42/ch1.html.

15. "'I Never Said I Didn't Want My Baby': Mom Won't Be Prosecuted," *Des Moines Register*, February 2, 2010, http://www.momlogic.com/2010/02/i_never_said_i_didnt_want_my_b.php.

16. Gibbs v. State of Mississippi Supreme Court Amicus Briefing, May 20, 2010.

17. Interview, Lynn Paltrow, executive director, National Advocates for Pregnant Women, August 10, 2012.

18. Carla Zanoni, Shayna Jacobs and Ben Fractenberg, "Mother of Fetus Found in Alley Charged with Self-Abortion," DNA Info, Dec 1, 2011, http://www.dnainfo.com/new-york/20111201/washington-heights-inwood/mother-of-fetus-found-alley-charged-with-selfabortion (retrieved January 6, 2013).

19. Interview, Pamela Merritt, reproductive justice activist, July 22, 2012.

20. Commonweath v. Pugh SJC-10895, Massachusetts Supreme Court, July 12, 2012, http://law.justia.com/cases/massachusetts/supreme-court/2012/sjc-10895.html.

6. OKLAHOMA: THE SOONER PROBE

1. Associated Press, "Oklahoma: Abortion Law Overturned," *New York Times*, August 19, 2009, http://www.nytimes.com/2009/08/19/us/19brfs-ABORTIONLAWO_BRF.html?_r=0.

2. Interview, Michelle Movahed, attorney for Center for Reproductive Rights, July 22, 2012.

3. Amie Newman, "New Oklahoma Law Forces Ultrasounds," RH Reality Check, April 25, 2008, http://www.rhrealitycheck.org/blog/2008/04/25/new-oklahoma-law-forces-women-to-view-ultrasounds.

4. Ryan Sibley, "Virginia ultrasound law is the image of a few others," Sunlight Foundation Reporting Group, March 7, 2012 http://reporting.sunlightfoundation.com/2012/virginia-ultrasound-law-image-few-others/

5. Alex Spillius, "Oklahoma Forces Women to Have Ultrasound Before Abortion," *Telegraph*, April 28, 2010, http://www.telegraph.co.uk/news/worldnews/northamerica/usa/7647166/Oklahoma-forces-women-to-have-ultrasound-before-abortion.html.

6. Interview, Curtis Boyd, July 24, 2012.

7. Oklahoma HB 2870, Section 2.c.,https://www.sos.ok.gov/documents/legislation/52nd/2010/2R/HB/2780.pdf, retrieved January 8, 2013.

8. National Right to Life Committee, "Woman's Right to Know: States that offer ultrasound option," January 11, 2012 http://www.nrlc.org/WRTK/Ultrasound-Laws/StateUltrasoundLaws.pdf retrieved February 23, 2013

9. Ala. Code § 26-23A-4 (4);(5).

10. Focus on the Family: Be a Voice for Life, "Option Ultrasound: Revealing Life to Save Life," http://www.heartlink.org/oupdirectors.cfm, retrieved January 8, 2012.

11. Focus on the Family, "Focus on the Family Clarifies Option Ultrasound Numbers," October 18, 2011, http://www.focusonthefamily.com/about_us/news_room/news-releases/20111018-focus-on-the-family-clarifies-option-ultrasound-numbers.aspx, retrieved January 8, 2013.

12. "Ultrasound Initiative Guidelines," Knights of Columbus, http://www.kofc.org/un/en/prolife/ultrasound/guidelines.html, retrieved January 8, 2013.

13. Scott Noble, "Life Care Center Dedicates New Ultrasound," *Minnesota Christian Examiner*, October 2011, http://www.minnesota.christianexaminer.com/Articles/Oct11/Art_Oct11_02.html.

14. Jeanne Monahan, "Ultrasound Policy," Family Research Council, http://www.frc.org/onepagers/ultrasound-policy, retrieved January 8, 2013.

15. Kevin Sack, "In Ultrasound, Abortion Fight Has New Front," *New York Times*, May 27, 2010, http://www.nytimes.com/2010/05/28/health/policy/28ultrasound.html.

16. "Deception at Crisis Pregnancy Centers, the Crisis Project," Youtube video, http://www.youtube.com/watch?feature=player_embedded&v=b3aH8h3PWHc#!, retrieved January 8, 2013.

17. Tracy Weitz, "Oklahoma Gets Top Pro-Life Honors for Abortion Laws:

A Look at Ultrasound," Advancing New Standards in Reproductive Health, January 27, 2011, http://blog.ansirh.org/2011/01/oklahoma-abortion-laws-and-ultrasound/.

18. Associated Press, "Hearing Set on Oklahoma Law Suit," NewsOK, April 29, 2010, http://newsok.com/hearing-set-in-planned-parenthood-lawsuit-against-oklahoma/article/3730121.

19. Associated Press, "Judge Says Oklahoma Cannot Force Abortion Patients to View Ultrasound," *The Guardian*, March 28, 2012, http://www.guardian.co.uk/world/2012/mar/29/abortion-oklahoma-ultrasound-fetus-judge.

20. Barbara Hoberock "State AG Appeals Court's Ruling Tossing Abortion Ultrasound Bill," *Tulsa World*, June 22, 2012, http://www.tulsaworld.com/news/article.aspx?subjectid=336&articleid=20120622_16_A1_OKLAHO878149.

21. Corrie MacLaggan, "Texas Senate Approves Pre-Abortion Ultrasound Law," Reuters, February 17, 2011, http://www.reuters.com/article/2011/02/18/us-texas-abortion-idUSTRE71H03G20110218.

22. Jordan Smith, "Sparks Strikes Again in Abortion Case," *Austin Chronicle*, August 23, 2011, http://www.austinchronicle.com/blogs/news/2011-08-23/sparks-strikes-again-in-abortion-case/.

23. Jodi Jacobson, "Texas Sonogram Law Found to Violate the First Amendment," RH Reality Check, August 30, 2011, http://www.rhrealitycheck.org/blog/2011/08/30/texas-sonogram-found-violate-first-amendment.

24. Katherine Haenschen, "More on the Mandatory Sonogram Law and Chief Judge Edith Jones," Burnt Orange Report, January 11, 2012, http://www.burntorangereport.com/diary/11715/more-on-the-mandatory-sonogram-law-and-chief-judge-edith-jones.

25. Lakey at 14.

26. Interview, Michelle Movahed, attorney for Center for Reproductive Rights, July 22, 2012.

27. "How Abortion Harms Women's Health," Family Research Council, http://www.frc.org/content/how-abortion-harms-womens-health retrieved February 23, 2012

28. Interview, Curtis Boyd, July 24, 2012.

29. Bigelow v. Virginia, 421 US 809 (1975).

30. The Eighth Circuit also has addressed the "compelled speech" issue in Planned Parenthood v. Rounds, setting up another potential conflict of circuits that could prompt Supreme Court review; Casey at 882.

31. Carolyn Jones, "'We Have No Choice': One Woman's Ordeal with Texas' New Sonogram Law,' *Texas Observer*, March 15, 2012, http://www.texasobserver.org/we-have-no-choice-one-womans-ordeal-with-texas-new-sonogram-law/.

7. SOUTH DAKOTA: COME FOR THE CHRISTIANITY, STAY FOR THE CONVERSION

1. Amanda Robb, "Controversial South Dakota 'Crisis Pregnancy Center' Activist Leslee Unruh," More, April 6, 2010, http://www.more.com/news/womens-issues/leslee-unruhs-facts-life.

2. Andy Kospa, "Alpha Center and Their $2 Million Government Grant," Off the Record: On Religion, Politics and Equality, March 23, 2011, http://akopsa.wordpress.com/2011/03/23/south-dakotas-anti-abortion-law-cpc-djour-alpha-center-and-their-2-million-government-grant/.

3. Angela Kennecke, "Pro-Choice Groups Fight Abortion Ban Proposal," Keloland Television, March 12, 2008, http://www.keloland.com/newsdetail.cfm/pro-choice-group-fights-abortion-ban-proposal/?id=0,67375.

4. South Dakota HB 1217,http://legis.state.sd.us/sessions/2011/Bill.aspx?File=HB1217ENR.htm.

5. Nancy Gibbs, "When Is an Abortion Not an Abortion?" Time, March 6, 2006, http://www.time.com/time/nation/article/0,8599,1170368,00.html, retrieved January 11, 2013.

6. "When Is an Abortion Not an Abortion?", Time.

7. Interview, Alisha Sedor, executive director, NARAL Pro-Choice South Dakota, July 22, 2012.

8. Interview, Sunny Clifford, Lakota reproductive rights advocate.

9. South Dakota HB 1217, February 12, 2011.

10. South Dakota HB 1217, February 12, 2011.

11. Sofia Resnick, "Taxpayer-Funded Crisis Pregnancy Centers Using Religion to Oppose Abortion," American Independent, April 24, 2012, http://www.huffingtonpost.com/2012/04/24/abortion-religion-pregnancy-centers_n_1446506.html.

12. Robin Marty, "Will Draconian South Dakota Force Women to Visit Religious Pregnancy Centers Before Abortions?" Alternet, February 18, 2011, http://www.alternet.org/story/149969/will_draconian_south_dakota_force_women_to_visit_religious_pregnancy_centers_before_abortions?page=0%2C2&paging=off.

13. Rob Boston, "Pregnant Pause: Taxpayer Funding for Abortion 'Counseling' Subsidizes Fundamentalist Religion," Americans United, March 31, 2011, https://www.au.org/blogs/wall-of-separation/pregnant-pause-taxpayer-funding-for-abortion-%E2%80%98counseling%E2%80%99-subsidizes.

14. Mary Garrigan, "Pregnancy Centers Wait Out Daugaard's Decision," Rapid City Journal, March 17, 2011,

15. Mary Garrigan, "Pregnancy Centers Wait Out Daugaard's Decision."

16. Kristen Gosling, "Governor Signs 3-Day Wait for Abortion into Law," Associated Press, March 22, 2011, http://www.ksdk.com/news/article/250805/28/

SD-governor-signs-3-day-wait-for-abortion-into-law.

17. Kristen Gosling, "Governor Signs 3-Day Wait for Abortion into Law."

18. Robin Marty, "Just Who Is Paying to Defend Anti-Choice Laws in South Dakota?" RH Reality Check, March 27, 2011, http://www.rhrealitycheck.org/blog/2011/03/26/mysterious-money-south-dakota-abortion-will-cost-state-either.

19. Robin Marty, "Patron of Live Action Films Among Contributors to Defense of South Dakota's Newest Anti-Choice Bill," RH Reality Check, March 28, 2011.

20. Robin Marty, "Patron of Live Action Films Among Contributors to Defense of South Dakota's Newest Anti-Choice Bill."

21. Robin Marty, "Planned Parenthood, ACLU Sue South Dakota Over New Abortion Restrictions," RH Reality Check, May 27, 2011, http://www.rhreality-check.org/blog/2011/05/27/planned-parenthood-aclu-sues-south-dakota-over-unconstitutional-abortion-access-laws.

22. John Terbush, "Planned Parenthood Sues South Dakota Over Abortion Law," Talking Points Memo, May 28, 2011, http://tpmmuckraker.talkingpoints-memo.com/2011/05/planned_parenthood_sues_south_dakota_over_restrict.php.

23. Jodi Jacobson, "Court Blocks Anti-Choice Legislation in South Dakota," RH Reality Check, June 30, 2011, http://www.rhrealitycheck.org/blog/2011/06/30/court-blocks-antichoice-legislation-south-dakota-0.

24. Mary Garrigan, "Crisis Pregnancy Centers Enter Suit Over State Anti-Abortion Law," Rapid City Journal, January 17, 2012, http://rapidcityjournal.com/news/crisis-pregnancy-centers-enter-suit-over-state-anti-abortion-law/article_9041b29e-40d7-11e1-8729-0019bb2963f4.html.

25. Casey at 882.

26. Planned Parenthood v. Rounds, 530 F.3rd 724 (8th Cir. 2008).

27. Id.

28. Id. at 26, quoting Gonzales, 550 U.S. at 163.

29. Planned Parenthood v. Rounds Nos. 09-3231/3233/3262 (July 24, 20012).

30. Id. at 14.

31. Jodi Jacobson, "Journal Considering Retraction of Article Used to Support Federal Court Ruling on South Dakota Law," RH Reality Check, June 25, 2012, http://www.rhrealitycheck.org/article/2012/07/25/researchers-urge-retraction-by-journal-article-used-to-support-federal-court-ruli.

32. Interview, Heather Stringfellow, vice president of public policy at the Planned Parenthood Action Council of Utah, July 24, 2012.

33. "Planned Parenthood: We Continue to Fight for our Patients," Planned Parenthood Minnesota, North Dakota, South Dakota, December 21, 2012, http://www.plannedparenthood.org/about-us/newsroom/local-press-releases/planned-parenthood-we-continue-fight-our-patients-40730.htm, retrieved January 10, 2013.

8. WASHINGTON, DC: TUG OF WAR, MEDICAID-STYLE

1. Carolyn Dryer, "Groups Protest Franks Anti-Abortion Bill," Glendale Star, March 15, 2012, http://www.glendalestar.com/news/headlines/article_730c1366-6d48-11e1-894d-0019bb2963f4.html.

2. Laura Bassett, "Trent Franks, Arizona Congressman, Targets D.C. Abortion Rights," Huffington Post, May 16, 2012, http://www.huffingtonpost.com/2012/05/16/trent-franks-dc-abortion-rights_n_1521667.html.

3. Interview, Gloria Feldt, July 25, 2012.

4. "D.C. Abortion Ban Lifted by House of Representatives: Effort Moves to Senate," RH Reality Check, July 17, 2009.

5. The ban is not automatic but enacting it is usually one of the first things Republicans do when they take over the House, either by introducing it as a standalone bill or tacking it on to some other bill.

6. Press release: "Norton Urges President to Not Allow D.C. to Be Used as Bargaining Chip in CR Negotiations," March 29, 2011, http://www.norton.house.gov/index.php?option=com_content&task=view&id=2056&Itemid=99999999, retrieved January 17, 2013.

7. Sabrina Tavernise, "Abortion Limit Is Renewed, as Is Washington Anger," New York Times, April 10, 2011, http://www.nytimes.com/2011/04/11/us/politics/11district.html?_r=0.

8. Interview, Val Vilott, executive director, DC Abortion Funds, July 27, 2012.

9. Robin Marty, "A Minnesota Decision Shows Every Woman Has the Right to Choose," RH Reality Check, June 7, 2010, http://www.rhrealitycheck.org/blog/2010/06/03/minnesotans-gomez-shows-every-woman-right-choose.

10. "Are You in the Know? Abortion Costs in the United States," Guttmacher Institute, http://www.guttmacher.org/in-the-know/abortion-costs.html, retrieved January 17, 2013.

11. "How Can I Find All of the Money I Need?" National Network of Abortion Funds, http://www.fundabortionnow.org/get-help/financial-counseling, retrieved January 17, 2013.

12. "Restrictions on Medicaid Funding for Abortions: A Literature Review," Guttmacher Institute, 2009, http://www.guttmacher.org/pubs/MedicaidLitReview.pdf, retrieved January 17, 2013.

13. 42 U.S.C. §§ 1396a(a)(13)(B) (1970 ed., Supp. V), 1396d(a)(1)-(5) 91970 ed. and Supp. V).

14. 42 U.S.C. § 1396a(a)(17) (1970 ed., Supp. V).

15. 3 Penn. Bulletin 2207, 2209 (September 29, 1973).

16. Beal, 432 U.S. at 445.

17. Id.

18. Id. (summarizing plaintiffs' arguments).

19. Beal, 432 U.S. at 445.

20. Id.

21. Beal, 432 U.S. at 444.

22. Id. at 444-45 (emphasis in original).

23. Id. at 450.

24. Id. at 450-51.

25. Beal at 453-54 (Brennan, J., dissenting).

26. Beal, 432 U.S. at 454-62 (Marshall, dissenting).

27. Beal, 432 U.S. at 462-63 (Blackmun, J., dissenting).

28. Id. at 470 (summarizing plaintiffs' argument).

29. Maher, 432 U.S. at 469.

30. Id. at 469-70.

31. Maher, 432 U.S. at 470-471.

32. Id. at 471.

33. Maher, 432 U.S. at 478 (citation and internal quotation marks omitted).

34. Id. (quoting Roe, 410 U.S. at 162-63).; Id. (quoting Beal v. Doe, 432 U.S. 438, 446 (1977).

35. Id. at 478-79.

36. Id. at 479.

37. Id. at 483.

38. Zbaraz v. Quern, 469 F.Supp. 1212, 1221 (N.D. Ill. 1979).

39. Williams v. Zbaraz, 448 U.S. at 369.

40. Facts on Induced Abortion in the United States, Guttmacher Institute. http://www.guttmacher.org/pubs/fb_induced_abortion.html, retrieved January 19, 2013.

41. Sharon Jayson, "Abortion Rates Fall, Except Among Poor Women," *USA Today*, May 23, 2011, http://usatoday30.usatoday.com/NEWS/usaedition/2011-05-24-Abortion-stats-story-for-Tuesday-print-Monda_ST_U.htm.

42. Women's Medical Fund, Stories, http://womensmedicalfund.org/index.php/stories, retrieved January 17, 2013.

43. "Emergency Funding Request, Woman with Multiple Cancers Needs Your Help," New York Abortion Access Fund, June 7, 2012, http://www.nyaaf.org/2012/06/emergency-funding-request-woman-with-multiple-cancers-needs-your-help/, retrieved January 17, 2013.

44. Associated Press, "Abortion Insurance Bill Dies in Washington Senate," *Columbian*, March 2, 2012, http://www.columbian.com/news/2012/mar/02/abortion-insurance-bill-dies-in-wash-senate/.

45. Press release: "Statement of Congresswoman Eleanor Holmes Norton on H.R. 3, the No Taxpayer Funding for Abortion Act," House Committee on the Judiciary Sub-

committee on the Constitution, February 8, 2011, http://www.norton.house.gov/index. php?option=com_content&task=view&id=1994&Itemid=88, retrieved January 17, 2013.

9. TEXAS: AN INACCESSIBLE MEDICAL SYSTEM FOR POOR WOMEN

1. Rick Perry, "Prepared Remarks for 'Light of Life Dinner and Gala,'" September 26, 2009, http://governor.state.tx.us/news/speech/13747, retrieved January 25, 2013.

2. Danielle Connolly, "Shelby Commission Votes for Family-Planning Contract with Christ Community," *Commercial Appeal*, October 11, 2011, http://www.commercialappeal.com/news/2011/oct/17/shelby-county-commission-votes-family-planning-con.

3. Robin Marty, "Planned Parenthood Greater Memphis Region Receives $395,000 Title X Grant to Make Up for Funds Given to Religious Health Group," RH Reality Check, July 5, 2012, http://www.rhrealitycheck.org/article/2012/07/05/planned-parenthood-greater-memphis-region-receives-395000-title-x-grant-to-make-u.

4. Robin Marty, "Ohio Republicans Attempting to Defund Planned Parenthood, Give Money to Groups that Don't Provide Birth Control," RH Reality Check, April 17, 2011, http://www.rhrealitycheck.org/article/2012/04/17/ohio-republicans-attempting-to-defund-planned-parenthood.

5. "The Uninsured in Texas," Texas Medical Association, http://www.texmed. org/Uninsured_in_Texas, retrieved January 25, 2013.

6. "The Uninsured in Texas," Texas Medical Association.

7. Interview, Veronica Bayetti Flores, July 27, 2012.

8. Adam Thomas, "Policy Solutions for Preventing Unplanned Pregnancies," Brookings Institute, March 2012, http://www.brookings.edu/research/reports/2012/03/unplanned-pregnancy-thomas, retrieved January 25, 2013.

9. Pam Belluck and Emily Ramshaw, "Women in Texas Losing Options for Health Care in Abortion Fight," *New York Times*, March 8, 2012, http://www.nytimes.com/2012/03/08/us/texas-womens-clinics-retreat-as-finances-are-cut. html?pagewanted=all&_r=0.

10. Belluck and Ramshaw, "Women in Texas Losing Options for Health Care in Abortion Fight."

11. Wade Goodwyn. "Gov. Perry Cut Funds For Women's Health In Texas." NPR, September 20, 2011. http://www.npr.org/2011/09/20/140449957/gov-perry-cut-funds-for-womens-health-in-texas

12. Belluck and Ramshaw, "Women in Texas Losing Options for Health Care in Abortion Fight."

13. Belluck and Ramshaw, "Women in Texas Losing Options for Health Care in Abortion Fight."

14. Jordan Smith, "Rick Perry's War on Women," *The Nation*, December 19, 2011, http://www.thenation.com/article/164880/rick-perrys-war-women#.

15. Patrick Brendel, "State Abortion-Alternatives Program Funds Christian Nonprofits in Houston," Washington Independent, March 15, 2011, http://americanindependent.com/174776/texas-anti-abortion-program-serves-fewer-clients-than-targeted.

16. Editorial, "Rick Perry: Women's Health vs. Abortion Politics," *Abilene Reporter News*, March 12, 2012, http://www.reporternews.com/news/2012/mar/08/rick-perry-womens-health-vs-abortion-politics.

17. "Gov. Perry Pledges State Will Take Care of Texas Women if Obama Administration Ends Women's Health Program Funding, as Threatened," office of Governor Rick Perry, March 8, 2012, http://governor.state.tx.us/news/press-release/17020, retrieved January 25, 2013.

18. Texas Catholic Conference, "Texas Bishops Support True, Comprehensive Women's Health Programs," http://www.txcatholic.org/the-church-in-texas/134-texas-bishops-support-true-comprehensive-womens-health-program, retrieved January 25, 2013.

19. Interview, Jon O'Brien, August 7, 2012.

20. Andrea Grimes, "All Those Alternatives to Planned Parenthood? In Texas, at Least, They Don't Exist," RH Reality Check, April 5, 2011, http://www.rhrealitycheck.org/blog/2011/04/05/where-will-health-care-when-family-planning-funds-thing-past.

21. Planned Parenthood, "Federal Judge in Texas Rules in Favor of Women's Health," April 30, 2012, http://www.plannedparenthood.org/about-us/newsroom/press-releases/federal-judge-texas-rules-favor-womens-health-39241.htm, retrieved January 25, 2013.

22. In the United States Court of Appeals for the Fifth Circuit. http://www.ca5.uscourts.gov/opinions/pub/12/12-50377-CV0.wpd.pdf

23. Hollie O'Connor, "Medical Groups Oppose Women's Health Program Rule," Texas Tribune, August 6, 2012, http://www.texastribune.org/2012/08/06/tma-rejects-rule-banning-discussion-abortion.

24. "Governor's Letter to HHS Secretary Kathleen Sebelius," July 9, 2012, http://governor.state.tx.us/files/press-office/O-SebeliusKathleen201207090024.pdf, retrieved January 25, 2013.

25. 42 U.S.C. § 300(a).

26. 53 Fed. Reg. 2923-24 (1988).

27. Id § 59.8(a)(3).

28. Id. § 59.8(b)(5).

29. Rust v. Sullivan 500 U.S.183 (1991).

30. Rust, 500 U.S. at 183-91.

31. Rust, 500 U.S. at 192.

32. Id. at 194.

33. Rust, 500 U.S. at 196.

34. Id.

35. Id.

36. Id.

37. Carolyn Jones, "One Year Later, Cuts to Women's Health Have Hurt More than Just Planned Parenthood," *Texas Observer*, August 15, 2012, http://www.texasobserver.org/one-year-later-cuts-to-womens-health-have-hurt-more-than-just-planned-parenthood.

38. Jones, "One Year Later, Cuts to Women's Health Have Hurt More than Just Planned Parenthood."

39. On August 21, 2012, the Fifth Circuit held in *Planned Parenthood v. Suehs* that the Texas rule defining abortion affiliate to include any clinic tied to Planned Parenthood, regardless if they performed abortions, and cutting off state and federal grant money to those clinics could be implemented.

10. KANSAS: ALWAYS LET YOUR CONSCIENCE BE YOUR GUIDE

1. Michael Clancy, "Nun at St. Joseph's Hospital Rebuked Over Abortion to Save Woman," *Arizona Republic*, May 19, 2010, http://www.azcentral.com/news/articles/2010/05/15/20100515phoenix-catholic-nun-abortion.html.

2. St. Joseph's Hospital and Medical Center, "St. Joseph's Statement Regarding the Bishop's Announcement," http://www.stjosephs-phx.org/Who_We_Are/Press_Center/211990, retrieved January 25, 2013.

3. Associated Press, "Arizona Hospital Loses Status Over abortion Case," *USA Today*, December 22, 2010, http://usatoday30.usatoday.com/news/religion/2010-12-21-phoenix-catholic-hospital_N.htm.

4. "ACLU Asks Government to Ensure that Religiously-Affiliated Hospitals Provide Emergency Reproductive Health Care," American Civil Liberties Union, July 1, 2010, http://www.aclu.org/reproductive-freedom/aclu-asks-government-ensure-religiously-affiliated-hospitals-provide-emergency, retrieved January 25, 2013.

5. This is the paradox created by Casey. Since, according to Casey, women do not have an absolute right to terminate a pregnancy prior to viability because even then the state retains some interest in promoting potential fetal life, an abortion restriction may be "particularly burdensome" on women by creating an increase in cost and potential delays and still not create an "undue burden" on the right to terminate a pregnancy.

6. See generally: Hobby Lobby Stores v. Sebelius, O'Brien v. HHS, Legatus v. Sebelius, and Autocam Corp. v. Sebelius, all of which are pending in U.S. Courts of Appeals.

7. See generally: ACLU, Conflicts Between Religious Refusals and Women's Health: How the Court Responds I (2002) for the spectrum of religious refusal lawsuits and constitutional arguments and the shifting legal landscape reflected in opinions such as Shelton v. Univ. of Med. & Dentistry, 223 F 3d 220 (3rd Cir 2000) and Valley Hosp. Ass'n Inv. v. Mat-Su Coal. for Choice, 948 P2d 963, 972 (Alaska 1997).

8. On the Issues, "Sam Brownback on Abortion," http://www.ontheissues.org/social/Sam_Brownback_Abortion.htm, retrieved January 25, 2013.

9. On the Issues, "Sam Brownback on Abortion."

10. Interview, Meghan Smith, state coordinator, Catholics for Choice, August 3, 2012.

11. Steven Kreytak, "Bus Driver Who Refused to Take Woman to Planned Parenthood Gets $21K in Settlement," *Austin American Statesman*, April 25, 2011, http://www.statesman.com/blogs/content/shared-gen/blogs/austin/courts/entries/2011/04/25/driver_who_refused_to_bring_wo.html/.

12. Kathleen Gilbert, "Interview: Bus Driver Fired for Refusing to Drive Woman to Abortion Clinic," Lifesitenews.com, July 20, 2010, http://www.lifesitenews.com/news/archive//ldn/2010/jul/10072008.

13. Seth Augenstein, "12 Nurses Accuse UMDNJ of Forcing Them to Assist in Abortion Cases Despite Religious and Moral Objections," *New Jersey Star Ledger*, November 14, 2011, http://www.nj.com/news/index.ssf/2011/11/12_nurses_accuse_umdnj_of_forc.html.

14. George Prentiss, "Planned Parenthood: Walgreens Pharmacist Refused to Fill Prescription," *Boise Weekly*, January 12, 2011, http://www.boiseweekly.com/CityDesk/archives/2011/01/12/planned-parenthood-walgreens-pharmacist-refused-to-fill-presciption.

15. George Prentiss, "No Law Requires a Pharmacist to Fill a Prescription," *Boise Weekly*, January 24, 2011, http://www.boiseweekly.com/CityDesk/archives/2011/01/24/no-law-requires-pharmacist-to-fill-a-prescription.

16. Interview, Jon O'Brien, president, Catholics for Choice, August 3, 2012.

17. Stephen Webster, "Kansas Republicans Look to Profit off Abortion Taxes," Raw Story, March 9, 2012, http://www.rawstory.com/rs/2012/03/09/kansas-republicans-look-to-profit-off-abortion-taxes/.

18. The Healthcare Rights of Conscience Act -House Substitute for SB 62 by Committee on Judiciary—Concerning medical care facilities; relating to abortion; sterilization sb62_enrolled.pdf

19. Interview, Holly Weatherford, ACLU Kansas, August 8, 2012.

20. Food and Drug Administration: Ella Labeling Information, http://www.accessdata.fda.gov/drugsatfda_docs/label/2010/022474s000lbl.pdf, retrieved January 26, 2013.

21. Pam Belluck, "Abortion Qualms on Morning-After Pill May Be Unfounded," *New York Times*, June 5, 2012, http://www.nytimes.com/2012/06/06/health/research/morning-after-pills-dont-block-implantation-science-suggests.html?pagewanted=all&_r=0.

22. Interview, Gabrielle Goodrick, July 29, 2012.

23. Marimer Matos, "Rape Victim Can Sue for Denied Contraception," Courthouse News, June 25, 2012, http://www.courthousenews.com/2012/06/25/47785.htm.

24. Michael Winter, "Anti-Abortion Group Obtains Kansas Clinic Records from Trash," *USA Today*, May 4, 2012, http://content.usatoday.com/communities/ondeadline/post/2012/05/anti-abortion-group-obtains-kansas-clinic-records-from-trash/1#.UQOdueim5e4.

25. Donald Bradley and Alan Baverly, "Kansas Investigates Operations Rescue's Child Sexual Abuse Claim Against Abortion Clinic," *Kansas City Star*, May 4, 2012, http://www.mcclatchydc.com/2012/05/04/v-print/147705/kansas-investigates-operation.html.

11. MISSISSIPPI: CLOSE THE CLINICS, BRING BACK THE HANGER

1. Emily Wagster Pettus and Laura Tillman, "New Law Targets Lone Abortion Clinic in Mississippi," Associated Press, April 12, 2012, http://news.yahoo.com/law-targets-lone-abortion-clinic-miss-205336423.html

2. Emily Wagster Pettus, "Mississippi 'Personhood' Amendment Vote Fails," Associated Press, November 8, 2011, http://www.huffingtonpost.com/2011/11/08/mississippi-personhood-amendment_n_1082546.html.

3. "Letter from Diane Derzis," Wakeupmississippi.org, October 7, 2011, retrieved February 3, 2013.

4. Irin Carmon, "Personhood's Mississippi Moment of Truth," Salon.com, November 8, 2011, http://www.salon.com/2011/11/08/personhoods_mississippi_moment_of_truth.

5. Emily Wagster Pettus, "1 Abortion Reg Survives, 2 Die in Miss. Senate," Associated Press, April 3, 2012, http://www.necn.com/04/03/12/1-abortion-reg-survives-2-die-in-Miss-Se/landing_politics.html?&apID=dcd659638770487f811db1ad4f189b6d.

6. Kate Sheppard, "Abortion Foes' Latest Backdoor Ban," *Mother Jones*, June 27, 2012, http://www.motherjones.com/politics/2011/06/abortion-foes-latest-backdoor-ban.

7. Emily Wagster Pettus, "Tate Reeves Blocking Nomination Because of Candidate's Ties to Abortion Clinic," Associated Press, April 24, 2012, http://www.10tv.com/content/stories/apexchange/2012/04/24/ms--mississippi-abortion.html.

8. Jen Gunter, "The Medical Nonsense and Dangerous Precedent of Mississippi's Abortion Bill HB 1390," Dr. Jen Gunter, June 29, 2012, http://drjengunter. wordpress.com/2012/06/29/the-medical-nonsense-and-terrible-precedent-of-mississippis-abortion-bill-hb-1390.

9. Pettus and Tillman, "New Law Targets Lone Abortion Clinic in Mississippi."

10. Laura Tillman, "Mississippi Senate Passes Abortion Regulation Bill," Associated Press, April 5, 2012, http://finance.yahoo.com/news/mississippi-senate-passes-abortion-regulation-125042579.html.

11. Laura Conaway, "Mississippi Lawmaker: Coat Hanger Abortions Might Come Back. 'But Hey . . .'" The Maddow Blog, May 14, 2012, http://maddowblog. msnbc.com/_news/2012/05/14/11702049-mississippi-lawmaker-coat-hanger-abortions-might-come-back-but-hey?lite.

12. MJ Lee, "Bill Dooms Only Miss. Abortion Clinic," Politico, April 5, 2012, http://www.politico.com/news/stories/0412/74871.html.

13. Steven Ertelt, "Mississippi Could Become First Abortion-Free State," Lifenews.com, April 5, 2012, http://www.lifenews.com/2012/04/05/mississippi-could-become-first-abortion-free-state.

14. Esme Deprez and Elizabeth Waibel, "Mississippi May Be First U.S. State with No Abortion Clinic," Bloomberg News, June 22, 2012, http://www.businessweek.com/news/2012-06-22/mississippi-may-become-first-u-dot-s-dot-state-with-no-abortion-clinic.

15. Deprez and Waibel, "Mississippi May Be First U.S. State with No Abortion Clinic."

16. Emily Wagster Pettus, "Quick Enforcement Sought for Mississippi Abortion Law," Associated Press, June 22, 2012, http://www.10tv.com/content/stories/apexchange/2012/06/22/ms--abortion-mississippi.html.

17. Emily Le Coz, "Update 1 – Mississippi's Sole Abortion Clinic Sues Over New Law," Reuters, June 27, 2012, http://in.reuters.com/article/2012/06/27/usa-abortion-mississippi-idINL2E8HRBZY20120627.

18. "Center for Reproductive Rights Takes Legal Action to Keep Last Abortion Clinic in Mississippi Open," press release, June 27, 2012.

19. "Center for Reproductive Rights Takes Legal Action to Keep Last Abortion Clinic in Mississippi Open," press release, June 27, 2012.

20. CNN Wire Staff, "Mississippi Sole Abortion Clinic Can Stay Open, for Now," CNN, July 13, 2012, http://www.cnn.com/2012/07/13/justice/mississippi-abortion-clinic-ruling.

21. Interview, Michelle Movahed, Center for Reproductive Rights, July 28, 2012.

22. Mississippi Department of Health, "Infant Mortality in Mississippi," http://msdh.ms.gov/msdhsite/_static/23,4569,266,291.html, retrieved February 3, 2013.

23. Interview, Willie Parker, July 24, 2012.

24. Women's Legislative Network of NCSL, National Conference of State Legislatures, http://www.ncsl.org/legislatures-elections/wln/women-in-state-legislatures-2011.aspx, retrieved February 3, 2013.

25. Interview, Pamela Merritt, July 22, 2012.

26. Emily Le Coz, "Abortion Clinic Gets Letter, Revocation Process Starts," *Jackson Clarion Ledger*, January 28, 2013, http://www.clarionledger.com/article/20130129/NEWS/301280034/Abortion-clinic-gets-letter-revocation-process-starts.

12. ARIZONA: BANNING EVERYTHING BUT THE KITCHEN SINK

1. Elizabeth Nash, "Another Busy Year: State Legislative Trends on Reproductive Health and Abortion in 2009," Guttmacher Institute, January 21, 2010, http://rhrealitycheck.org/article/2010/01/21/another-busy-year-state-legislative-trends-reproductive-health-and-abortion-2009.

2. Alia Beard Rau, "Court Asked to Block New Arizona Abortion law," Arizona Republic, October 27, 2011, http://www.azcentral.com/news/election/azelections/articles/2011/10/26/20111026arizona-abortion-law-court-case-domestic-violence-group.html?nclick_check=1.

3. Interview, Veronica Bayetti Flores, August 2, 2012.

4. E.J. Montini, "Legislature, Anti-Abortion and Anti-Child," Arizona Republic, July 7, 2011, http://www.azcentral.com/arizonarepublic/local/articles/2011/07/07/20110707Montini0707.html.

5. Jorge Rivas, "Arizona Law Could Allow Employers to Fire Workers for Using Birth Control," Colorlines, March 14, 2012, http://colorlines.com/archives/2012/03/arizonas_hb_2625_could_allow_bosses_to_fire_employees_for_using_birth_control.html.

6. Betsy Russell, "Closing Debate: Winder Compares Abortion to U.S. War Casualties," *Idaho Spokesman*, March 19, 2012, http://www.spokesman.com/blogs/boise/2012/mar/19/closing-debate-winder-compares-abortion-us-war-casualties.

7. Interview, Gabrielle Goodrick, July 28, 2012.

8. Jessica Mason Pieklo, "Anti-Choice Medical Malpractice Shields Threaten to Permanently Alter Medical Care for Women," RH Reality Check, April 5, 2012, http://www.rhrealitycheck.org/article/2012/04/02/medical-malpractice-shields-threaten-to-permanently-alter-medical-care-women.

9. Evan Wyloge, "Arizona Bill Would Prevent 'Wrongful Birth' Lawsuits," *AZ Capitol Times*, February 8, 2012, http://azcapitoltimes.com/news/2012/02/08/bill-would-prevent-wrongful-birth-lawsuits.

10. To be absolutely certain that doctors in Arizona understood their directive

was to coerce women out of having an abortion, the state passed SB 1365, which prohibits the state from denying, revoking, or suspending a professional or occupational license based on any action deriving from a person's religious convictions. It's a broad expansion of the state's conscience clause that already allows pharmacists, doctors, and other health care workers to refuse to perform abortions or to prescribe emergency contraception (though it is contraception, not an abortifacient) based on religious objections. Now, any licensed professional can deny services to anyone by declaring that his or her "sincerely held" religious belief is in conflict with otherwise prohibited and discriminatory conduct and be insulated from professional repercussions for doing so. That means, for example, that attorneys can now decline to represent health care workers facing complaints related to the delivery of reproductive health care, or they can refuse to represent an individual simply because he or she happens to be gay. http://www.rhrealitycheck.org/article/2012/05/16/arizona-law-endorses-malpractice-and-discrimination-in-defense-religious-liberty.

11. HB 2036 Women's Health and Safety Act Fact Sheet, Center for Arizona Policy, January 2012.

12. "Dr. Isaacson Letter to Senate President and House Speaker re H.B. 2036," March 7, 2012.

13. "Center for Reproductive Rights, ACLU Launch New Legal Challenge to Block Arizona's Cruel, Unconstitutional Abortion Ban," Center for Reproductive Rights, July 12, 2012, http://reproductiverights.org/en/press-room/center-for-reproductive-rights-aclu-launch-new-legal-challenge-to-block-arizonas-cruel-un.

14. Editorial, "Anti-Abortionists on Trial," *New York Times*, July 25, 2012 http://www.nytimes.com/2012/07/26/opinion/anti-abortionists-on-trial.html?_r=2&ref=opinion,.

15. Order p. 9 of 15.

16. See Gonzales, 550 U.S. at 157–58 ("the fact that a law which serves a valid purpose, one not designed to strike at the right itself, has the incidental effect of making it more difficult or more expensive to procure an abortion cannot be enough to invalidate it.") (quoting Roe v. Wade, 505 U.S. at 874), p.11.

17. Jessica Mason Pieklo and Robin Marty, "Goodbye, Trimesters: How the Arizona Court Ruling May Turn Roe on Its Head," RH Reality Check, July 31, 2012, http://www.rhrealitycheck.org/article/2012/07/31/good-bye-trimesters-how-arizona-court-ruling-will-turn-roe-on-its-head.

18. Ayotte v. Planned Parenthood 546 U.S. 320 (2006).

19. Ayotte, 546 U.S. at 328-29 (citing cases).

20. The Ninth Circuit Court of Appeals heard arguments in November, 2012 and as of publication had not yet ruled.

21. Howard Fischer, "County Attorney Says Lawmakers Entitled to Ban Abortions at 20 Weeks," Capitol Media Services, July 26, 2012, http://cvbugle.

com/Main.asp?SectionID=1&SubSectionID=1&ArticleID=35423.

22. Robin Marty, "The Real Reason Anti-Choice Advocates Are Pushing Fetal Pain Laws," RH Reality Check, May 30, 2011, http://rhrealitycheck.org/article/2011/05/30/real-reason-antichoice-activists-pushing-fetal-pain-laws.

TAKING BACK CONTROL

1. Interview, Gloria Feldt, July 18, 2012.

2. Jacqueline Rabe Thomas, "Abortion to Be Considered Essential Health Benefit," *Connecticut Mirror*, June 8, 2012, http://www.ctmirror.org/story/16602/abortion-be-considered-essential-health-benefit.

3. Anne Galloway, "Shumlin Signs Nation's First Single Payer Health Care Bill into Law," Vtdigger.org, May 27, 2011, http://vtdigger.org/2011/05/27/shumlin-signs-nations-first-single-payer-bill-into-law.

4. "Public Funding for Abortion: Medicaid and the Hyde Amendment," National Abortion Federation, http://www.prochoice.org/about_abortion/facts/public_funding.html, retrieved February 20, 2013.

5. Interview, Veronica Bayetti Flores, July 24, 2012.

6. Interview, Stephanie Poggi, August 8, 2012.

7. "Accessibility of Abortion in the United States, 2001," *Perspectives on Sexual and Reproductive Health*, vol. 31, no. 1, January/February 2003, http://sparky.guttmacher.org/pubs/journals/3501603.html#26, retrieved February 20, 2013.

8. Michael New, "Mississippi Still Has a Chance to Become Abortion Free," Lifenews.com, July 6, 2012, http://www.lifenews.com/2012/07/06/mississippi-still-has-a-chance-to-become-abortion-free.

9. R.K. Jones and K. Kooistra, "Abortion Incidence and Access to Services in the United States, 2008," *Perspectives on Sexual and Reproductive Health*, 2011, 43(1):41–50.

10. "Access to Abortion," National Abortion Federation, http://www.prochoice.org/about_abortion/facts/access_abortion.html#1, retrieved February 20, 2013.

11. Medical Students for Choice, http://www.medicalstudentsforchoice.org/index.php?page=sitemap, retrieved February 20, 2013.

12. Peter Kasperowicz, "House to Vote Tonight on Abortion Training Program," *The Hill*, May 24, 2011, http://thehill.com/blogs/floor-action/house/163013-house-preps-for-controversial-abortion-vote-tuesday-night.

13. California SB No. 1501, http://www.leginfo.ca.gov/pub/11-12/bill/sen/sb_1501-1550/sb_1501_bill_20120224_introduced.pdf

14. Political, "Bill to Allow Some Non-Physician Abortions Is Pulled," *Los Angeles Times*, May 4, 2012, http://latimesblogs.latimes.com/california-politics/2012/05/california-abortion-bill-pulled-back.html.

15. Political, "California Lawmaker Wants to Expand Abortion Access," *Los Angeles Times*, January 23, 2013, http://latimesblogs.latimes.com/california-politics/2013/01/lawmaker-wants-to-expand-abortion-access.html.

16. HHS Mandate Information Central, Becket Fund for Religious Liberty, http://www.becketfund.org/hhsinformationcentral, retrieved February 20, 2013.

17. "AB 2348 Would Increase Access to Birth Control for Thousands of Women in California by Allowing Registered Nurses to Dispense Self-Administered Hormonal Contraceptives," California Women's Law Center, July 3, 2012, http://www.cwlc.org/women-reproductive-justice/3817_ab-2348-increase-access-birth-control-thousands-women-california-allowing-registered-nurses-dispense-selfadministered-hormonal-contraceptives, retrieved February 20, 2013.

18. Jenna Chandler, "Governor Signs Holly Mitchell's Bill Easing Access to Birth Control," *Culver City Patch*, September 25, 2012, http://culvercity.patch.com/articles/governor-signs-holly-mitchell-s-bill-easing-access-to-birth-control.

19. Steven Ertlelt, "Pawlenty Credited with Helping Minnesota Abortions Drop Again," LifeNews.com, July 26, 2011, http://www.lifenews.com/2011/07/26/pawlenty-credited-with-helping-minnesota-abortions-drop-again.

20. Kate Harding, "Stupak: Two More Years?!?" Salon, January 14, 2010, http://www.salon.com/2010/01/14/stupak_reelection.

21. Interview, Stephanie Schriock, August 6, 2012.

22. She Should Run, Mission, http://www.sheshouldrun.org/pages/about/about-she-should-run.html, retrieved February 20, 2013.

23. Off the Sidelines: How You Can Get Off the Sidelines, http://www.off-thesidelines.org/act/how-you-can-get-off-the-sidelines, retrieved February 20, 2013.

24. Interview, Todd Beeton, August 10, 2012.

25. Jessica Mason Pieklo, "Why Dark Money in Politics is Bad for Women," RH Reality Check, July 24, 2012, http://www.rhrealitycheck.org/article/2012/07/22/why-dark-money-in-politics-is-bad-women.

26. Laws Affecting Reproductive Health and Rights, 2012 State Policy Review, Guttmacher Institute, http://www.guttmacher.org/statecenter/updates/2012/statetrends42012.html, retrieved February 20, 2013.

27. Jessica Mason Pieklo, "How James Bopp Is Using Citizens United and Campaign Finance Law to Promote the Anti-Choice Agenda," RH Reality Check, March 19, 2012, http://www.rhrealitycheck.org/article/2012/03/19/how-james-bopp-is-using-citizens-united-and-campaign-finance-law-to-promote-anti-.

28. Dave Levinthal, "Still a Man's World When It Comes to Political Donations," OpenSecrets Blog, March 8, 2011, http://www.opensecrets.org/news/2011/03/still-a-mans-world-when-it-comes-to.html.

29. Dave Levinthal, "Still a Man's World When It Comes to Political Donations."

30. United States Courts, Judicial Emergencies as of 2/25/2013 http://www.uscourts.gov/JudgesAndJudgeships/JudicialVacancies/JudicialEmergencies.aspx retrieved February 25, 2013

31. Denis Steven Rutkus & Susan Navarro Smelcer, Cong. Research Serv., R41942, *Vacancies on Article III District and Circuit Courts, 1977–2011: Data, Causes, and Implications* 5 (2011), http://www.nwlc.org/resource/vacancy-crisis-federal-judiciary-whats-stake-women#_edn2.

32. United States Courts, Judicial Emergencies as of 2/25/2013 http://www.uscourts.gov/JudgesAndJudgeships/JudicialVacancies/JudicialEmergencies.aspx retrieved February 25, 2013

33. Interview, Erin Mattson, August 3, 2012.

34. Olympia Meola, "Update: 31 Arrested in Women's Rights Demonstration at State Capitol," *Times Dispatch*, March 3, 2012, http://www.timesdispatch.com/news/update-arrested-in-women-s-rights-demonstration-at-state-capitol/article_c398c779-b1a8-5f4a-a7bc-76ceca00dcb3.html.

35. Dahlia Lithwick, "Virginia's Proposed Ultrasound Bill Is an Abomination," *Slate*, February 16, 2012, http://www.slate.com/articles/double_x/doublex/2012/02/virginia_ultrasound_law_women_who_want_an_abortion_will_be_forcibly_penetrated_for_no_medical_reason.html.

36. Andy Kopsa, "UPDATE: Virginia Delegate Says Mandatory Ultrasound Bill Will Turn Doctors into 'Criminals' Under the Law," RH Reality Check, February 17, 2012, http://rhrealitycheck.org/article/2012/02/17/virginia-ultrasound-bill-will-turn-doctors-into-criminals-under-law-says-delegate.

37. Julian Walker, "Poll: Virginians Give Gov. McDonnell Positive Review," *Virginian-Pilot*, March 22, 2012, http://hamptonroads.com/2012/03/poll-virginians-give-gov-mcdonnell-positive-review.

38. Tarina Keene, "McDonnell's Forced Ultrasound Bill Awakens a Sleeping Giant—Pro-Choice Virginians—and They Are Going to the Polls," RH Reality Check, April 17, 2012, http://rhrealitycheck.org/article/2012/04/16/virginian-women-are-awake-and-ready-to-vote/?quicktabs_popular=0.

39. Melissa Davlin, "Abortion Bill Raises Ultrasound Costs Questions," magicvalley.com, March 11, 2012, http://magicvalley.com/news/local/govt-and-politics/abortion-bill-raises-ultrasound-cost-questions/article_73d60657-baea-51cb-9bda-d6ea974c65a2.html.

40. Betsy Russell, "Party-Line Vote Passes Pre-Abortion Ultrasound Bill," *Spokesman-Review*, March 14, 2012, http://www.spokesman.com/stories/2012/mar/14/party-line-vote-passes-pre-abortion-ultrasound-bil.

41. Interview, Hannah Brass Greer, August 20, 2012.

42. John Miller, "Abortion Foes Do Live Ultrasounds in Idaho Capitol," *Idaho Press Tribune*, March 21, 2012, http://www.idahopress.com/news/state/anti-abor-

tion-activists-hold-ultrasound-exhibition/article_59c6dbf6-5766-545d-8715-07facb28525b.html.

43. Jay Bookman, "The Fanaticism Behind Ga.'s Pending Abortion Law," *Atlanta Journal Constitution*, March 20, 2012, http://blogs.ajc.com/jay-bookman-blog/2012/03/20/the-fanaticism-behind-ga-s-pending-abortion-law/?cp=12.

44. Christopher Quinn and Kristina Torres, "Georgia Lawmakers Pass Abortion Bill on Last, Emotional Day," *Atlanta Journal Constitution*, March 29, 2012, http://www.ajc.com/news/news/state-regional-govt-politics/georgia-lawmakers-pass-abortion-bill-on-last-emoti/nQSfD.

45. Quinn and Torres, "Georgia Lawmakers Pass Abortion Bill on Last, Emotional Day."

46. Quinn and Torres, "Georgia Lawmakers Pass Abortion Bill on Last, Emotional Day."

47. Lisa Coston, "Doctors Challenge Georgia's 'Fetal Pain' Law," Courthouse News, December 5, 2012, http://www.courthousenews.com/2012/12/05/52845.htm.